THE LANGUAGE GYM
SPANISH TRILOGY II

THE LANGUAGE GYM
SPANISH TRILOGY II

SPANISH
SENTENCE BUILDERS
TRILOGY

A lexicogrammar approach
Beginner to Pre-Intermediate

PART II

About the authors

Gianfranco Conti taught for 25 years at schools in Italy, the UK and in Kuala Lumpur, Malaysia. He has also been a university lecturer, holds a Master's degree in Applied Linguistics and a PhD in metacognitive strategies as applied to second language writing. He is now an author, a popular independent educational consultant and professional development provider. He has written around 2,000 resources for the TES website, which have awarded him the Best Resources Contributor in 2015. He has co-authored the best-selling and influential book for world languages teachers, "The Language Teacher Toolkit" and "Breaking the sound barrier: Teaching learners how to listen", in which he puts forth his Listening As Modelling methodology. Gianfranco writes an influential blog on second language acquisition called The Language Gym, co-founded the interactive website language-gym.com and the Facebook professional group Global Innovative Language Teachers (GILT). Last but not least, Gianfranco has created the instructional approach known as E.P.I. (Extensive Processing Instruction).

Dylan Viñales has taught for 15 years, in schools in Bath, Beijing and Kuala Lumpur in state, independent and international settings. He lives in Kuala Lumpur. He is fluent in five languages, and gets by in several more. Dylan is, besides a teacher, a professional development provider, specialising in E.P.I., metacognition, teaching languages through music (especially ukulele) and cognitive science. In the last five years, together with Dr Conti, he has driven the implementation of E.P.I. in one of the top international schools in the world: Garden International School. This has allowed him to test, on a daily basis, the sequences and activities included in this book with excellent results (his students have won language competitions both locally and internationally). He has designed an original Spanish curriculum, bespoke instructional materials, based on Reading and Listening as Modelling (RAM and LAM). Dylan co-founded the fastest growing professional development group for modern languages teachers on Facebook, Global Innovative Languages Teachers, which includes over 12,000 teachers from all corners of the globe. He authors an influential blog on modern language pedagogy in which he supports the teaching of languages through E.P.I. Dylan is the lead author of Spanish content on the Language Gym website and oversees the technological development of the site. He completed the NPQML qualification in 2021 and is now planning to pursue a Masters in second language acquisition.

Ryan Cockrell has taught for nine years in British secondary schools and has served as Head of English and Head of Languages. Though born in Germany, Ryan is actually a native speaker of English and Spanish, having grown up in Alicante, Liverpool and Coventry. He is currently also learning German and dabbles with other Romance languages. With a first-class BSc (Hons) degree in Psychology, Ryan's passion for language and learning in general steered him towards a career in teaching. Initially trained as an English teacher, Ryan's transition to teaching languages was made easier with the E.P.I. training provided by Dr Conti and the wonderfully supportive community that has emerged as a result. Ryan co-produced the PowerPoint resources for the Spanish Trilogy Part I and was overjoyed to make his co-authoring debut with Spanish Trilogy Part II. Ryan has completed the NPQLT qualification and plans to continue providing support to language teachers who, like him, see the clear benefits of using E.P.I. to teach languages.

Acknowledgements

We would like to thank our editors, **Paloma Lozano García** and **Jaume Llorens**, for their tireless work, proofreading, editing and advising on this book. They are talented, accomplished professionals who work at the highest possible level and add value at every stage of the process. Not only this, but they are also lovely, good-humoured colleagues who go above and beyond, and make the hours of collaborating a real pleasure.

Our sincere gratitude to all the people involved in the recording of the listening audio files: **Ana del Casar, Paloma Lozano García, Tomás Lozano, Manu Hinojosa, Candela Hinojosa, Ariella Viñales, Leonard Viñales & José Luis Larrosa**. Your energy, enthusiasm and passion comes across clearly in every recording and is the reason why the listening sections are such a successful and engaging resource, according to the many students who have been alpha and beta testing the book.

Our sincere thanks to **Simona Gravina** and **Stefano Pianigiani** for their ongoing support, since the very beginning of the Sentence Builder books project. Some important structural elements in this book, such as the inclusion of a listening element at the start of every unit, are inspired by their excellent work as lead authors of the Primary Sentence Builders series.

Dylan would like to thank his eagle-eyed students **David Gazeau, Gemma Gobinath, Siya Gupta, Sixte de Pascal, Kobus Elbers, Chaejun Kim, Zion Kim, Aiman Moosa Rasheed, Dev Sutha, Ruiyi Wang, Muyuan Zhang, Xi Chen, Wei Chen Hui, Julia Yan, Salma Abouraya, Meera Takru, Ayush Salunkhe, Charlotte & Oliver Cooper and Grace Golding-Solomons** for their contributions to the proofreading of this edition.

Finally, our gratitude to the MFL Twitterati for their ongoing support of E.P.I. and the Sentence Builders book series. In particular a shoutout to our team of incredible educators who helped in checking all the units: **María Cristina Caroprese, Barry Agnew, Bárbara Rodríguez Montero, Catalina Petre, María Valverde, Ben Levi, Hannah Foote, Ana Amores Márquez, Christopher Pye, Regina Vara Corella, Anneliese Yafai, Lorène Martine Carver, Aurélie Lethuilier, Joe Barnes-Moran, Jérôme Nogues, Ester Borin, Simona Gravina & Roberto Jover Soro**. It is thanks to your time, patience, professionalism and detailed feedback that we have been able to produce such a refined and highly accurate product.

Gracias a todos,
Gianfranco, Dylan & Ryan

Dedication

For Catrina
-Gianfranco

For Ariella, Leonard, Natasha & Lily
-Dylan

For Harriet, Louis & Ada
-Ryan

Introduction

Hello and welcome to the first 'text' book designed to be an accompaniment to a Spanish, Extensive Processing Instruction course. The book has come about out of necessity, because such a resource did not previously exist.

How to use this book

This book was originally designed as a resource to use in conjunction with our E.P.I. approach and teaching strategies. Our course favours flooding comprehensible input, organising content by communicative functions and related constructions, and a big focus on reading and listening as modelling. The aim of this book is to empower the beginner-to-pre-intermediate learner with linguistic tools - high-frequency structures and vocabulary - useful for real-life communication.

What's inside

The book contains 13 macro-units which concern themselves with specific communicative functions, such as 'Saying what I do at home', 'Talking about my weekend plans' or 'Making after-school plans with a friend'.

Each unit includes:

- a sentence builder modelling the target constructions;
- a set of listening activities to model and input-flood the target language
- a set of vocabulary building activities which reinforce the material in the sentence builder;
- a set of narrow reading texts exploited through a range of tasks focusing on both the meaning and structural levels of the text;
- a set of translation tasks aimed at consolidation through retrieval practice;
- a set of writing tasks targeting essential writing micro-skills such as spelling, functional and positional processing, editing and communication of meaning.
- a "Bringing it all together" section to recycle and interleave the target language seen in previous units

At the end of each term, there is also an End of Term - Question Skills unit. These units are designed to model asking and answering the key questions which have been studied throughout the term. This is also an additional opportunity for structured production as students move towards routinising the language and producing spontaneous speech by the end of the term.

Listening files

These can be accessed by going to **language-gym.com/listening** – access is free, and you can also share this link with students if you want to set a listening homework.

Each sentence builder at the beginning of a unit contains one or more constructions which have been selected with real-life communication in mind. Each unit is built around that construction <u>but not solely on it</u>. Based on the principle that each E.P.I instructional sequence must move from modelling to production in a seamless and organic way, each unit expands on the material in each sentence builder by embedding it in texts and graded tasks which contain both familiar and unfamiliar (but comprehensible and learnable) vocabulary and structures.

The point of all the above micro-units is to implement lots of systematic recycling and interleaving, two techniques that allow for stronger retention and transfer of learning.

Gianfranco, Dylan & Ryan

SENTENCE BUILDERS TRILOGY
PART 2 - TABLE OF CONTENTS

TERM 1 – OVERVIEW

This term you will learn:

Unit 1 – Talking about the weather & free time
• To say what free-time activities you do in different types of weather
• To say where you do them **and** who with
• Words for places in town

Unit 2 – Talking about my daily routine & activities
• To say what daily activities you do
• To say at what time you do things
• To say what you "can", "must" and "want" to do

Unit 3 – Saying what I do at home
• To say what activities you do as part of your daily routine
• To say what you do in different rooms of the house

Unit 4 – Talking about the clothes I wear
• To say what clothes you wear in various circumstances and places
• To say what you wear when it is cold/hot
• A wide range of words for clothing items and accessories
• A range of words for places in town

Unit 5 – My weekend plans: food & leisure
• To describe future activities
• To predict how the future event will be
• To say what you will eat at different times of the day

TERM 1 - KEY QUESTIONS

¿Qué haces en tu tiempo libre?	*What do you do in your free time?*
¿Qué hace tu amigo en su tiempo libre?	*What does your friend do in his/her free time?*
¿Adónde vas los fines de semana?	*Where do you go at the weekend?*
¿A qué hora te levantas entre semana?	*What time do you get up during the week?*
¿Qué haces antes/después del colegio?	*What do you do before/after school?*
¿Qué haces para ayudar en casa?	*What do you do to help at home?*
¿Qué haces en tu dormitorio?	*What do you do in your bedroom?*
¿Con qué frecuencia (lo haces)?	*How frequently (do you do it)?*
¿Qué ropa llevas en casa?	*What clothes do you wear at home?*
¿Qué ropa llevas cuando hace frío/calor?	*What do you wear when it's cold/hot?*
¿Qué ropa llevas cuando sales?	*What do you wear when you go out?*
Describe tu uniforme escolar.	*Describe your school uniform.*
¿Qué vas a hacer este fin de semana?	*What are you going to do this weekend?*
¿Qué vas a tomar para el desayuno?	*What are you going to have for breakfast?*
¿Qué sueles comer para el almuerzo?	*What do you usually eat for lunch?*
¿Qué te gusta beber?	*What do you like to drink?*

UNIT 1
Talking about the weather & free time

In this unit you will learn:

- To say what free-time activities you do in different types of weather
- To say where you do them **and** who with
- Words for places in town

You will revisit:

- Free-time activities
- The verbs 'hacer', 'ir' and 'jugar' in the present indicative
- Family members & pets
- Places in town

Unit 1. Talking about the weather & free time

¿Qué haces en tu tiempo libre?	*What do you do in your free time?*
¿Qué haces cuando hace buen/mal tiempo?	*What do you do when it's good/bad weather?*
¿Qué hace tu amigo en su tiempo libre?	*What does your friend do in his/her free time?*
¿Adónde vas los fines de semana?	*Where do you go at the weekend?*

A veces *Sometimes*	**juego** *I play*	**al ajedrez**	*chess*
		a las cartas	*cards*
Entre semana		**al baloncesto**	*basketball*
During the week	**mi amiga María juega**	**al fútbol**	*football*
	my friend Maria plays	**al tenis**	*tennis*
Los fines de semana		**con mis amigos**	*with my friends*
At the weekends		**con sus amigos**	*with his/her friends*
Cuando tengo tiempo		**ciclismo**	*cycling*
When I have time		**deporte**	*sport*
		equitación	*horse riding*
Cuando está despejado	**hago** *I do*	**escalada**	*rock climbing*
When the sky is clear		**esquí**	*skiing*
		footing	*jogging*
Cuando está nublado	**mi amigo Lionel hace**	**los deberes**	*homework*
When the sky is cloudy	*my friend Lionel does*	**natación**	*swimming*
		senderismo	*hiking*
Cuando hace buen tiempo		**vela**	*sailing*
When the weather is good			
Cuando hace mal tiempo		**a casa de mi amigo**	*to my friend's house*
When the weather is bad		**a casa de su amigo**	*to his/her friend's house*
Cuando hace calor		**a la montaña**	*to the mountain*
When it's hot	**voy** *I go*	**a la piscina**	*to the pool*
		a la playa	*to the beach*
Cuando hace frío	**mi amigo va**	**al campo**	*to the countryside*
When it's cold	*my friend (m) goes*	**al centro comercial**	*to the shopping mall*
		al gimnasio	*to the gym*
Cuando hace sol		**al parque**	*to the park*
When it's sunny	**mi amiga va**	**al polideportivo**	*to the sports centre*
Cuando hace viento	*my friend (f) goes*		
When it's windy		**de marcha**	*clubbing*
		de paseo	*for a walk*
Cuando hay niebla		**de pesca**	*fishing*
When it's foggy		**en bici**	*on a bike ride*
Cuando hay tormenta	**me quedo** *I stay*	**en mi casa**	*in my home*
When it's stormy		**en mi dormitorio**	*in my bedroom*
Cuando llueve *When it rains*	**Felipe** **se queda**	**en su casa**	*in his/her home*
Cuando nieva *When it snows*	**María** *stays*	**en su dormitorio**	*in his/her bedroom*

1. Listen and fill in the gaps

a. Cuando tengo _____________ juego al ajedrez.

b. Cuando está _____________ hago ciclismo.

c. Cuando hace __________ _____________ hago footing.

d. Cuando hace _____________ voy a la playa.

e. Cuando _____________ voy al centro comercial.

f. Entre _____________ no hago deporte.

g. Cuando hay _____________ no voy en bici.

h. Cuando hay _____________ me quedo en casa.

i. Cuando hace ________ _____________ hago los deberes.

2. Mystery WORDS: guess the words, then listen and see how many you guessed right

a. La   _ _ _ b _ _

b. El   _ _ l _ _

c. El   _ _ e _ _ _

d. El   _ _ l

e. _ _ _ _ _ j _ _ _

f. Cuando   _ _ _ _ v _

g. Está   _ _ b _ _ _ _

h. El   _ _ _ o

3. Listening for detail: tick the activities these three people do at the weekend

a. **Pablo**	Does jogging
	Goes to the shopping mall
	Does horse riding
	Does his homework
	Goes clubbing
b. **Ana**	Does swimming
	Goes to the shopping mall
	Goes to the sports centre
	Plays on the computer
	Goes to the restaurant
c. **Conchi**	Does jogging
	Goes to the shopping mall
	Does horse riding
	Plays chess
	Goes to her friend's house

4. Fill in the blanks

¿Qué hago en mi tiempo libre? Muchas cosas. Cuando hace buen tiempo siempre voy al __________. Me gusta _________. Entonces hago __________, solo o con mi _________. A él también le gusta correr. Además me _____________ hacer escalada y _____________. Por lo tanto, cuando no __________, hago senderismo en el bosque cerca de mi casa (vivo en el __________). Cuando está _____________ y hace _________, me voy a la __________. Me encanta la _____________ y tomar el __________. Cuando hace ______ _________, sobre todo cuando __________, me quedo en casa. Me meto en __________, hago los deberes, juego al __________ con mi hermano mayor o leo una __________. Me encanta pasar tiempo en __________.

<table>
<tr><td colspan="4">

5. Write in English what each person thinks about different types of weather

</td></tr>
<tr><td></td><td>Opinion</td><td>Weather</td><td>Activity</td></tr>
<tr><td>e.g.</td><td>Loves</td><td>Hot</td><td>Beach</td></tr>
<tr><td>a.</td><td></td><td></td><td></td></tr>
<tr><td>b.</td><td></td><td></td><td></td></tr>
<tr><td>c.</td><td></td><td></td><td></td></tr>
<tr><td>d.</td><td></td><td></td><td></td></tr>
<tr><td>e.</td><td></td><td></td><td></td></tr>
<tr><td>f.</td><td></td><td></td><td></td></tr>
<tr><td>g.</td><td></td><td></td><td></td></tr>
</table>

6. Sentence puzzle: listen and rewrite correctly

a. hace me cuando quedo frío en casa

b. hace centro cuando comercial tiempo voy de al mal compras

c. cuando yo mi llueve y padre al jugamos ajedrez

d. mi cuando calor la hace familia a va playa

e. hace damos un en el paseo parque buen tiempo cuando

f. nieva cuando esquí en la hacemos montaña

g. con cuando cielo está hago footing mi el perro despejado

---

7. Listen, spot and correct the grammar and spelling mistakes

Me llamo Patricio. Soy di Barcelona pero vivo en Cádiz, en sur de Espana. Soy alto y delgada. Vivo con mi padres y mi hermano major, Jorge. Me llevo muy bien con mis padre. Pasamos muy tiempo junto. Me gusta mucho jugar al ajedrez con mi padre y a la cartas con mi madre. Paso mucho tiempo con mi hermano tambien. Hago deporte juntos, como footing, natación y pesos. En el fin de semana vamos a marcha juntos.

---

8. Listen to Denisse and answer the questions in English

a. Which country is she from? Where is this country located?

b. Where does she live?

c. What is the weather like?

d. What does she do when the weather is bad? (three details)

e. What does she do when the weather is nice? (three details)

Unit 1. Talking about the weather & free time: VOCABULARY BUILDING

1. Match

Cuando	It's cold
Hace frío	It's hot
Hace calor	The sky is clear
Hace buen tiempo	When
Hace mal tiempo	It's good weather
Está despejado	It's raining
Llueve	It's bad weather

2. Translate into English

a. Cuando hace frío

b. Cuando llueve

c. Está despejado

d. Cuando hace calor

e. Cuando nieva

f. Cuando hace buen tiempo

g. Cuando hay niebla

h. Juego al tenis

i. Hago esquí

j. Cuando hace mal tiempo

3. Complete with the missing word

a. Cuando hace___________ tiempo.
When it's bad weather.

b. Cuando __________ y hace ________.
When it rains and is cold.

c. Cuando ________ sol y hace ________.
When it's sunny and hot.

d. Cuando hay tormenta me __________en casa.
When it's stormy I stay at home

e. Cuando hace___________ tiempo voy al parque.
When it's good weather I go to the park.

f. Cuando __________ hago esquí en la montaña.
When it snows I do skiing on the mountain.

g. Cuando hace _________ mi amigo se queda en casa.
When it's windy my friend stays at home.

h. Me gusta cuando hace ________.
I like it when it's sunny.

4. Anagrams: weather

a. fíor	e. desadopej	i. yah blaine
b. orcal	f. lam tempoi	j. blanudo
c. nieav	g. ceha slo	k. toentarm
d. luelve	h. vtoien	l. benu tpoime

5. Associations: match each weather word below with the clothes/activities in the box

a. Mal tiempo: tormenta, viento, lluvia –

b. Hace buen tiempo: sol y calor –

c. Nieva y hace frío –

Botas de nieve	**Me quedo en casa**	**Hago esquí**	**La playa**
No hago nada	**Pantalón corto**	**Veo la tele**	**Sombrero**
La montaña	**Bufanda**	**Pijama**	**Bañador**

6. Complete

a. Hace buen ________.   *It's good weather.*

b. Me quedo en c_____.   *I stay at home.*

c. Cuando l________.   *When it rains.*

d. Cuando hace __________.   *When it's hot.*

e. ______ a la playa.   *I go to the beach.*

f. Cuando ______ tormenta.   *When it's stormy.*

g. Cuando _______ despejado.   *When the skies are clear.*

h. Cuando está ___________.   *When it's cloudy.*

Unit 1. Talking about the weather & free time: VOCABULARY BUILDING

7. Match

Juego al tenis	I go clubbing
Juego a las cartas	In his bedroom
Hago equitación	She goes fishing
Voy de marcha	I play tennis
Ella va de pesca	I do horseriding
En su dormitorio	I play cards
Me quedo en casa	Swimming
La natación	I stay at home

9. Translate into English

a. La casa de mi amigo.

b. Hago equitación.

c. Está despejado.

d. Hago escalada.

e. Hace footing.

f. Va al polideportivo.

g. Voy a la piscina.

h. Hago deporte.

8. Complete with the missing word

a. Me quedo en ____ dormitorio. *I stay in my bedroom.*

b. Mi amigo ____ a la playa. *My friend goes to the beach.*

c. Voy a _______ de mi _________. *I go to my friend's house.*

d. Voy al _______________. *I go to the sports centre.*

e. ____________ semana siempre hago mis deberes.
During the week I always do my homework.

f. Me gustan los fines de ___________. *I like the weekends.*

g. Juego con mis __________. *I play with my friends.*

h. Mi amiga Vero siempre ____ a casa de ___ amigo.
My friend Vero always goes to her friend's house.

i. Siempre hago _________________. *I always go hiking.*

10. Anagrams: activities

a. foinotg

b. naciatón

c. sendsmerio

d. equtiacinó

e. bonalcesto

f. búftol

g. tracas

h. ajeezdr

i. cernto corcmeial

j. de chamra

k. de pecsa

l. poderte

11. Broken words

a. J_________ a___f________ c_____ mis a_______s.
I play football with my friends.

b. M_ t_____ M______ j______ a l__ c________ .
My aunt Maria plays cards.

c. V____ a c_______ d____ m____ a__________.
I go to my friend's house.

d. J_________ v____ a_ p___________________ .
Joaquín goes to the sports centre.

e. H________ e_______________ c____m__ c___________.
I do horse riding with my horse.

f. Mi a______ se q______ en c_____ y h_____ los d_________.
My friend stays at home and does homework.

12. Complete

a. Hago los __________. *I do homework.*

b. Se __________ en casa.
He/She stays at home.

c. Hace _______________.
He/She does swimming.

d. Voy ______ gimnasio. *I go to the gym.*

e. ______ a la piscina *I go to the pool.*

f. Me quedo en _______. *I stay home.*

g. Hago _______________. *I do climbing.*

h. Hago __________ en la ___________.
I do skiing in the mountain.

i. En mi _______________. *In my bedroom.*

Unit 1. Talking about the weather & free time: READING

Me llamo Pietro. Soy de Italia. Tengo once años. Soy muy deportista, entonces me gusta cuando hace buen tiempo. Cuando hace sol siempre voy al parque con mis amigos y juego al fútbol. También, cuando hace calor siempre voy a la playa con mi perro. Es pequeño y negro, y muy simpático. Yo llevo un bañador, sandalias y un sombrero cuando voy a la playa.
Pietro, 11 años. Venecia, Italia

Me llamo Chloé. Soy de Francia. Tengo catorce años. Cuando hace calor y está despejado voy a la piscina y hago natación. También voy de pesca con mi padre en su barco. Es un poco aburrido pero me gusta de todas formas. Por la noche voy de marcha con mis amigos. Cuando voy a la discoteca por lo general llevo una camiseta y vaqueros. Mi amiga se llama Sofía. Es simpática e inteligente. Si hace mal tiempo y llueve ella siempre se queda en su casa y hace sus deberes.
Chloé, 14 años. Niza, Francia

Me llamo Isabela. Soy de Roma, en Italia. Tengo quince años. Me encanta comprar camisetas y chaquetas. Me encanta cuando hay tormenta porque me quedo en casa con mi hermano mayor y juego a videojuegos o a las cartas con él. Las tormentas son muy bonitas y divertidas. No me gusta cuando hace frío porque no me gusta llevar abrigos ni bufandas. ¡En casa tengo un perro, un gato y un loro que habla italiano!
Isabela, 15 años. Roma, Italia

1. Find the Spanish equivalent in Pietro's text

a. I am from

b. I am 11

c. I like it

d. When

e. It's sunny

f. I go to the park

g. With my dog

h. Small and black

i. A swimsuit

j. The beach

2. Find the Spanish equivalent in Chloe's text

a. When it's hot

b. The sky is clear

c. I do swimming

d. I go fishing

e. A bit boring

f. I go clubbing

g. A t-shirt

h. Is called

i. Stays

j. In her house

3. Complete the following statements about Isabela

a. She is __________ years old

b. She loves buying ______________ and ______________

c. She loves it when it's ____________

d. When it's stormy she plays ____________ or __________ with her ____________ brother

e. Isabela does not like __________ weather

f. Her pet can ______________ Italian

Me llamo Ana Laura. Soy de Brasil. Tengo doce años. Me encanta cantar en mi tiempo libre. Cuando hace frío voy al centro comercial con mis amigas. Llevo un abrigo, una bufanda y unas botas. ¡Me encanta el frío! Mi película favorita es Frozen II. No me gusta cuando hace calor así que me quedo en casa. Nunca voy a la playa. ¡Odio la playa!
Ana Laura, 12 años, Brasil

4. Answer the questions about Ana Laura in Spanish

a. ¿De dónde es?

b. ¿Cuántos años tiene?

c. ¿Qué hace en su tiempo libre?

d. ¿Qué tiempo le encanta?

e. ¿Adónde va cuando hace frío?

f. ¿Qué hace cuando hace calor?

g. ¿Le gusta el calor?

h. ¿Cuál es su película favorita?

5. Find someone who...

a. ...likes to go fishing
b. ...is from France
c. ...loves cold weather
d. ...has three pets at home
e. ...thinks that storms are pretty
f. ...wears jeans to go out
g. ...goes to the beach with an animal
h. ...never goes to the beach
i. ...owns a boat

Unit 1. Talking about the weather & free time: WRITING

1. Split sentences

Me gusta	sol voy a la playa.
No me	abrigo y una bufanda.
Cuando hace	cuando hace frío.
Cuando hace frío llevo un	gusta la lluvia.
Las tormentas son	hago esquí.
Cuando hace mal tiempo	me quedo en casa.
Cuando hace buen	muy bonitas.
Cuando nieva	tiempo voy al parque.

2. Complete with the correct option

a. __________ hace frío llevo una bufanda. ¡No me __________!

b. __________ semana hago los deberes.

c. Cuando ________ mal tiempo me ________ en casa.

d. Cuando ________ niebla no voy a la ___________.

e. Cuando hace __________ voy a la playa.

f. Cuando _______ despejado hago senderismo en el campo.

g. Cuando hace mal tiempo mi amigo Pepe se queda en _______ casa.

calor	hay	quedo	montaña	entre
gusta	hace	cuando	está	su

3. Spot and correct the grammar and spelling mistakes

a. Cuando hace viento voy a la gimnasio con mi amigo.

b. Cuando esta nublado mi amiga Juana juega al tenis.

c. Me encantan la tormentas, son muy bonita.

d. Cuando hace malo tiempo mi amigo me queda en casa.

e. Cuando hace niebla no juego al baloncesto.

f. Los fins de semana voy ala playa con mi perro.

g. Cuando hace sol voy al campo y lleva una camiseta blanco.

h. (yo) Siempre lleva zapatillos de deporte cuando juego al fútbol.

4. Complete the words

a. F__________	*Cold*
b. C__________	*Hot*
c. N__________	*Cloudy*
d. C__________	*When*
e. T__________	*Storms*
f. V__________	*Wind*
g. N__________	*Fog*

5. Guided writing: write 3 short paragraphs in the first person (I) using the details below

Person	Lives	Weather	Activity	With
Elías	Sevilla	Good weather	Go to the park	Friends
Santino	Córdoba	Hot and sunny	Go to the beach	Dog
Julieta	Huelva /welva/	Cold and rainy	Stays at home	Older sister

6. Describe this person using the 3ʳᵈ person (she)

Name: Paula

Lives in: Mérida

Age : 13

Pet: A white dog

Weather: Sunny and good weather

Always: Goes to the countryside and does hiking

Never: Stays at home and does homework

TERM 1 - BRINGING IT ALL TOGETHER – 1

1. Me llamo Jaime y tengo doce años. Mi cumpleaños es el veintitrés de junio. Soy de Madrid pero ahora vivo en Bath, en el suroeste de Inglaterra, con mi familia. En mi familia hay cuatro personas: mis padres, mi hermano Noel y yo. Vivimos en una casa pequeña en las afueras de Bath.

2. Entre semana hago muchas cosas. Cuando hace buen tiempo hago footing en el parque de mi barrio o juego al tenis con mi hermano Noel en el polideportivo. Me llevo bien con él porque es muy deportista y tranquilo. Jugar al tenis es muy divertido, pero bastante agotador *(exhausting)*. También, cuando hace sol y no hace viento a veces voy a la montaña y hago senderismo con mi perro. Mi perro se llama Chug y es muy guapo.

3. Cuando hace mal tiempo me gusta ir al gimnasio y a la piscina. La natación es agotadora pero muy relajante y emocionante porque me encanta el deporte. Cuando llueve o hay tormenta me quedo en casa, en mi dormitorio, y veo la televisión. También me gusta mucho jugar a la Play con mis amigos, ¡me encantan los videojuegos!

4. Mi mejor amigo se llama Samuel. Los lunes después del colegio siempre voy a su casa y juego a las cartas con él *(with him)*. También jugamos al baloncesto en su jardín *(garden)*. Me gusta mucho porque es divertido y su casa es grande. Samuel es muy alto, amable y gracioso. Es un buen amigo porque es muy simpático y siempre me ayuda.

5. En su tiempo libre mi amigo Samuel también hace mucho deporte. Su deporte favorito es la escalada; hace escalada todos los días en el polideportivo. ¡A veces hace escalada en las montañas! También juega al fútbol y al rugby los fines de semana.

6. Sin embargo *(however)*, cuando hace mal tiempo no le gusta hacer deporte. Cuando hace frío se queda en su casa y juega a videojuegos con sus amigos. Cuando hay tormenta juega al ajedrez con su madre o su abuela.

Jaime, 12 años. Bath, Inglaterra

1. Answer the following questions in English

a. Where is Jaime from?

b. Where does Jaime live now?

c. Why does he get on with his brother?

d. What does Jaime do when it's sunny?

e. Where does he go when the weather is bad?

f. When does he stay in his bedroom and watch TV?

g. When does he go to Samuel's house?

h. Why is Samuel a good friend?

i. When/where does Samuel go climbing?

j. What does Samuel do when there are storms?

2. Find the Spanish equivalent in Jaime's text

a. I am from (1)

b. On the outskirts (1)

c. I do many things (2)

d. With my brother (2)

e. ...but quite tiring (2)

f. He is very handsome (2)

g. When it rains (3)

h. I stay (3)

i. I always go (4)

j. In his garden (4)

k. His house (4)

l. Sometimes (5)

m. He doesn't like (6)

3. Complete the translation of paragraphs 5 & 6

In his free time, my friend Samuel also does a lot of __________. His favourite sport is _____________; he goes climbing every _________ at the ___________ ____________. ____________ he goes climbing in the ______________! He also plays football and rugby at _______________.

However, when the weather is ___________, he doesn't like to do sport. When it's ___________, he stays at home and plays __________ with his friends. When it's _____________, he plays _____________ with his mum or his _____________.

TERM 1 - BRINGING IT ALL TOGETHER – 1

Ramón y Liam son amigos y viven en Madrid. Están en el patio *(playground)* y están hablando de lo que hacen en su tiempo libre.	
Ramón	¿Qué haces en tu tiempo libre, Liam?
Liam	Bueno *(well)*, en mi tiempo libre hago muchas cosas. Todos los días juego al fútbol en el parque con mis amigos y mi hermano David. ¿Y tú, Ramón?
Ramón	También me gusta jugar al fútbol, pero no juego todos los días. Cuando hace buen tiempo voy al campo a hacer ciclismo.
Liam	¿Y cuando hace mal tiempo? ¿Qué haces?
Ramón	Pues, cuando hace mal tiempo hago natación después del colegio. Siempre voy al polideportivo y hago natación en la piscina municipal. Es mi lugar *(place)* favorito.
Liam	¡Qué bien! Suena muy divertido.
Ramón	Sí, gracias, es muy divertido. ¿Y tú, Liam? ¿Qué haces cuando hace mal tiempo?
Liam	Cuando llueve juego al fútbol en el polideportivo porque hay una pista cubierta *(covered pitch)*.
Ramón	¿Y qué hace tu hermano David?
Liam	Mi hermano David va a casa de su amigo a jugar a videojuegos en la Play. A mí no me gustan los videojuegos así que me quedo en mi casa.
Ramón	¿No te gustan los videojuegos? Entonces, ¿qué haces tú cuando hay tormenta?
Liam	Cuando hay tormenta me quedo en casa y veo la televisión o hago los deberes. A veces juego al ajedrez o a las cartas con mi padre.
Ramón	¿Y qué haces cuando nieva?
Liam	Cuando nieva siempre me voy a las montañas a jugar en la nieve. ¿No te gusta la nieve?
Ramón	¡No! ¡Qué va! *(no way)*. Odio la nieve. Cuando nieva nunca salgo de mi casa. Prefiero el calor.

4. True (T), False (F) or Not Mentioned (NM)?

a. Liam doesn't do much in his free time.	
b. Liam plays rugby every day.	
c. Ramón has a brother named David.	
d. Ramón cycles when it rains.	
e. Ramón swims after school.	
f. Liam thinks swimming sounds fun.	
g. Liam plays football when it rains.	
h. Liam's brother plays videogames at home.	
i. Liam loves videogames.	
j. Liam stays at home when there it's stormy.	
k. Ramón plays chess when it's stormy.	
l. Liam plays cards with his brother.	
m. Ramón hates the snow.	

5. Complete the statements

a. Liam plays football in the ________________ every day.

b. Ramón goes to the ________________________ to cycle.

c. Ramón does swimming at the ____________ __________________.

d. When it rains, Liam plays football on the ______________ __________ .

e. Liam ______________ __________ videogames.

f. Liam plays __________ with his dad.

g. Liam goes to the ________________ to play in the snow.

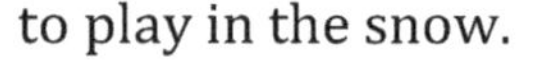

UNIT 2
Talking about my daily routine & activities

In this unit you will learn:
- To say what daily activities you do
- To say at what time you do things
- To say what you 'can', 'must' and 'want' to do

You will revisit:
- Daily routine activities
- Times of day
- Time markers

UNIT 2. Talking about my daily routine & activities

¿A qué hora te levantas entre semana?	*What time do you get up during the week?*
¿Qué haces antes del colegio?	*What do you do before school?*
¿Qué haces cuando vuelves a casa?	*What do you do when you return home?*
¿Qué haces para ayudar en casa?	*What do you do to help at home?*

Entre semana *During the week*	**me acuesto**	*I go to bed*	**a la una**			
	me ducho	*I shower*				
	me lavo los dientes	*I brush my teeth*	**a las**	**dos** **tres** **cuatro** **cinco**	**y cuarto** *quarter past*	
	me levanto	*I get up*				
	me meto en internet	*I go on the internet*				
	me peino	*I brush my hair*				
	me pongo el uniforme	*I put on my uniform*				
Antes del colegio *Before school*	**me visto**	*I get dressed*		**seis** **siete** **ocho** **nueve** **diez** **once**	**y media** *half past* **menos cuarto** *quarter to*	
Por la mañana *In the morning*	**almuerzo**	*I have lunch*				
	ceno	*I have dinner*				
	descanso	*I rest*				
	desayuno cereales	*I have cereal for breakfast*				
	hago mis deberes	*I do my homework*				
	hago pesas	*I lift weights*				
Por la tarde *In the afternoon/ evening*	**juego a videojuegos**	*I play videogames*				
	leo un libro	*I read a book*				
	miro escaparates	*I go window shopping*				
	preparo mi mochila	*I get my bag ready*	**a**	**mediodía** *midday*		
Por la noche *At night*	**salgo de casa**	*I leave the house*				
	tomo el desayuno	*I have breakfast*				
	voy al colegio	*I go to school*		**medianoche** *midnight*		
	veo la tele	*I watch television*				
	vuelvo a casa	*I return home*				

pero *but* **sin embargo** *however* **y** *and*	**hoy** *today* **esta tarde** *this afternoon / evening*	**(no) debo** *I must (not)* **puedo** *I can* **quiero** *I want to* **tengo que** *I have to* **voy a** *I'm going to*	**ayudar en casa** **hacer la cama** **hacer las tareas domésticas** **hacer mis deberes** **ir al colegio** **levantarme temprano**	*help at home* *make the bed* *do the chores* *do my homework* *go to school* *get up early*	
			salir *go out*	**con** *with*	**mi amigo** *my friend (m)* **mi amiga** *my friend (f)*

Author's notes:

1) The verbs ***debo/puedo/quiero*** fall into a special category known as "modal verbs". These are used to say what you "must", "can" or "want to" do. ***"Voy a"*** is used for the near future.

2) The activities have been arranged by reflexives and non-reflexives. They are organised alphabetically for ease of use. This means that "me acuesto" is first on the list... although usually the last activity in the day :)

1. Multiple choice: tick the activity you hear

e.g.	Go to school ✔	Read a book	Get dressed
a.	Brush teeth	Shower	Get dressed
b.	Rest	Have lunch	Have breakfast
c.	Watch TV	Return home	Go to school
d.	Use the internet	Brush teeth	Get up
e.	Prepare my bag	Brush hair	Do homework
f.	Leave the house	Read a book	Get up
g.	Play videogames	Go to bed	Put on uniform

2. Complete the words

a. Ma _ a _ a	*Morning*
b. N _ c _ e	*Night*
c. Ce _ e _ l _ s	*Cereal*
d. M _ chi _ a	*Backpack*
e. Co _ e _ io	*School*
f. A l _ s s _ _ s	*At six*
g. Las die _ y _ ua _ to	*10:15*
h. De _ e _ e _	*Homework*
i. La un _ men _ s cuart _	*12:45*

3. Fill in the blanks

a. Hoy _____________ ayudar en casa.

b. Esta tarde _____________________ ir al colegio.

c. Hoy _____________________ salir con mis amigos.

d. Sin embargo, _____________ hacer la cama.

e. Por la noche _______________ hacer mis deberes.

f. Hoy _________________ ir al colegio.

g. Mañana _____________ levantarme temprano.

4. Spot the intruders

Hola, mi soy José Luis. Entre el semana tengo que ir voy al colegio. Por la mañana, me levanto a las seis y la media y me desayuno a las siete menos cuarto. Debo Salgo de casa a las siete y media. Por la tarde, veo vuelvo a casa a las tres y media y veo la radio tele hasta *(until)* las cinco porque debo ayudo ayudar en casa a las cinco y cuarto. Por la noche, me yo acuesto a las nueve y una media.

5. Faulty translation: listen and identify the errors

e.g.	~~After school~~ *In the afternoon*	**I arrive home**	**at 5:30**
a.	In the morning	I brush my hair	at 7:15
b.	In the afternoon	I read a book	at 8:30
c.	In the afternoon	I have to do my homework	at 4:45
d.	Before school	I get up	at 6:45
e.	In the afternoon	I can go out with my friends	at 5:00
f.	At night	I eat dinner	at 10:30
g.	In the afternoon	I have lunch	at 1:30
h.	At night	I play football	until 11:00

6. What is their daily routine?

	In the morning	In the afternoon	At night	Today
a. **Raquel**				
b. **Raúl**				
c. **Sara**				

7. Narrow listening: gapped translation

a. Hello, my name is Alexis. I am from ___________ but I live in Argentina with my ___________.
I _________ 18 years old. In my ______________, I don't like my ___________ _____________. During the
___________, I have to get up _________ because ___ _________ ___ go to school. ____________ school, I
___________ at ____________ and I put on my uniform at _______________ – I _____________ my uniform!

b. In the afternoon, _____ _____________ __________ at _____________ and _____________ do chores and
_____________. However, ___________ afternoon I am _____________ to do my homework;
_____________ I am going _______________ with my ___________.

8. Listen to Omar and answer the questions in English

PART 1 – a.
1. How does he feel about his daily routine?
2. What does he have to do during the week?
3. When does he get up on school days?
4. When does he get to school?

PART 2 – b.
1. When does he get home from school?
2. What does he do until 18:00?
3. Why does he stop this activity at 18:00?
4. What does he think about helping at home?
5. What does he do at weekends?
6. Why is he able to do this?

Unit 2. Talking about my daily routine & activities: VOCAB BUILDING

1. Match

Tomo el desayuno	I go to bed
Hago mis deberes	I wash my face
Salgo de casa	I read a book
Me levanto	I do my homework
Llego al colegio	I have breakfast
Me acuesto	I rest
Leo un libro	I want
Me lavo la cara	I leave my home
Me visto	I arrive at school
Me ducho	I get dressed
Descanso	I can
Almuerzo	I have lunch
Quiero	I shower
Puedo	I get up

2. Missing letters

a. To _ o el desa _ uno

b. Descan _ o

c. Me la _ o

d. Pue _ o

e. Quie _ o

f. Me le _ anto

g. Sal _ o de ca _ a

h. Le _ un lib _ o

i. L _ ego al cole _ io

j. Me vi _ to

k. Me duc _ o

l. V _ elvo _ cas _

3. Multiple choice: choose the correct translation

		1	2	3
a.	**I get dressed**	Me lavo	Preparo la mochila	Me visto
b.	**I have lunch**	Almuerzo	Desayuno	Ceno
c.	**I have dinner**	Como algo	Ceno	Almuerzo
d.	**I wash**	Me lavo	Me visto	Me despierto
e.	**I want**	Me gusta	Debo	Quiero
f.	**I read a book**	Leo un libro	Leo una revista	Voy al cine
g.	**I watch a film**	Voy de compras	Veo una película	Leo un libro
h.	**I have to**	Tengo que	Me gusta	Debo
i.	**I am going to do**	Me gustaría	Voy a hacer	Voy a ir
j.	**I arrive**	Llego	Voy	Vuelvo

4. Complete with the missing verb

a. _ _ _ _ _ _ _   *I get dressed*

b. _ _ _ _ _ _   *I wash*

c. _ _ _ _ _ _ _ _   *I have lunch*

d. _ _ _ _ _ _ _ _ _ _   *I read a book*

e. _ _ _ _ _ _   *I want*

f. _ _ _ _ _ _ _ _ _   *I am going to do*

g. _ _ _ _   *I must*

h. _ _ _ _ _ _ _ _ _   *I go to bed*

5. Match action and place

Me lavo		mi dormitorio
Almuerzo		el gimnasio
Me visto		el cuarto de baño
Hago footing		el centro comercial
Hago pesas	en	la piscina
Veo una película		el restaurante
Voy de compras		el cine
Hago natación		el parque

Unit 2. Talking about my daily routine & activities: VOCAB BUILDING

6. Arrange the actions below in the correct chronological order

Me despierto	1
Almuerzo	
Ceno	
Me levanto	
Tomo el desayuno	
Salgo del colegio	
Voy al colegio	
Llego al colegio	
Después de cenar, veo la tele	

7. Faulty translation: correct the English

a. Me levanto a las seis y media.	*I get up at 6:15.*
b. Me ducho enseguida.	*I shower much later.*
c. Me visto.	*I have breakfast.*
d. Me pongo el uniforme.	*I take off my uniform.*
e. Llego al colegio.	*I go to school.*
f. Hago footing.	*I have feet.*
g. Almuerzo.	*I have dinner.*
h. Salgo del colegio.	*I go to school.*
i. Descanso.	*I read.*
j. Me acuesto.	*I shower.*

8. Complete with the options below

a. Por lo general me levanto a las seis y ___________.   *I usually get up at 6:30.*

b. Tomo el desayuno a eso de la siete menos __________.   *I have breakfast around 6:40.*

c. Salgo de casa a eso de las siete y ________.   *I leave my home around 7:10.*

d. Cojo el autobús a las siete y ____________.   *I catch the bus at 7:15.*

e. Llego al colegio a las ocho ____________ cuarto.   *I get to school at 7:45.*

f. Las clases empiezan a las ocho menos ____________.   *Lessons start at 7:55.*

g. Almuerzo a __________________.   *I have lunch at midday.*

h. Vuelvo a casa en el autobús de las cuatro y ___________.   *I get back home on the 4:20 bus.*

i. Ceno a ________ de las ocho de la tarde.   *I have dinner around 8:00 p.m.*

j. Me acuesto a _____________.   *I go to bed at midnight.*

veinte	veinte	cuarto	menos	mediodía
media	diez	medianoche	eso	cinco

9. Match

A las ocho y cuarto	A las ocho y diez	A las ocho y media	A las ocho y cinco	A las nueve menos cinco	A las nueve menos diez	A las nueve menos cuarto
8:05	8:10	8:15	8:30	8:50	8:45	8:55

Unit 2. Talking about my daily routine & activities: READING & WRITING

Silvio: Mañana no puedo salir con mi novia porque tengo muchos deberes.

Marina: El próximo fin de semana voy a ir a la fiesta de Amparo.

Gabriel: El próximo domingo quiero ir a la playa.

Elena: Hoy por la tarde voy a ir de compras con mi madre.

Fernando: Hoy no quiero hacer las tareas. Estoy cansadísimo.

Roberto: Todos los días después de levantarme tengo que hacer mi cama.

Susana: Por lo general ayudo a mi madre en casa, pero hoy no puedo porque tengo que repasar para un examen.

Ana Laura: Este fin de semana quiero pasarlo con mi familia. Vamos a ir a un parque de atracciones y luego a un restaurante italiano en el centro.

Pedro: Hoy no puedo hacer ciclismo de montaña con mis amigos porque hace mal tiempo.

Carla: El sábado que viene no voy a hacer nada. Solo voy a descansar.

1. Find someone who…

a. …must revise for an exam.

b. …can't go mountain biking today.

c. …has a lot of homework so can't go out with his girlfriend.

d. …wants to spend the weekend with their family.

e. …is going to go shopping with their mother.

f. …is going to an amusement park with their family.

g. …mentions bad weather.

h. …who has to make their bed after getting up.

i. …wants to go to the beach at the weekend.

j. …is planning to go to a party.

k. …is planning to only rest at the weekend.

2. Sentence puzzle: rewrite the sentences in the correct order

a. no Hoy hacer mis tengo que deberes — *Today I don't have to do my homework*

b. que tengo temprano levantarme no Mañana — *Tomorrow I don't have to get up early*

c. Esta salir puedo tarde mis con amigos — *This evening I can go out with my friends*

d. tengo Mañana que no colegio ir al — *Tomorrow I don't have to go to school*

e. de fin Este voy semana al ir a estadio — *This weekend I am going to go to the stadium*

f. El debo viernes las próximo hacer tareas — *Next Friday I must do the chores*

g. sábado El próximo puedo tarde acostarme — *Next Saturday I can go to bed late*

h. domingo El próximo la puedo a ir de fiesta Paco — *Next Sunday I can go to Paco's party*

Unit 2. Talking about my daily routine & activities: TRANSLATION

1. Gapped translation

a. Mañana no puedo salir con mi novia porque tengo muchos deberes.

Tomorrow I _________ go out with my girlfriend because I have ___ _________ ____ _________________.

b. El próximo fin de semana voy a ir a la fiesta de Amparo.

Next _____________ I am going to go to Amparo's _______________.

c. El próximo domingo quiero ir a la playa.

Next _____________ I _________ to go to the beach.

d. Hoy por la tarde voy a ir de compras con mi madre.

Today in the __________________ I am going to go _______________ with my mother.

e. Hoy no quiero hacer las tareas. Estoy cansadísimo.

_______________ I don't want to do the chores. I am very _____________.

f. Todos los días después de levantarme tengo que hacer mi cama.

Every day, after _________________ _______ I ____________ _______ make my bed.

g. Hoy no puedo hacer ciclismo de montaña porque hace mal tiempo.

Today I _____________ go mountain biking because ______ _______________ ____ _________.

h. El sábado que viene no voy a hacer nada. Solo voy a descansar.

Next _________________ I am not going to do anything. I am only going to _____________.

---

2. Sort the activities below in the appropriate box

a. Hacer ciclismo
b. Hacer los deberes
c. Repasar para un examen
d. Hacer la cama
e. Mirar escaparates
f. Ir de tiendas
g. Comprar ropa
h. Jugar al baloncesto
i. Lavar los platos
j. Ir a clase de español
k. Hacer pesas
l. Cocinar

Los deportes *(Sports)*	Las compras *(Shopping)*

Los estudios *(Studies)*	Las tareas domésticas *(Chores)*

3. Complete with a suitable word

a. Hoy tengo que hacer mis _____________.

b. Mañana quiero ir de _______________.

c. Esta tarde voy a ayudar a mi

_______________.

d. Esta mañana no voy a _______ al colegio.

e. Hoy quiero comer _______________.

f. Tengo que _________________ para el examen.

g. Quiero _____________ en bici.

h. Llego al _________________ a las ocho.

i. Tomo el _______________ en la cocina.

j. No hago _______________.

k. Leo un _____________ en mi dormitorio.

Unit 2. Talking about my daily routine & activities: READING 1

Por lo general, entre semana me levanto muy temprano, a eso de las seis, porque debo coger el autobús para el instituto a las siete menos cuarto. Me ducho enseguida y desayuno unas tostadas con miel y un zumo de naranja.

Después del desayuno me pongo el uniforme y salgo de casa para coger el autobús. Por lo general llego al instituto a eso de las siete y media. Las clases empiezan a las ocho menos cuarto y terminan a las tres y cuarto.

Vuelvo a casa a eso de las cuatro. Luego me ducho enseguida y descanso un poco antes de hacer mis deberes.

Hoy tengo que repasar para mis exámenes, así que no puedo salir con mis amigos. Por lo general, entre las cinco y las siete y media vamos al centro comercial para mirar escaparates y dar un paseo. En cambio, hoy voy a estudiar hasta las once. ¡Será muy aburrido!

Eduardo, 14 años. Cáceres, España

1. Find the Spanish equivalent in Eduardo's text

e.g. During the week   ***Entre semana***

a. Early

b. I must catch

c. I shower right away

d. Some toast with honey

e. After breakfast

f. I arrive at

g. Lessons start

h. I rest a bit

i. I cannot go out

j. To go window shopping

k. I am going to study

2. Complete the sentences

a. During the week I get up ________________.

b. At 6.45 I must ____________________

   to go to school.

c. For breakfast I have ______________

   with ____________.

d. After breakfast I put on my uniform and

   ____________________ to catch the bus.

e. Lessons start at ____________ and

   end at ______________.

f. At around 4:00 I

   ________________________________.

g. Before doing my homework I __________

   ________________________________.

h. Today I must revise for my exams, so I

   ________________________________.

i. Between 5:00 and 7.30 we go to the

   shopping mall to __________________.

3. Find in the text and write below

a. Two reflexive verbs:

b. Two modal verbs:

c. Two names of food:

d. Two verbs associated with school:

e. Two activities you can do in a shopping mall:

f. Two time phrases:

g. Two sequencers:

h. Two times of day:

4. Answer the questions in Spanish in full sentences, as if you were Eduardo

a. ¿A qué hora te levantas, Eduardo?

b. ¿A qué hora coges el autobús?

c. ¿Qué desayunas?

d. ¿Cuándo te pones el uniforme?

e. ¿A qué hora empiezan las clases?

f. ¿Por qué no puedes salir con tus amigos?

g. ¿Qué haces en el centro comercial con tus amigos?

h. ¿Qué vas a hacer esta noche?

Unit 2. Talking about my daily routine & activities: READING 2

Entre semana suelo levantarme bastante temprano. Tengo que levantarme a eso de las seis y media, porque debo coger el autobús para el instituto a las siete y cuarto. Me ducho enseguida y después desayuno unas tostadas con mermelada y un zumo de manzana. Después del desayuno me lavo los dientes y antes de salir de casa me pongo el uniforme. Luego salgo de casa para coger el autobús.

Por lo general, llego al instituto a eso de las siete y media. Las clases empiezan a las ocho menos cuarto y terminan a las tres y cuarto. Antes de salir del instituto, por lo general, paso una hora o dos repasando en la biblioteca. Es bastante difícil y aburrido, pero mi mejor amiga Laura estudia conmigo, así que nos ayudamos cuando no comprendemos algo.

Vuelvo a casa a eso de las cinco. Luego me ducho enseguida y descanso un poco antes de hacer mis deberes. A causa de los exámenes no puedo ni salir con mis amigas ni chatear con ellas en internet. Cuando salgo con ellas me divierto mucho. Nos contamos chistes *[we tell each other jokes]* y hablamos de chicos y de nuestros novios. Compartir *[sharing]* secretos es muy divertido. ¡El cotilleo *[gossiping]* es nuestra pasión! En mi barrio hay muchas tiendas buenas, así que vamos de tiendas, miramos escaparates y compramos ropa. De vez en cuando tomamos algo en una cafetería del barrio. Mi novio se llama Roberto. Es muy guapo y gracioso. Por lo general, salgo con él los sábados y domingos.

Inés, 14 años. Sevilla

<table>
<tr><td>

1. Find the Spanish equivalent in Inés' text

a. During the week

b. I have to get up

c. Right away

d. I brush my teeth

e. I leave the house

f. I get to (secondary) school

g. Lessons start

h. I spend one hour

i. Before leaving (secondary) school

j. We help each other

k. Because of exams

l. Gossiping

m. We go window shopping

</td><td>

2. Translate into English the following extracts from the text above

a. Suelo levantarme bastante temprano.

b. Tengo que levantarme a eso de las seis y media.

c. Antes de salir de casa.

d. Antes de salir del instituto.

e. Nos ayudamos cuando no comprendemos algo.

f. Vuelvo a casa.

g. Descanso un poco antes de hacer mis deberes.

h. No puedo ni salir con mis amigas ni chatear con ellas.

i. Miramos escaparates y compramos ropa.

</td></tr>
</table>

3. Tick the phrases below that you can find in Inés' text

a. Tomamos algo	e. Tengo exámenes	i. Nos divertimos mucho
b. Tiendas buenas	f. Paso una hora	j. Antes de comer
c. Vamos al parque	g. Hacer vela	k. Es muy guapo
d. Conmigo	h. Hacer mis deberes	l. El viernes

Unit 2. Talking about my daily routine & activities: WRITING & TRANSLATION

1. Complete the text with one of the options below

Entre __________ suelo levantarme bastante temprano. Tengo que ______________ a eso de las seis y media porque __________ coger el autobús para el colegio a las siete y cuarto. Me ducho ____________ y después desayuno unas tostadas con __________ y un zumo de manzana. Después del desayuno me lavo los dientes y antes de ___________ de mi casa me pongo el uniforme. Luego salgo de casa __________ coger el autobús.

Por lo general ____________ al colegio a eso de las ocho. Las clases empiezan a las ocho menos cuarto y ______________ a las tres y cuarto. Antes __________ salir del colegio, por lo general, paso una hora o dos repasando en la ________________. Es bastante difícil y __________________, pero mi ______________ amiga Laura estudia conmigo, ______________ nos ayudamos cuando no comprendemos algo.

enseguida	para	debo	levantarme	terminan	mejor	aburrido
salir	semana	llego	de	miel	biblioteca	así que

2. Jigsaw reading: arrange the text in the correct order

Por lo general, me levanto temprano porque	
siete y media. Luego me ducho enseguida	
Hola. Me llamo Sergio y voy a	1
dos tostadas con mermelada y mantequilla. Luego	
debo coger el autobús para el colegio a las	
las tres y vuelvo a casa en autobús.	
hablarte de mi rutina diaria.	
salgo de casa y me voy al colegio. Llego al	
y me pongo el uniforme. Para el desayuno solo como	
colegio a eso de las ocho. Estoy en el colegio hasta	
Entonces descanso un poco y hago mis deberes.	

3. Translate the sentences below into Spanish using *tengo que* + infinitive

a. I have to get up early.

b. I have to do my homework.

c. I have to help my mother.

d. I have to go to school.

e. I have to make my bed.

f. I have to go to bed early.

g. I have to revise for the exams.

h. I have to help at home.

4. Translate the sentences below into Spanish using *(no) puedo* + infinitive

a. I can go out with my friends.

b. I cannot play on my computer.

c. I can ride a bike in the park.

d. I can go to bed late.

e. I cannot have breakfast.

f. I can get up early.

5. Translate the sentences below into Spanish using *quiero / tengo que / puedo* + infinitive

a. I have to work.

b. I don't want to shower.

c. I can't go to the party.

d. I have to tidy my bed room.

e. I want to watch TV.

f. I don't want to go fishing.

g. I can't get up early.

h. I want to eat pizza.

i. I don't want to play.

j. I have to go back home.

k. I don't want to study.

l. I have to do my homework.

6. Guided translation

a. M______________ t____________ q______ i____ d____ c____________ c_____ m____ m____________.
Tomorrow I have to go shopping with my mother.

b. E__________ t____________ n_____ p____________ s____________ c______ m_______ a____________.
This evening I can't go out with my friends.

c. H________ n______ p____________ j__________ a v__________________.
Today I can't play videogames.

d. H________ n______ q____________ h__________ m______ d______________.
Today I don't want to do my homework.

e. E__________ f______ d_____ s______________ q ________ p______ t________ c_____ m____ f__________.
This weekend I want to spend time with my family.

f. E____________ s____________ d________ l______________ t______________.
During the week I must get up early.

g. E__________ m______________ n______ p____________ i____ a______ c______________.
This morning I can't go to school.

h. M______________ n______ q____________ i____ a l_____ f________________.
Tomorrow I don't want to go to the party.

7. Translate the following text into Spanish

Hi. My name is Marisa. I am going to tell you about my daily routine.

During the week I have to get up early because I must catch the bus to go to school at 6:30. I get up at 6:00 and shower right away. I then have breakfast. Generally, I eat two eggs, a slice of toast and a banana. After breakfast I leave home and catch the bus to go to school.

Usually, I arrive at school at 7:30. Lessons start at 7:40 and end at 2:20. My favourite subject is Spanish because the teacher is very good, cool and funny.

I come back home at 3:00. After coming back I rest a bit, I shower and then I have to do my homework or I cannot go out. Around 6:00 I go out with my friends. Usually, we go to the shopping mall near my house. We go window shopping, buy clothes and gossip about the boys in our school.

I must come back home at 8:00 for dinner. After dinner I watch TV and then go to bed.

Marisa, 12 años. Coventry, Inglaterra

8. Write a 150 to 250 word text in which you:

- Briefly describe yourself and your family.
- Say where you live and where your town is located.
- Describe your neighbourhood and what one can do there.
- Say what you normally do on a typical weekday.
- Say what you normally do at the weekend and your plans for next weekend.
- Say what you did yesterday (3 things minimum).
- List three things you want to do today (feel free to make them up).
- List three things you must do today (feel free to make them up).

TERM 1 - BRINGING IT ALL TOGETHER – 2

1. Hola, soy Enrique y soy de Cuenca, una ciudad en España. Tengo doce años. Vivo en un piso bastante grande con mis padres y mi hermana menor. Mi hermana se llama Andrea y tiene ocho años. Vivimos en el centro de la ciudad.

2. En mi tiempo libre hago muchísimas cosas, ya que vivo en una ciudad. Cuando hace buen tiempo siempre voy al polideportivo con mis amigos a jugar al baloncesto. Sin embargo, si hace mal tiempo, vamos de compras en el centro comercial o vemos una película en el cine cerca de mi casa. Cuando hay tormenta o llueve, mi hermana se queda en casa.

3. Mi rutina diaria es muy simple. Entre semana tengo que ir al colegio, así que me levanto a las seis y media. Antes del colegio, me lavo los dientes y me ducho. Me pongo el uniforme y desayuno cereales con mi hermana a las siete y cuarto. A veces veo la tele con mi familia o leo un libro. Después salgo de casa con mi madre a las siete y media. Vuelvo a casa a las cinco y media.

4. Después del colegio hago mis deberes en mi dormitorio a las seis y juego a videojuegos con mi hermana a las seis y media. A las siete puedo salir con mis amigos si hace buen tiempo. Si llueve, leo un libro y preparo mi mochila.

5. Esta tarde hace mal tiempo así que no quiero salir con mis amigos, pero tampoco quiero leer un libro. Tengo que hacer las tareas domésticas y ayudar en casa, y después puedo jugar a videojuegos. Voy a jugar con mi mejor amigo José a las ocho, él también tiene que hacer sus tareas domésticas primero. Esta noche, tengo que acostarme a las diez porque mañana tengo que levantarme temprano.

6. Creo que José también tiene que acostarse temprano. Mañana tiene que ir al aeropuerto porque se va de vacaciones a Francia con su familia. Normalmente José se levanta a las ocho menos cuarto y desayuna cereales a las ocho. Después del colegio José siempre ve la tele y lee un libro antes de cenar.

Enrique, 12 años. Cuenca, España

1. Answer the following questions in English

a. Where is Enrique from?

b. Where does Enrique live?

c. What does Enrique do when it's good weather?

d. What does Enrique do when it's bad weather?

e. What does Enrique do before school?

f. Where does Enrique do his homework?

g. When can Enrique go out with his friends?

h. When will Enrique play videogames with José?

i. What is José doing tomorrow?

j. What does José do before dinner?

2. Find the Spanish equivalent in Enrique's text

a. My sister is called (1)

b. We live (1)

c. Given that (2)

d. However (2)

e. Sometimes (3)

f. After (3)

g. In my bedroom (4)

h. Therefore (5)

i. I want to read (5)

j. My best friend (5)

k. He also (5)

l. To the airport (6)

m. He always watches (6)

3. Complete the translation of paragraph 5

This ______________, the weather is ___________ therefore I don't want ______ _____ _________ with my _____________ but I also don't want to read a _____________. I _____________ to do chores and __________ at home and _____________ I can play __________________. I am going _____________ with my __________ friend José at ______, he also has to do his chores first. _____________, I have to go to bed at _______ because _____________ I have to get up _____________.

	Ana y Estela son amigas. Están hablando de sus rutinas diarias y de lo que hacen en casa.
Ana	¿Qué haces hoy después del colegio, Estela?
Estela	Hoy tengo que hacer mis deberes y ayudar en casa. Luego tengo que hacer las tareas domésticas. ¿Y tú, Ana?
Ana	También tengo que ayudar en casa, pero no quiero. Sin embargo, debo ayudar a mi madre. Después voy a ver la tele. ¿Tú qué vas a hacer después de las tareas?
Estela	Voy a salir con mi hermana al centro comercial para ir de compras y tomar un batido *(milkshake)*. Siempre tomamos un batido en el centro comercial los miércoles.
Ana	¡Qué chulo! Yo tengo que acostarme pronto esta noche porque mañana voy a levantarme temprano.
Estela	¿Por qué vas a levantarte temprano? ¿Qué quieres hacer?
Ana	Antes del colegio me gusta jugar a videojuegos o leer un libro. Luego tengo que salir de casa a las siete y media para ir al colegio. Suelo ir en autobús.
Estela	¡Madre mía! Eso es demasiado pronto para mí. Siempre salgo de casa a las ocho y cuarto. ¿Desayunas?
Ana	Sí, desayuno fruta en el autobús. ¿Y tú?
Estela	No, no desayuno, pero sí tomo un café mientras *(while)* preparo mi mochila.
Ana	¿Y qué haces cuando vuelves a casa?
Estela	Normalmente hago mis deberes a las cinco, me meto en internet a las seis, ceno a las ocho y media y me acuesto a las once. ¿Y tú?
Ana	Cuando vuelvo a casa descanso, leo un libro y me acuesto a las nueve.

4. True (T), False (F) or Not Mentioned (NM)?

Ana and Estela are not friends.	
Estela has to do homework today.	
Ana doesn't have to do homework today.	
Ana is going to a concert.	
Estela is going out with her sister.	
Estela always goes out with her sister on Tuesdays.	
Ana has to go to bed early tonight.	
Ana likes to play videogames before school.	
Ana takes the bus to school at 7:45.	
Estela would not like to wake up early.	
Ana eats fruit at home.	
Estela drinks milkshakes.	
Ana cooks dinner every night.	

5. Complete the statements

a. Ana must help ________________

________________.

b. Estela ____________ has a coffee with her sister on ________________.

c. Ana has to wake up early ________________.

d. ________________ takes the bus to school.

e. ________________ always leaves the house at 8:15.

f. Estela goes online at ____________ .

UNIT 3
Saying what I do at home

In this unit you will learn:
- To say what activities you do as part of your daily routine
- To say what you do in different rooms of the house

You will revisit:
- Time markers
- Activities in the present indicative

Unit 3. Saying what I do at home

¿Qué haces en tu tiempo libre?	*What do you do in your free time?*
¿Qué haces en tu dormitorio?	*What do you do in your bedroom?*
¿Con qué frecuencia (lo haces)?	*How frequently (do you do it)?*

Frequency	Action		Place
A eso de las seis de la mañana *At around 6 a.m.*	**charlo con mi madre**	*I chat with my mum*	**en la cocina** *in the kitchen*
	***chateo por Whatsapp**	*I chat on Whatsapp*	**en el comedor** *in the dining room*
A menudo *Often*	**desayuno**	*I have breakfast*	
	descanso	*I rest*	**en el cuarto de baño** *in the bathroom*
A veces *Sometimes*	**escucho música**	*I listen to music*	
	hago mis deberes	*I do my homework*	**en la habitación de mi hermano** *in my brother's room*
De vez en cuando *From time to time*	**juego a la Play**	*I play on the PlayStation*	
	leo revistas	*I read magazines*	**en el dormitorio de mis padres** *in my parents' bedroom*
Cuando tengo tiempo *When I have time*	**leo tebeos**	*I read comics*	
	me ducho	*I shower*	
Dos veces a la semana *Twice a week*	**me lavo**	*I wash*	**en mi dormitorio** *in my bedroom*
	me lavo los dientes	*I brush my teeth*	
	me meto en internet	*I go on the internet*	**en el garaje** *in the garage*
Nunca *Never*	**me visto**	*I get dressed*	
	monto en bici	*I ride my bike*	**en el jardín** *in the garden*
Por lo general *Usually*	**preparo la comida**	*I prepare food*	
	salgo de casa	*I leave the house*	**en la sala de juegos** *in the games room*
Raramente *Rarely*	**subo fotos a Instagram**	*I upload pics to Instagram*	
	veo la tele	*I watch television*	**en el salón** *in the living room*
Siempre *Always*	**veo películas**	*I watch films/movies*	
	veo series en Netflix	*I watch series on Netflix*	**en la terraza** *on the terrace*
Todos los días *Every day*			

Author's note: there are two verbs in Spanish, **"charlar"** and **"chatear"**, which both mean *to chat*. We use **"charlar"** to refer to a spoken conversation and as a synonym of **"hablar"** *to talk*. **"Chatear"** usually refers to an online, text-based messaging, kind of chat.

1. Mosaic listening: follow the speaker from <u>left</u> to <u>right</u> → and number accordingly

e.g.	**A eso de las siete (1)**	preparo la comida	y juego en el ordenador	en mi dormitorio
a.	Por lo general	**desayuno (1)**	películas	en la sala de juegos
b.	Cuando tengo tiempo	escucho música y	**en la cocina (1)**	en el salón
c.	A menudo	ayudo	con mi madre	**con mis hermanos (1)**
d.	A veces	me meto en internet	hago los deberes	en el jardín
e.	Todos los fines de semana	veo	a mi padre	en la cocina

2. Listen and fill in the gaps

a. ______________ con mi madre a menudo en la cocina.

b. De vez en cuando juego a la Play en la sala de ______________.

c. Dos veces a la semana ______________ en bici.

d. A menudo preparo la comida en la ______________.

e. Siempre hago mis deberes en el ______________.

f. Por lo general me ducho en el ______________ de baño de mis padres.

g. Cuando hace buen tiempo, ______________ revistas en el jardín.

h. Nunca ______________ la tele en ______ salón con mis padres.

3. Faulty translation: what, how often, where? Listen and correct the errors

		What does Dylan do, and how often does he do it?	Where
e.g.	**Often**	**chats with his brother**	*In the ~~kitchen~~ dining room*
a.	Helps father	once a week	in the garage.
b.	Watches TV	every day	in the games room.
c.	Does homework	five times a week	in the living room.
d.	Often	goes on the internet	in his parents' room.
e.	Has lunch	every day	in his bedroom.
f.	Sometimes	prepares food	in the kitchen.
g.	Never	rides his bike	in the garden.

4. Likely or Unlikely? Write L or U for each sentence you hear, explaining why

a.		
b.		
c.		
d.		
e.		
f.		
g.		
h.		

5. Narrow listening: gapped translation

a. __________ __________ I get up at five in the morning. Then, I __________ and have breakfast in the __________. After that I brush my teeth and __________ my __________. Then, I __________ and go to school at ______. Normally, I go by ______. When I __________ __________, I chat on Skype with my family in Australia and go on the internet in my __________.

b. Then, I ______ __ ______ in the garden with my two ______. Sometimes I watch __________ and upload photos to Instagram in my __________ ______. In general, I have dinner at around ______. After dinner I ______ ______ and then shower. Then, I read my favourite ______ and go to bed at ______.

6. Answer the questions about Maya
(EXTENSION: Write down some extra details that you hear)

a. At what time does she usually get up?

b. How does she go to school?

c. What is her favourite school subject?

d. What two sports does she usually do after school?

e. Where does she usually chat with her mother?

f. In which room does she do her homework?

g. What does she never do during dinner?

h. What three things does she always do after dinner?

i. What two things does she do before going to bed?

j. At what time does she go to bed?

Unit 3. Saying what I do at home: VOCABULARY BUILDING

1. Match

Leo tebeos	I chat with
Veo películas	I wash myself
Preparo la comida	I watch movies
Leo revistas	I prepare food
Me visto	I read magazines
Charlo con	I shower
Me lavo	I get dressed
Me ducho	I read comics

2. Complete with the missing words

a. Me ___________ *I get dressed*

b. Leo ___________ *I read comics*

c. Leo ___________ *I read magazines*

d. Me lavo los _________ *I wash my teeth*

e. Me ___________ *I shower*

f. ___________ la comida *I prepare food*

g. Me _______ en internet *I go on the Net*

h. Escucho ___________ *I listen to music*

i. _________ fotos a Instagram
I upload photos onto Instagram

3. Translate into English

a. Por lo general me ducho a eso de las siete de la mañana.

b. Nunca preparo la comida.

c. Normalmente leo revistas en el salón.

d. A eso de las siete de la mañana desayuno en el comedor.

e. De vez en cuando charlo con mi madre en la cocina.

f. A veces desayuno en la cocina.

g. A veces juego a la Play con mi hermano en la sala de juegos.

h. Siempre salgo de casa a las ocho de la mañana.

4. Complete the words

a. Me d______ *I shower* g. Me v______ *I get dressed*

b. L________ *I read* h. J________ *I play*

c. C________ *I chat* i. S________ *I leave*

d. P________ *I prepare* j. H________ *I do*

e. S________ *I upload* k. M________ *I ride*

f. Me l______ *I wash* l. V________ *I watch*

5. Classify the words/phrases below in the table below

a. **A eso de las seis**	i. Me lavo los dientes
b. Siempre	j. A veces
c. Nunca	k. Todos los días
d. Mi dormitorio	l. Escucho música
e. Veo la tele	m. Leo tebeos
f. Juego a la Play	n. Monto en bici
g. Me lavo	o. Dos veces a la semana
h. Subo fotos a Instagram	p. Chateo por Whatsapp

Time phrases	Rooms in the house	Things you do in the bathroom	Free-time activities
a.			

6. In which room would you do the following activities?

Juego a la Play	En mi dormitorio
Veo la tele	
Me ducho	
Hago mis deberes	
Me lavo los dientes	
Descanso	
Preparo la comida	

Unit 3. Saying what I do at home: VOCABULARY BUILDING

7. Complete the table

English	Español
I get dressed	
I shower	
	Hago mis deberes
I upload photos	
	Salgo de casa
	Charlo con mi hermano
I rest	

8. Multiple choice quiz

	A	B	C
Nunca	Always	Never	Sometimes
A veces	Sometimes	Always	Never
Dormitorio	Bedroom	Lounge	Garden
Me lavo	I shave	I wash	I go out
Me ducho	I shower	I go out	I rest
Descanso	I go out	I watch	I rest
Jardín	Garden	Garage	Kitchen
Cocina	Bedroom	Lounge	Kitchen
Juego	I rest	I play	I prepare
Leo	I watch	I read	I play
Salgo	I go out	I rest	I read
Siempre	Always	Never	Every day

9. Anagrams: unscramble & translate

e.g. Ncanu - *nunca* - *never*

a. cinoCa

b. goSal

c. oeL

d. emSipre

e. uboS tofos

f. oval eM

10. Broken words

a. La co_______________ *Kitchen*

b. Nun_______________ *Never*

c. A vec_______________ *Sometimes*

d. Sie_______________ *Always*

e. A men_______________ *Often*

f. Los te_______________ *Comics*

g. Mi dor_______________ *My bedroom*

h. Sa_______________ *I go out*

i. Ch_______________ *I chat*

11. Complete with the missing word

a. A e_____ d___ l____ s________ y media, m__ l________
l____ d____________. *At around 7:30, I brush my teeth.*

b. A e_____ d_____ l_____ o______ y cuarto, d__________.
At around a quarter past eight I have breakfast.

c. A v________ p____________ l___ c____________.
Sometimes I prepare the food.

d. S________ v______ l___ t______ mientras
d___________. *I always watch TV while I have breakfast.*

e. P___ l___ g__________, s_______ d__ c_____ a l____
o______ y media. *In general, I leave the house at 8:30.*

f. L____ t________ r____________. *I rarely read comics.*

g. A e___ d___ l____ c_______ h_______ m______
d____________. *At around 5:00 I do my homework.*

12. Gap-fill from memory

a. A veces ________ tebeos.

b. Siempre me _________ los dientes
después de comer.

c. ______ series en Netflix todos los días.

d. Nunca _______ revistas de moda.

e. Nunca _________ mis deberes.

f. ________ fotos a Instagram a menudo.

g. Los fines de semana _________ en bici.

h. _________ de casa a eso de las ocho.

i. _______________ música a menudo.

Unit 3. Saying what I do at home: READING

Me llamo Fabián. Soy de Gibraltar. Tengo un perro en casa. Siempre me levanto temprano, a las cinco y cuarto. Luego, voy al gimnasio y hago deporte. Me ducho cuando vuelvo a casa. Mi hermano Joe es muy trabajador e inteligente. Se levanta a las siete. Joe nunca juega al fútbol, y nunca hace deporte. Por eso está tan gordo. Por la tarde, leo tebeos en mi dormitorio o escucho música. Entre semana cuando vuelvo a casa hago mis deberes en el salón con mi madre. Me gusta porque ella es muy inteligente y siempre me ayuda. Finalmente me acuesto a las nueve en mi dormitorio.

Fabián, 12 años. Gibraltar

Me llamo Eduardo y vivo en Dinamarca. Todos los días me levanto a las cinco de la mañana. Luego me ducho y tomo el desayuno en el jardín. Salgo de casa a las siete y voy al colegio a caballo. Cuando vuelvo a casa chateo por Whatsapp con mi familia en Inglaterra y me meto en internet, en mi dormitorio. Luego monto en bici en el jardín con mis dos perros. A veces veo dibujos animados y subo fotos a Instagram en el dormitorio de mi hermano. Mi hermano Samuel sube videos a TikTok de sus bailes nuevos. Me gusta mucho mi hermano porque es muy divertido y activo. ¡Baila muy bien! Siempre charlo y juego a las cartas con él. Samuel es el mejor amigo del mundo mundial *(in the whole wide world)*.

Eduardo, 13 años. Copenhague, Dinamarca

Me llamo Valentino. Soy italiano. Siempre me despierto temprano, a eso de las seis. Luego me ducho y me lavo los dientes en el cuarto de baño. No desayuno nada por la mañana pero mi hermana Valeria desayuna cereales en el comedor. Voy al colegio a pie. Vuelvo a casa a eso de las tres y media y luego me relajo un poco. Por lo general veo la tele en el salón. Luego navego por internet, veo una serie en Netflix o veo videos de TikTok en mi dormitorio. Luego, a las ocho, preparo la comida con mi madre en la cocina. Me encanta preparar ensaladas porque son deliciosas. Me acuesto tarde, a las diez.

Valentino, 16 años. Milán, Italia

1. Answer the following questions about Fabián

a. Where is he from?

b. What animal does he have?

c. What does he do after he wakes up?

d. Why is Joe fat?

e. Where does he do his homework on weekdays?

f. Who helps him with his homework?

g. Where does he go to bed?

2. Find the Spanish equivalent in Eduardo's text

a. I get up.

b. Then I shower.

c. I go to school.

d. By horse.

e. I go on the internet.

f. (He) uploads videos to TikTok.

g. New dances.

h. I always chat.

3. Find someone who...

a. ...wakes up earliest.

b. ...gets help with their homework from a family member.

c. ...likes to watch videos of people dancing.

d. ...has nothing for breakfast.

e. ...has a really clever brother.

f. ...likes to prepare healthy food.

g. ...has a family member that is their best friend.

h. ...goes to school in the most exciting way.

4. Find the Spanish equivalent in Valentino's text

a. I am Italian.

b. I wake up early.

c. I have nothing for breakfast.

d. Valeria eats cereal for breakfast.

e. In the dining room.

f. In the living room.

g. I watch TikTok videos.

Unit 3. Saying what I do at home: WRITING

1. Split sentences

Charlo	comida.
Descanso en	temprano.
Preparo la	con mi madre.
Subo fotos	mi dormitorio.
Hago mis	los dientes.
Me levanto muy	a Instagram.
Juego en mi	ordenador.
Me lavo	deberes.

2. Complete with the correct option

a. Me levanto a las seis de la _______________.

b. Juego al fútbol en el _______________.

c. Veo la tele en el _______________.

d. Escucho música en mi _______________.

e. Preparo la _____________ con mi padre.

f. Me _____________ los dientes.

g. _____________ dibujos animados.

h. _____________ al colegio a caballo.

salón	mañana	lavo	dormitorio
voy	comida	veo	jardín

3. Spot and correct the grammar and spelling mistakes (including missing words)

a. Me ducha en el cuarto de bano.

b. Desayuno en el coccina.

c. En mi dormitoria.

d. Juego en la ordenator.

e. Salga casa a ocho.

f. Hago mi deberes.

g. Veo serias en Netflix.

h. Voy a la colegio a cabballo.

i. El dormitorio mi hermano.

4. Complete the words

a. Des___________ — *I have breakfast*

b. La co___________ — *The kitchen*

c. Mi d___________ — *My bedroom*

d. El g_________ — *The garage*

e. S________ de c_______ — *I leave the house*

f. En el s_________ — *In the living room*

g. En el c___________ — *In the dining room*

h. En el c___________d____ b_______
In the bathroom

i. V______p____________ e___ e___
d____________ d___ m___ h____________
I watch films in my brother's bedroom

5. Guided writing: write 3 short paragraphs in the first person (I) using the details below

Person	Gets up	Showers	Has breakfast	Goes to school	Evening activity 1	Evening activity 2
Gonzalo	6.15	In bathroom	Kitchen	With brother	Watch TV in living room	Prepare food in the kitchen
Mauricio	7.30	In shower	Dining room	With mother	Read book in bedroom	Chat to friend on Whatsapp
Isidora	6.45	In bathroom	Living room	With Uncle	Listen to music in garden	Upload photos to Instagram

TERM 1 - BRINGING IT ALL TOGETHER – 3

1. Buenos días. Soy Pedro y tengo dieciséis años. Soy de Buenos Aires, la capital de Argentina. Vivo en una casa pequeña en las afueras de la ciudad. En mi familia somos seis: mis padres, mi hermano mayor, mi hermana menor y mi abuela. Me llevo bien con mi hermano mayor porque es muy simpático y me llevo bien con mi hermana porque es muy amable y graciosa.

2. En mi tiempo libre juego al fútbol en el parque con mis amigos o a veces jugamos en el polideportivo. Cuando hace mal tiempo no puedo jugar al fútbol, así que juego a videojuegos en casa con mis hermanos. Cuando hace calor me gusta ir a la playa con mi familia. Sin embargo, cuando llueve, me gusta jugar al ajedrez con mi abuela.

3. Antes del colegio tengo que levantarme pronto porque tengo que ayudar en casa. Me levanto a las seis y me ducho a las seis y cuarto. A las seis y media desayuno cereales y una taza de chocolate caliente y empiezo *(I begin)* a hacer las tareas domésticas. Salgo de casa a las ocho para llegar al colegio. Después del colegio puedo salir con mis amigos.

4. Los fines de semana desayuno fruta en la terraza con mi madre a las nueve y leo tebeos en el salón. Después juego a la Play en mi dormitorio o a veces veo series en Netflix. Todos los sábados preparo la comida en la cocina a las doce y media porque me gusta cocinar *(to cook)*. ¡Mi hermano nunca me ayuda!

5. Los domingos siempre monto en bici con mis hermanos y mi padre y vamos a las montañas. Después tomamos un café en una cafetería en mi barrio y hablamos. Cuando llegamos a casa vemos una película en el salón.

6. Hoy no puedo salir en bici con mi familia porque voy a casa de mi amigo para celebrar su cumpleaños. Vamos a ir al centro comercial a las doce y cuarto y luego vamos a comer en un restaurante. Mi amigo nunca come en restaurantes porque prefiere comer en casa, pero hoy sí va a venir a comer con nosotros.

Pedro, 16 años. Buenos Aires, Argentina

1. Answer the following questions in English

a. Who does Pedro live with?

b. Who does Pedro get on with and why?

c. What does Pedro do in his free time?

d. What does Pedro do when the weather is bad?

e. Why does Pedro have to get up early?

f. When does Pedro leave for school?

g. Where does Pedro eat breakfast at weekends?

h. What does Pedro do every Saturday?

i. What is the last thing Pedro does on Sundays?

j. Why is Pedro going to his friend's house?

2. Find the Spanish equivalent in Pedro's text

a. My younger sister (1)

b. Because she is (1)

c. In the sports centre (2)

d. When it rains (2)

e. I have to (3)

f. I shower (3)

g. At weekends (4)

h. Every Saturday (4)

i. Never helps me (4)

j. We go (5)

k. In my neighbourhood (5)

l. Today (6)

m. He never eats (6)

3. Complete the translation of paragraph 4

At ________________, I eat ____________ for breakfast

on the ________________ with my mum at __________

and I _____________ _____________ in the living room.

________________, I play on the PlayStation in my

________________ or, at times, I watch _____________

on Netflix. ____________ Saturday, I ________________

food in the ________________ at __________

because I like to cook. My ________________ never

________________ me!

TERM 1 - BRINGING IT ALL TOGETHER – 3

Laura y Álvaro están en la misma clase. Tienen que hablar de lo que hacen en su tiempo libre y sus rutinas diarias.	
Álvaro	Bueno, Laura. Eh... ¿Qué haces cuando tienes tiempo libre?
Laura	Pues, supongo que *(I suppose that)* hago varias cosas. Cuando tengo tiempo veo series en Netflix en el salón con mi hermana. ¿Y tú?
Álvaro	Yo también veo series. Me gusta *Bob Esponja*. Sin embargo, primero hago mis deberes y entonces *(then)* puedo ver la tele en mi dormitorio.
Laura	¿Y qué haces los fines de semana?
Álvaro	Todos los sábados leo tebeos por la mañana y escucho música en mi dormitorio. Después ceno con mi familia en el comedor. ¿Y tú?
Laura	¡Yo también! Me encantan los tebeos. Después, a las once, monto en bici y luego descanso en el salón.
Álvaro	¡Qué guay! Yo también monto en bici pero, por lo general, nunca cuando hace mal tiempo. Cuando llueve me quedo en casa y juego a la Play en mi dormitorio con mi primo.
Laura	¿Cómo se llama tu primo? ¿A él le gustan los tebeos también?
Álvaro	Se llama Jorge. Él prefiere las revistas de deporte. Jorge lee revistas todos los días.
Laura	¿Y dónde lee revistas? ¿En su dormitorio?
Álvaro	No, él lee revistas en la cocina mientras su madre prepara la cena.
Laura	¡Qué mono! *(How cute!)*. Hoy tengo que comprar un tebeo nuevo. ¿Quieres acompañarme a la librería a comprarlo?
Álvaro	¿En serio? Bueno... sí. Tengo que pedirle permiso *(ask for permission)* a mi madre.
	Álvaro llama a su madre para pedir permiso.
Álvaro	Laura, sí puedo ir contigo a la tienda. ¡Qué bien!

4. True (T), False (F) or Not Mentioned (NM)?

Laura watches films with her sister.	
Álvaro does his homework before watching TV.	
Álvaro watches Netflix in the living room.	
Álvaro reads comics every Sunday morning.	
Álvaro eats dinner with his family in the dining room.	
Laura loves comics as well.	
Laura reads books at 11:00.	
Laura's cousin is called Tomás.	
Álvaro has a cousin.	
Álvaro reads comics while his mum makes dinner.	
Laura wants to buy two new comics.	
Álvaro needs to ask for permission.	
Álvaro is allowed to go with Laura to the book shop.	

5. Complete the statements

a. Laura relaxes in the _______________ ______________ after riding her bike.

b. Álvaro ________________ rides his bike when it's raining.

c. ______________ cousin reads sports magazines every day.

d. Alvaro's cousin reads sports magazines in the ________________.

e. ________________ invited ___________________ to the bookshop.

TERM 1 – MIDPOINT – RETRIEVAL PRACTICE

1. Answer the following questions in Spanish

¿Qué haces en tu tiempo libre?	
¿Qué hace tu amigo en su tiempo libre?	
¿Adónde vas los fines de semana?	
¿A qué hora te levantas entre semana?	
¿Qué haces antes/después del colegio?	
¿Qué haces para ayudar en casa?	
¿Qué haces en tu dormitorio?	
¿Con qué frecuencia (lo haces)?	

2. Write a paragraph in the first person singular (I) using the details below

a. Your name is Mike. You are 14 and are from England.

b. When the weather is good you like to play football.

c. When it's stormy you stay at home and do your homework.

d. Your friend Miguel goes to the beach when it's hot.

e. During the week you get up at 7:00, you shower and you brush your teeth.

f. You have cereal for breakfast at 8:00.

g. Today you cannot go to the cinema with your friend…

h. …because you have to do the chores and help at home.

i. This afternoon/evening you want to watch television.

j. When you have time you read magazines in your bedroom.

k. Every day you watch films in the living room.

UNIT 4
Talking about clothes & the weather

In this unit you will learn:

- To say what clothes you wear in various circumstances and places
- To say what you wear when it it cold/hot
- A wide range of words for clothing items and accessories
- A range of words for places in town

You will revisit:
- Time markers
- Frequency markers
- Colours
- Adjectival agreement

UNIT 4. Talking about the clothes I wear

¿Qué ropa llevas en casa?	What clothes do you wear at home?
¿Qué ropa llevas cuando hace frío/calor?	What do you wear when it's cold/hot?
¿Qué ropa llevas cuando sales con tus amigos?	What do you wear when you go out with your friends?
Describe tu uniforme escolar	Describe your school uniform

Cuando *When*		llevo *I wear*	un abrigo — a coat	amarillo — yellow

Cuando *When*

hace calor *it's hot*

hace frío *it's cold*

juego al fútbol *I play football*

salgo con mi novio/novia *I go out with my boyfriend/girlfriend*

salgo con mis amigos *I go out with my friends*

salgo con mis padres *I go out with my parents*

llevo *I wear*

un abrigo	a coat
un bañador	a swimsuit
un chándal	a tracksuit
un cinturón	a belt
un collar	a necklace
un jersey	a jumper
un reloj	a watch
un sombrero	a hat
un traje	a suit
un uniforme	a uniform
un vestido	a dress

una bufanda	a scarf
una camisa	a shirt
una camiseta	a t-shirt
una chaqueta	a jacket
una chaqueta deportiva	a sports jacket
una corbata	a tie
una falda	a skirt
una gorra	a cap

amarillo	yellow
blanco	white
morado	purple
negro	black
rojo	red

*azul	blue
gris	grey
marrón	brown
naranja	orange
rosa	pink
verde	green

amarilla	yellow
blanca	white
morada	purple
negra	black
roja	red

lleva *he/she wears*

En casa	At home
En la discoteca	At the nightclub
En la playa	At the beach
En el colegio	At school
En el gimnasio	At the gym
Nunca	Never
Por lo general	Usually
Siempre	Always

botas	boots
calcetines	socks
chanclas	flip-flops
pantalones	trousers
pantalones cortos	shorts
pantuflas	slippers
pendientes	earrings
sandalias	sandals
vaqueros	jeans
zapatos	shoes
zapatos de tacón	high-heeled shoes
zapatillas (de deporte)	trainers

amarillos/as	yellow
azules	blue
blancos/as	white
dorados/as	golden
grises	grey
marrones	brown
morados/as	purple
naranjas	orange
negros/as	black
rojos/as	red
verdes	green

***Author's note:** The adjectives in this section (azul/gris/marrón/naranja/verde) stay the same regardless of the gender of the noun: e.g. Un traje verd<u>e</u> / Una falda verd<u>e</u>.

1. Listen and fill in the gaps

a. En casa __________ un chándal.

b. En la playa llevo un ____________.

c. En el gimnasio llevo una __________.

d. Nunca llevo __________.

e. Cuando hace frío llevo una __________.

f. En la discoteca llevo una __________.

g. Mi hermano siempre lleva zapatillas de ____________.

h. Mi novia __________ ropa elegante.

2. Mystery WORDS: guess the words, then listen and see how many you guessed right

a. Una b _ _ _ _ _ _

b. Una _ _ _ _ s _

c. Una _ _ _ d _

d. Un _ b _ _ _ _

e. Un _ _ _ _ _ y

f. Un _ _ _ j _

g. Un _ _ ñ _ _ _ _

3. Listening for detail: tick the clothes Dylan wears

Lo que llevo cuando hace frío:	Una bufanda
	Un jersey
	Un abrigo
	Botas
	Un bañador
Lo que llevo cuando salgo con mi novia:	Una camisa
	Un cinturón
	Pantalones
	Sandalias
	Zapatos elegantes
Lo que llevo cuando salgo con mis amigos:	Una chaqueta deportiva
	Una falda
	Un sombrero
	Una gorra
	Zapatillas de deporte
Lo que llevo cuando me quedo en casa:	Un jersey
	Una camiseta
	Un sombrero
	Unos vaqueros
	Pantuflas

4. Spot the differences and correct your text

Me llamo Alejandra. Tengo diecisiete años. Soy bastante deportista y tengo ropa de muchos colores y tipos diferentes.

Prefiero la ropa de mala calidad pero no muy barata. Por lo general, en casa llevo un chándal o una camiseta, pantalones y zapatillas de deporte o botas.

Cuando voy al gimnasio, llevo un abrigo y zapatillas de deporte blancas. Tengo seis chándales diferentes. Son de marca porque las marcas me encantan.

Cuando salgo con mis amigos me pongo una chaqueta negra, vaqueros y zapatillas de deporte.

Cuando salgo con mi hermano me pongo vestidos elegantes y aburridos y mis patos favoritos. También son feos y cómodos.

5. Narrow listening: gapped translation

a. Usually, in the winter at home I wear a _________, _________ trousers and _________. In the summer, instead, I wear a _________, _________ and _________. I have a lot of _________ _________ but also some _________ clothes. I like _________ clothes but they are very expensive so, I don't have _________.

b. When I go out with my friends or with my _________ in the _________, I wear a _________ t-shirt, _________, trainers and _________. However, in the _________, I wear a coat, Levi's jeans and _________.

6. Listen to Diego's description of himself and his family and answer the questions in English

a. Where is he from?

b. How many siblings has he got?

c. What are his favourite foods? (3 details)

d. Why?

e. What does he usually wear? (3 details)

f. What are his favourite shoes? (2 details)

g. Who wears jeans and trainers all the time?

h. Who wears elegant clothes?

7. What are they wearing?

	Four details each
a. Paola	
b. Eva	
c. Silvio	

8. Fill in the grid: what did they buy?

	Item bought	**What for**	**Colour**	**Opinion**	**Price**
a. Vero			navy blue		
b. Ana	trainers				
c. Pepe			dark grey		
d. Maite					87 euros

Unit 4. Talking about the clothes I wear: VOCABULARY BUILDING

1. Match

Unos pendientes	A baseball cap
Una camiseta	Some shoes
Un vestido	Some trousers
Unos zapatos	A suit
Unos pantalones	A t-shirt
Un traje	Some earrings
Una gorra	A dress

2. Translate into English

a. Llevo una camiseta negra.

b. Llevo un traje gris.

c. No llevo zapatillas de deporte.

d. Llevo una gorra azul.

e. No llevo un reloj.

f. Nunca llevo pendientes.

g. Llevo un chándal.

h. Nunca llevo trajes.

i. Siempre llevo sandalias.

j. Nunca llevo sombreros.

k. Mi hermano siempre lleva vaqueros.

3. Complete with the missing word

a. En casa __________ una __________________.
At home I wear a t-shirt.

b. En el colegio llevo un ________________ _________.
At school I wear a black uniform.

c. En el gimnasio ___________ un chándal _________.
At the gym I wear a pink tracksuit.

d. En la ___________ llevo un _______________.
At the beach I wear a swimsuit.

e. _____ _____ discoteca llevo un _______________ negro.
In the club I wear a black dress.

f. Raramente __________ zapatillas _____ ____________.
I rarely wear trainers.

g. Nunca ____________ trajes. *I never wear suits.*

4. Anagrams clothes and accessories

a. Una rrago

b. Un lojre

c. Un jetra

d. Unos dntieespen

e. Unos topasza

f. Una setacami

g. Unos roquesva

h. Una casami

i. Unas puntaflas

j. Un stidove

k. Un brerosom

l. Un llarco

5. Associations: match each body part below with the words in the box

a. La cabeza *(head)* – e.g. **gorra**

b. Los pies *(feet)* –

c. Las piernas *(legs)* -

d. El cuello *(neck)* –

e. El torso *(upper body)* –

f. Las orejas *(ears)* –

g. La muñeca *(wrist)* –

bufanda	corbata	zapatos	botas
chaqueta	camisa	calcetines	**gorra**
pendientes	pantalones	falda	sombrero
zapatillas	reloj	collar	camiseta

6. Complete

a. Llevo bo___________.   *I wear boots.*

b. En c_____________.   *At home.*

c. Tengo un r_________.   *I have a watch.*

d. Llevo una c_________ roja.   *I wear a red tie.*

e. Llevo un t_________ azul .   *I wear a blue suit.*

f. Mi hermano lleva una c___________blanca.
My brother wears a white shirt.

g. Ella siempre lleva vestidos n___________s.
She always wears black dresses.

Unit 4. Talking about the clothes I wear: READING

Me llamo Conchita. Soy de España. Tengo quince años. Soy muy deportista, entonces tengo mucha ropa de colores y estilos diferentes. Prefiero la ropa de buena calidad pero no muy cara. Por lo general, en casa llevo un chándal. Tengo cuatro o cinco chándales diferentes. Cuando salgo con mi novio llevo pendientes, un collar, un vestido rojo o negro y zapatos de tacón.

Conchita, 15 años. Madrid, España

Me llamo Renaud. Soy de Francia. Tengo trece años. Me encanta comprar ropa, sobre todo zapatos. Tengo muchos zapatos de marca. Me encanta la ropa italiana. Cuando hace frío, por lo general llevo un abrigo y pantalones negros o morados. A veces llevo una chaqueta deportiva. Cuando hace calor llevo camisetas cómodas, vaqueros y sandalias o zapatillas de deporte. Tengo un caballo que se llama Jacques Chirac.

Renaud, 13 años. Lila, Francia

Me llamo Gerda. Soy de Alemania. Tengo doce años. Siempre compro la ropa de Zara. Me gusta la ropa bonita pero no demasiado cara. La ropa de marca no me gusta. Siempre llevo ropa deportiva como chándales, camisetas y zapatillas de deporte. Cuando hace frío llevo una chaqueta deportiva y un chándal. Cuando hace calor llevo una camiseta y pantalones cortos.

Gerda, 12 años. Dorsten, Alemania

Me llamo Miguel. Soy de Argentina. Tengo catorce años. Cuando voy al colegio llevo una camisa, pantalones y zapatos. En casa por lo general llevo una camiseta y vaqueros. Tengo muchas camisetas y vaqueros en casa. Cuando voy al gimnasio llevo una camiseta blanca, pantalones cortos y zapatillas de deporte. Cuando voy al centro comercial con mis amigos llevo una chaqueta, una camisa, unos pantalones negros o grises, y zapatos negros.

Miguel, 14 años. Rosario, Argentina

1. Find the Spanish equivalent in Conchita's text

a. I am from

b. Sporty

c. Many clothes

d. Good quality clothes

e. A tracksuit

f. When I go out

g. With my boyfriend

h. Earrings

i. A red or black dress

j. High-heeled shoes

2. Find the Spanish equivalent in Miguel's text

a. When I go

b. I wear a shirt

c. A t-shirt and jeans

d. At home

e. In general

f. A white t-shirt

g. Trainers

h. With my friends

i. A jacket

j. Black trousers

3. Complete the following statements about Renaud

a. He is _________ years old.

b. He loves buying _____________.

c. He has many branded _____________.

d. When it's cold he wears a coat and a pair of ___________ or _________ _______________.

e. Sometimes he wears a _____________ _________________.

4. Answer the questions about Gerda (in Spanish)

a. ¿Cómo se llama?

b. ¿De dónde es?

c. ¿Cuántos años tiene?

d. ¿Qué le gusta?

e. ¿Dónde compra su ropa?

f. ¿Qué ropa lleva cuando hace frío?

g. ¿Qué ropa lleva cuando hace calor?

5. Find someone who...

a. ...loves branded clothes.

b. ...is from Germany.

c. ...wears a white t-shirt in the gym.

d. ...wears earrings when she goes out with her boyfriend.

e. ...has four or five different tracksuits.

f. ...has a lot of t-shirts and jeans at home.

g. ...is very sporty.

h. ...wears grey or black trousers at the shopping mall.

Unit 4. Talking about the clothes I wear: WRITING

1. Split sentences

En	camiseta y pantalones cortos.
Cuando hace	casa llevo un chándal.
En el gimnasio llevo una	llevo zapatos de tacón.
Cuando hace calor llevo	frío llevo una bufanda.
Nunca llevo vaqueros	una camiseta azul.
Cuando voy a la discoteca	Levi's.
Llevo pantalones	negra.
Llevo una camisa	negros.

2. Complete with the correct option

a. ___________ salgo con mi ____________ llevo ropa bonita pero cómoda.

b. En el colegio __________ un uniforme azul.

c. En el gimnasio llevo ____________ de deporte.

d. En la playa llevo un ______________.

e. Cuando __________ calor llevo una ______________ blanca.

f. En casa llevo ____ chándal.

g. Cuando hace mucho frío llevo un _____________.

h. ___________ llevo botas.

abrigo	novio	un	llevo	cuando
zapatillas	nunca	hace	bañador	camiseta

3. Spot and correct the grammar and spelling mistakes (including missing words)

a. Cuando salgo mis padres llevo un vestido elegante.

b. En casa llevo una chándal.

c. Tengo mucho zapatos.

d. Mi hermano siempre llevo vaqueros.

e. En el colegio un uniforme gris.

f. Me da igual las ropas de marca.

g. Cuando voy al centro commercial, por lo general llevo un chaqueta deportiva.

h. Siempre llevo zapatillas deporte.

4. Complete the words

a. F____________ *Skirt*

b. T____________ *Suit*

c. P____________ *Earrings*

d. P____________ *Trousers*

e. Z____________ *Shoes*

f. B____________ *Scarf*

g. C____________ *Tracksuit*

6. Describe this person using the 3ʳᵈ person (he)

Name: Juan

Lives in: London

Age : 20

Pet: A black spider

Hair: Blond

Eyes: Green

Always wears: A suit

Never wears: Jeans

At the gym wears: An Adidas tracksuit

5. Guided writing: write 3 short paragraphs in the first person (I) using the details below

Person	Lives	Always wears	Never wears	Hates wearing
Amparo	Madrid	Black dresses	Trousers	Earrings
Jorge	Pamplona	White t-shirts	A coat	A watch
Julio	Valencia	Jeans	Shorts	Scarves

TERM 1 - BRINGING IT ALL TOGETHER – 4

1. ¿Qué pasa, tío? Soy Tomás. Tengo catorce años y vivo en Cádiz, una ciudad en el sur de España. Vivo en un piso en el centro de la ciudad. Vivo con mi madre, mis hermanos y mi abuelo. Mis hermanos se llaman Antonio e Iván y son gemelos *(twins)*. Me llevo bien con mis hermanos porque son divertidos pero Antonio puede ser bastante terco e Iván puede ser muy pesado *(annoying)*.

2. Todos los días me levanto a las siete menos cuarto. Primero me lavo los dientes y me peino. Después desayuno cereales y tomo un chocolate caliente. Salgo de casa a las ocho y cuarto y vuelvo a las tres y media. Después del colegio, siempre voy al polideportivo a jugar al tenis con mis amigos. Por la noche cenamos en casa a las nueve.

3. En el colegio no tengo que llevar uniforme, ¡qué bien! Sin embargo, tengo que elegir *(choose)* ropa todos los días. Cuando hace calor llevo una camiseta y pantalones cortos con zapatillas. Mis zapatillas son blancas y mi camiseta favorita es roja. Sin embargo, cuando hace frío, llevo un chándal o vaqueros.

4. En casa, me gusta llevar ropa cómoda *(comfortable)*, así que nunca llevo ni camisa ni traje. Por lo general, llevo una camiseta blanca, pantalones cortos y sandalias. A veces llevo una gorra azul. Mi camiseta favorita es mi camiseta de fútbol del Cádiz; es amarilla y lleva el dorsal de "MÁGICO 11".

5. Cuando hace buen tiempo, llevo una camiseta verde y unos pantalones cortos negros para jugar al tenis. También llevo mis zapatillas blancas y mi gorra azul. Cuando llueve llevo una chaqueta deportiva blanca también.

6. Como son gemelos, mis hermanos siempre llevan la misma *(same)* ropa, es muy gracioso. En el colegio siempre llevan una camiseta de fútbol y un chándal. Cuando hace frío también llevan camiseta de fútbol pero con un abrigo. La única diferencia es que Antonio lleva la camiseta local *(home shirt)* e Iván la de visitante *(away)*.

Tomás, 14 años. Cádiz, España

1. Answer the following questions in English

a. Where is Cádiz?

b. Who does Tomás live with?

c. What does Tomás do every day?

d. What does Tomás do after school?

e. Does Tomás wear uniform to school?

f. What does Tomás wear when it's cold?

g. What does Tomás never wear at home?

h. What colour is his hat?

i. What does he wear when it rains?

j. What do Tomás' brothers always wear?

2. Find the Spanish equivalent in Tomás' text

a. They are fun (1)

b. He can be (1)

c. I brush my hair (2)

d. We eat dinner (2)

e. Every day (3)

f. When it's cold (3)

g. I never wear (4)

h. It is yellow (4)

i. To play (5)

j. When it rains (5)

k. They always wear (6)

l. Very funny (6)

m. The only difference (6)

3. Complete the translation of paragraph 4

At _______________, I _______________ to wear _______________________ clothing, therefore I _______________ wear a shirt nor a _____________. _______________, I wear a _________ _________, shorts and _____________. _______________, I wear a _________ baseball cap. My _______________ t-shirt is _______ Cádiz jersey; it is _______________________ and _______________ "MÁGICO 11" on the back.

Diego y José David son amigos pero van a colegios diferentes. Están hablando de la ropa y el uniforme.

Diego	Vas al instituto Jaume II, ¿verdad? ¿Tienes que llevar uniforme?
José David	Sí, voy a ese instituto *(secondary school)*. Sin embargo, no tengo que llevar uniforme. Puedo llevar lo que me dé la gana *(whatever I feel like)*.
Diego	¡Qué envidia! *(I'm jealous!)*. Yo voy a un instituto privado, así que tengo que llevar uniforme.
José David	¿Cómo es el uniforme?
Diego	Es asqueroso. Tengo que llevar un chándal verde, una camiseta blanca y verde y zapatillas de deporte blancas.
José David	Díos mío *(my God)*. ¿Tienes que llevar el chándal completo todos los días?
Diego	Bueno, no. Cuando hace calor llevo una camiseta con unos pantalones cortos verdes. Ah, también llevo una gorra verde. ¿Y tú?
José David	Cuando hace calor llevo unos pantalones cortos, una camiseta y zapatillas de deporte, como tú.
Diego	¿Y cuando hace frío qué llevas?
José David	Pues un chándal o algo *(something)*, como tú. En el colegio llevamos ropa muy similar, aunque tú tienes que llevar uniforme.
Diego	Es verdad. Aunque los colores de mi uniforme son muy feos.
José David	El uniforme de mi primo es peor *(worse)*. Él tiene que llevar un traje gris con camisa blanca y una corbata verde. También lleva zapatos negros y cinturón negro.

4. True (T), False (F) or Not Mentioned (NM)?

Diego must wear uniform.	
José David chooses what to wear to school.	
Diego would prefer not to wear uniform.	
Diego likes his uniform.	
Diego has to wear orange trousers.	
José David wears uniform to church.	
Diego doesn't have to wear uniform when it's hot.	
Diego wears an orange hat.	
José David wears trainers to school.	
José David wears a tracksuit when it´s cold.	
The boys wear similar clothes to school.	
Diego thinks José David is ugly.	
José David's cousin wears a green suit to school.	

5. Complete the statements

a. Diego is ___________________ of José David.

b. Diego's uniform is white and ___________________ .

c. Diego wears a green ___________________ when it's hot.

d. José David wears ___________ and t-shirt when it's ___________ .

e. José David's cousin's suit is ___________ and his tie is ___________ .

UNIT 5
My weekend plans – food & leisure

In this unit you will learn:

- To describe future tense activities
- To predict how the future tense event will be
- To say what you will eat at different times of the day

You will revisit:

- Time markers
- Free-time activities
- Present indicative of 'hacer', 'ir' and 'jugar'
- Adjectives for giving opinions
- Food and drink

UNIT 5. My weekend plans – food & leisure

¿Qué vas a hacer este fin de semana?	*What are you going to do this weekend?*
¿Cómo crees que será?	*What do you think it will be like?*
¿Qué vas a tomar para el desayuno?	*What are you going to have for breakfast?*
¿Qué sueles comer para el almuerzo?	*What do you usually eat for lunch?*
¿Qué te gusta beber?	*What do you like to drink?*

		hacer *to do*	deporte	*sport*
			los deberes	*homework*
			muchas cosas	*many things*
Este fin de semana *This weekend*	**voy a** *I am going*	**ir** *to go*	a un restaurante	*to a restaurant*
			a un concierto	*to a concert*
			al centro comercial	*to the mall*
			de compras	*shopping*
El sábado/domingo que viene *Next Saturday/Sunday*	**mi familia y yo vamos a** *my family and I are going*	**jugar** *to play*	al fútbol	*football*
			a videojuegos	*videogames*
Este sábado/domingo *This Saturday/Sunday*		**tocar** *to play (instrument)*	el piano	*the piano*
			la guitarra	*the guitar*
		ver *to see*	un partido	*a match*
			una película	*a film*
			una serie en Netflix	*a series on Netflix*

Creo que será *I think it will be*	**bastante** *quite* **muy** *very* **un poco** *a bit*	**aburrido** *boring*
		agotador *exhausting*
Creo que no será nada *I think it won't be … at all*		**divertido** *fun*
		emocionante *exciting*
		interesante *interesting*

Para el desayuno *For breakfast*		**comer** *to eat*	cereales con leche	*cereal with milk*
			fruta	*fruit*
			jamón	*ham*
			miel	*honey*
	me gusta *I like*		pescado	*fish*
		tomar *to have*	pollo asado	*roast chicken*
			queso	*cheese*
Para el almuerzo *For lunch*	**suelo** *I usually*		un bocadillo	*a sandwich*
			una ensalada	*a salad*
			una magdalena	*a cupcake*
	voy a *I am going (to)*		una tostada	*a slice of toast*
Para la cena *For dinner*		**beber** *to drink*	agua	*water*
			café	*coffee*
			chocolate caliente	*hot chocolate*
		tomar *to have*	un vaso de leche	*a glass of milk*
			té	*tea*
			zumo de naranja	*orange juice*

1. Multiple choice: tick the activity you hear

e.g.	**Do sport** ✔	**Do homework**	**Play football**
a.	Watch a series	Go to the mall	Go to a concert
b.	Do many things	Play the guitar	Play videogames
c.	Go shopping	Watch a series	Go to a restaurant
d.	Play videogames	Play the piano	Play football
e.	Do homework	Play football	Watch a football match
f.	Play the piano	Watch a match	Watch a series
g.	Go shopping	Go to the mall	Do homework

2. Complete the words

a. S _ ba _ o   *Saturday*

b. Gu _ ta _ _ a   *Guitar*

c. C _ nc _ e _ to   *Concert*

d. Abu _ _ i _ o   *Boring*

e. A _ m _ er _ o   *Lunch*

f. _ n _ ala _ a   *Salad*

g. Po _ _ o a _ ad _   *Roast chicken*

h. Un _ as _ de le _ h _   *Glass of milk*

3. Fill in the blanks

a. Para el __________ me gusta _________ una tostada.

b. Para el almuerzo __________ comer un ____________.

c. Para _______ cena voy a comer _________________.

d. Para el _______________ me gusta beber ________.

e. Para ____ desayuno suelo _________ chocolate caliente.

f. Después de la __________, me gusta beber __________.

g. Voy a desayunar _____________ con ____________.

4. Spot the intruders

Hola, soy me Manu. Soy de Santa Cruz del la Comercio. Este el fin de semana voy vamos a hacer deporte y jugar al el fútbol con mis los amigos. Creo que será muy un poco divertido y no será nada interesante aburrido. Después, ir voy a comer el la almuerzo. Para el almuerzo me gusta gusto comer fruta y beber agua. Para la cena voy a comer pollo y asado.

5. Faulty translation: one column contains a mistake - listen and correct the errors

e.g.	~~This Saturday~~ *This weekend*	**I am going**	**to play football.**
a.	This weekend	I am going	to play the piano.
b.	I don't think it will be	very	fun.
c.	For lunch	I like to eat	fruit.
d.	For dinner	I tend to drink	a glass of milk.
e.	This Sunday	I am going	to watch a football match.
f.	For lunch	I like to eat	a sandwich.
g.	I think that it will be	quite	exciting.
h.	For dinner	I am going to eat	roast chicken.

6. Narrow listening: fill in the grid in English

Person	Activity	Opinion	Breakfast	Lunch	Dinner
a. Tomás					
b. Sandra					
c. Samuel					

7. Gapped translation: fill in the blanks

_____________, my name is José Luis and I am ____________ Elche, a ____________ in the ________________of

Spain. I love ____________! This ______________ I am going to play the ____________ and the ____________

and I think that ________________________________ very ____________ and interesting. It won't be

________________ at all. I also like ____________. For ________________, I ____________ to have ______________

with milk and a mug of ________________________. For ____________, I am going to eat a ____________ and

cheese ____________ and ____________ lots of ____________. For dinner, I like to eat at ____________ and I

tend to eat ____________ ____________ or ________________ with rice – how ____________!

8. Listen to Leo and answer the questions in English

PART 1 – a.
1. Where does Leo live?
2. What is the first thing he will do this weekend?
3. What else will he do this weekend (2 details)
4. What does he think it will be like? (2 details)

PART 2 – b.
1. What does he drink at breakfast?
2. What does he eat at lunch? (2 details)
3. What does he drink at lunch?
4. What will he eat for dinner?
5. What will he eat for dessert *(postre)* afterwards?
6. What will he drink at dinner?

UNIT 5. My weekend plans – food & leisure: VOCAB BUILDING

1. Match

Este fin de semana	I am going to
Mi familia y yo	For breakfast
Hacer deporte	I like
Creo que será	My family and I
Voy a	To drink water
Ver un partido	Quite fun
Muy aburrido	I think it will be
Para el desayuno	To watch a match
Me gusta	For dinner
Suelo tomar	This weekend
Beber agua	I tend to have
Para la cena	To do sport
Bastante divertido	Very boring

2. Complete the words

a. E _ s _ _ _ do — *Saturday*

b. V _ _ a — *I am going to*

c. Toc _ _ e _ p _ an _ — *To play the piano*

d. I _ d _ c _ mpr _ _ — *To go shopping*

e. J _ g _ _ al f _ tb _ l — *To play football*

f. Cre _ q _ _ ser _ — *I think it will be*

g. P _ ra _ _ desa _ un _ — *For breakfast*

h. E _ a _ m _ _ rz _ — *Lunch*

i. B _ b _ _ z _ m _ — *To drink juice*

j. Com _ _ j _ m _ _ — *To eat ham*

k. H _ c _ _ l _ s deb _ r _ _ — *To do homework*

3. Break the flow

a. Voyahacerdeporte.

b. Creoqueserámuyinteresante.

c. Megustacomerpescado.

d. Voyajugaralfútbol.

e. Novoyatocarlaguitarra.

f. Suelotomarunvasodeleche.

g. Voyacomerpolloasado.

h. Novoyabebercafé.

i. Vamosairdecompras.

5. Spot and correct the nonsense sentences

a. Este semana de fin voy a jugar al fútbol.

b. Este sábado voy a hacer el fútbol.

c. Mi familia y yo vamos a comer el piano.

d. Este fin de semana voy a jugar al queso.

e. Creo que será muy bocadillo.

f. Para al desayuno voy a comer café.

g. Para la fruta voy a comer cena.

h. No voy a ver los deberes.

4. Complete with the missing words in the table below (2 words have no match)

a. ¿Qué vas a hacer este ___________ de semana?

b. Este fin de semana voy a hacer __________________.

c. Este sábado voy a ________________ a videojuegos.

d. El domingo que viene voy a tocar la ________________.

e. ¿Cómo crees que ______________?

f. Creo ______________ será muy emocionante.

g. ¿Qué vas a ________________ para el desayuno?

h. Voy a comer ________________ y queso.

i. Para la ______________ voy a comer un bocadillo.

j. ¿Qué te ________________ beber?

k. Me gusta beber ______________ de naranja.

l. También voy a ______________ al centro comercial.

m. Mi familia y yo vamos a ir a un ________________.

jugar	deporte	ir	será	concierto
jamón	divertido	comer	cena	guitarra
fin	zumo	que	ver	gusta

UNIT 5. My weekend plans – food & leisure: VOCAB BUILDING

6. Sentence puzzle

a. de jugar fútbol semana Este fin voy al a

b. voy a domingo la Este guitarra tocar

c. será Creo que un poco aburrido

d. familia de y yo Mi compras vamos a ir

e. comer el desayuno Para voy a fruta

f. un almuerzo suelo bocadillo Para el comer

g. no voy comer pescado a Para cena la

h. ¿ sueles comer para el almuerzo Qué?

i. ¿ este vas hacer de fin Qué semana a?

j. no que divertido Creo será nada

8. Translate into English

a. Este fin de semana

b. Voy a hacer los deberes

c. Voy a jugar a videojuegos

d. Vamos a ver un partido

e. Creo que será aburrido

f. Este sábado

g. Para el desayuno

h. Me gusta comer pollo asado

i. Voy a beber chocolate caliente

j. No suelo beber un vaso de leche

7. Gapped translation

a. *Este fin de semana voy a tocar la guitarra.*

This ______________ I am going to play the ___________.

b. *Este sábado voy a ver un partido.*

This ______________ I am going to ___________ a match.

c. *Creo que será emocionante e interesante.*

I __________ that it will be exciting and _____________.

d. *Creo que no será nada aburrido.*

I don't think that it __________ be _____________ at all.

e. *Para el desayuno me gusta comer cereales con leche.*

For _____________ I like to eat cereal with ___________.

f. *Para el amuerzo suelo comer una tostada.*

For lunch I ___________ eat a slice of _____________.

g. *Para la cena no me gusta comer pollo asado.*

For _____________ I don't like to _________ roast chicken.

h. *Mi familia y yo vamos a ir a un concierto.*

My ___________ and I are going to go to a ___________.

i. *El sábado que viene voy a ir de compras.*

___________ Saturday I am going to go _____________.

j. *Este domingo voy a hacer muchas cosas.*

_________ Sunday I am going to do ___________ things.

k. *¿Qué sueles comer para el almuerzo?*

What do ___________ tend to eat for _____________?

9. Guided translation

a. *Este sábado voy a tocar la trompeta.*

b. *El domingo que viene voy a ir a un concierto.*

c. *Creo que será bastante interesante.*

d. *Para el desayuno me gusta comer miel.*

e. *Para el almuerzo voy a comer una ensalada.*

f. *Para la cena no suelo comer pollo.*

g. *Este fin de semana voy a ver un partido.*

h. *El sábado que viene voy a ir de compras.*

i. *Este domingo voy a tocar el piano.*

j. *Creo que no será nada aburrido.*

This ___________ I am going to play the _________.

________ Sunday I am going to ____ ____ a concert.

I _________ that it will be __________ interesting.

For _______________ I like to eat ____________.

For ___________ I am going to eat a ____________.

For ___________ I don't _________ to eat chicken.

________ weekend I am going to watch a _________.

Next _____________ I am going to go ___________.

This _________ I am going to _________ the piano.

I don't think it _________ be _____________ at all.

UNIT 5. My weekend plans – food & leisure: READING 1

1. Hola, soy Mónica. Tengo diecisiete años y soy de Salobreña, un pueblo en Granada, en el sur de España. Vivo en un piso con mi familia. En mi familia hay cinco personas: mis padres, mi hermana mayor, mi hermano menor y yo. Me llevo bien con mi familia porque todos son simpáticos y hacemos muchas cosas juntos *(together)*.

2. Este fin de semana tengo muchos planes. El viernes por la noche voy a tocar la guitarra en mi dormitorio. Me encanta la música y lo que más me gusta es tocar la guitarra eléctrica. Será muy divertido y bastante interesante. Después voy a ver una serie en Netflix sobre mi grupo favorito, La Oreja de Van Gogh, un grupo musical de género pop rock.

3. Este sábado por la mañana mi familia y yo vamos a ir de compras al centro comercial de mi barrio. Quiero comprar ropa nueva y mi hermano quiere comprar un videojuego nuevo. Cuando vamos de compras suelo tomar un café con leche en mi cafetería favorita con mi madre. Ella suele comer fruta también o una magdalena para la merienda *(snack)*.

4. Por la noche tengo planes con mis amigas. Vamos a ir a un concierto de Rosalía en el estadio en el centro de la ciudad. El concierto empieza a las ocho y media, así que vamos a llegar al estadio a las ocho menos cuarto para comprar una camiseta o una pulsera *(bracelet)*. Después del concierto vamos a ir a una cafetería a tomar un zumo de naranja o un té.

5. Este domingo no tengo muchos planes, pero suelo hacer los deberes por la mañana con mi hermano. Para el desayuno me gusta comer cereales con leche y una magdalena y suelo tomar un té o un café. Mi padre prefiere comer unas tostadas y tomar un café sin leche. Después de los deberes mis hermanos y yo vamos a jugar a videojuegos en el salón.

6. El sábado que viene voy a ir al polideportivo a hacer deporte con mis primas. Vamos a jugar al tenis y hacer natación. Luego vamos a ir a un restaurante italiano a comer pizza. Finalmente vamos a ir a la casa de mi amiga Andrea a dormir *(sleep)*.

Mónica, 17 años. Salobreña, España

1. Answer the following questions

a. Where is Salobreña?

b. Who does Mónica live with?

c. Why does she get on with her family?

d. What is she going to do first on Friday night?

e. What will she do after?

f. What is 'La Oreja de Van Gogh'?

g. What will she do on Saturday morning?

h. What does she want to buy?

i. What is she going to do on Saturday night?

j. When will she do her homework?

k. What does she like to eat for breakfast?

l. What sports will she do next Saturday?

2. Complete the translation of paragraph 4

At ____________, I ____________ plans with my ______________. We are going to ______ ______ a Rosalía ______________ at the ______________ in the ______________ ______________. The concert starts at __________ so __________ are __________ to arrive at the stadium at ________ to __________ a ____________ or a bracelet. ____________ the concert, __________ are going to ________ to a café to __________ an ____________ juice or a ____________.

3. Find the Spanish equivalent in Mónica's text

a. A town	j. I have plans
b. In a flat	k. In the city centre
c. We do many things	l. The concert starts
d. Friday night	m. But I tend to
e. My favourite group	n. With my brother
f. We are going to go	o. My dad prefers
g. When we go	p. Black coffee
h. She tends to	q. With my cousins
i. A cupcake	r. My friend's house

1. Buenos días. Soy Luisa. Tengo trece años y soy de Besalú, un pueblo pequeño en el noreste de España. Vivo en una casa antigua en el campo. Vivo con mis padres, mi hermano mayor y mi abuela. Mi abuela se llama Rocío y me llevo muy bien con ella porque es muy simpática y divertida. Sin embargo, no me llevo bien con mi hermano porque es muy pesado.

2. En mi tiempo libre me gusta hacer muchas cosas. Normalmente suelo hacer deporte en el polideportivo o ir de compras con mis amigas. Este fin de semana voy a ir de compras con mi abuela al centro comercial. También vamos a ir a una cafetería a tomar un café aunque yo prefiero tomar chocolate caliente. A mi abuela le encanta el café con leche y una magdalena para merendar *(to snack)*.

3. El sábado por la noche voy a ir a un concierto en la plaza mayor con mis amigas. Creo que será muy divertido y emocionante y no será nada aburrido. Primero vamos a ir a casa de mi amiga a ver una serie en Netflix y después vamos a ir a la plaza mayor en taxi. Para la cena voy a comer una ensalada y tomar agua.

4. Este domingo por la mañana voy a desayunar unas tostadas con queso y jamón. También voy a tomar una magdalena y fruta y beber zumo de naranja. Normalmente suelo tomar solo un vaso de leche. Para el almuerzo voy a ir a casa de mi amiga y vamos a comer pescado. Creo que será delicioso. Después vamos a ir al polideportivo a hacer deporte. Vamos a jugar al tenis y al bádminton.

5. El fin de semana que viene no tengo muchos planes así que no voy a hacer muchas cosas. El viernes por la noche voy a comer en casa con mi familia. Vamos a cenar pollo asado y ensalada, mi plato favorito. Luego vamos a ver un partido de fútbol en el salón y tomar chocolate caliente. Después voy a tocar el piano en mi dormitorio antes de acostarme. El sábado por la mañana voy a jugar a videojuegos con mi hermano. Creo que será bastante divertido aunque me imagino que mi hermano será pesado como siempre.

Luisa, 13 años. Besalú, España

1. Find the Spanish equivalent in Luisa's text

a. The north-east of Spain

b. I get on with her

c. He is very annoying

d. In my free time

e. We are also going

f. She loves

g. I am going to go to a concert

h. It won't be

i. We are going to go

j. This Sunday morning

k. I tend to have

l. I think it will be delicious

m. I don't have many plans

n. My favourite dish

2. Answer in English

a. Who does Luisa live with?

b. Why does she get on with her grandmother?

c. What does she usually do in her free time?

d. What does Luisa prefer to drink?

e. What does her grandmother love to eat?

f. Who is Luisa going to a concert with?

g. What are they going to do before this?

h. What will Luisa eat for dinner afterwards?

i. What will she eat for breakfast on Sunday?

j. What will be delicious?

k. When will Luisa eat roast chicken and salad?

l. What will Luisa watch in the living room?

m. What will Luisa do next Saturday morning?

3. Translate the following into English

a. Vivo con mis padres

b. Sin embargo, no me llevo bien

c. Normalmente suelo hacer deporte

d. El sábado por la noche

e. No será nada aburrido

f. Vamos a ir a la plaza mayor en taxi

g. Con queso y jamón

h. Suelo tomar solo un vaso de leche

i. Así que no voy a hacer muchas cosas

j. Antes de acostarme

UNIT 5. My weekend plans – food & leisure: WRITING

1. Multiple choice: choose the correct translation

		1	2	3
a.	**Este fin de semana**	This weekend	Next weekend	Last weekend
b.	**Este sábado**	Last Saturday	This Saturday	This Sunday
c.	**Tocar la guitarra**	To play guitar	To play chess	To play piano
d.	**Creo que será**	I like it	I want to be	I think it will be
e.	**Hacer los deberes**	To do homework	To do chores	To do sport
f.	**Comer jamón**	To eat soap	To have cheese	To eat ham
g.	**Para el desayuno**	For lunch	After lunch	For breakfast
h.	**Ver un partido**	To watch a concert	To match a watch	To watch a match
i.	**Tomar fruta**	To eat fruit	To have fruit	To drink juice
j.	**Para la cena**	Before dinner	To eat dinner	For dinner
k.	**Beber agua**	To have water	To drink water	To drink milk

2. Complete with the correct option

a. ¿Qué _______________ a hacer este fin de semana?

b. Este fin de semana voy a _______________ un partido de baloncesto.

c. Este domingo no voy a _______________ la guitarra.

d. El sábado que _______________ voy a hacer deporte.

e. Creo que será _______________ divertido.

f. Creo que no será nada _______________.

g. Para el desayuno me _______________ comer cereales con leche.

h. Para el almuerzo _______________ comer un bocadillo.

i. Para la ___________ voy a comer pescado.

j. Este sábado no voy a _______________ café.

k. El domingo que viene voy a tomar ______.

l. _______________ que será muy interesante.

gusta	creo	suelo	vas
cena	ver	aburrido	beber
tocar	té	viene	muy

3. Spot and correct the grammar and spelling mistakes

a. ¿Qué vas a hago este fin de semana?

b. Este fin de semana voy a ir a compras.

c. El sabado que viene voy a ir a un concierto.

d. Este domingo voy a jugaré a videojuegos.

e. Creo que sera un poco interesante.

f. Este fin de semana voy a tocar el guitarra.

g. Creo que será no muy aburrido.

h. Para el desayuno me gusto comer fruta.

i. Para el almuerzo suelo comer una bocadillo.

j. Para el cena voy a beber un vaso de leche.

k. ¿Qué vas tomar para el desayuno?

l. ¿Qué tú gusta beber?

m. Mi familia y mi vamos a ir a un restaurante.

n. Este sábado no voy a ver un serie en Netflix.

o. Creo que nada será no emocionante.

p. Mi familia y yo vamos a desayuno fruta.

q. Para la cena suelo comer asado pollo y queso.

r. Para el almuerzo me no gusta comer pescado.

UNIT 5. My weekend plans – food & leisure: WRITING & TRANSLATION

1. Complete the table

	English	Spanish
a.	This weekend	
b.		Jugar al fútbol
c.		Voy a ver
d.	This Saturday	
e.		Creo que
f.		Bastante divertido
g.	For breakfast	
h.		Ir a un concierto
i.	To eat cheese	
j.		Beber café
k.		Para la cena
l.		Tocar la guitarra
m.	To do homework	
n.	A bit boring	

2. Complete with a suitable word

a. Este finde voy a _____________ los deberes.

b. Este _______________ voy a tocar la guitarra.

c. Creo que _____________ muy aburrido.

d. Para _________ desayuno voy a comer fruta.

e. Para la cena voy a _____________ pescado.

f. Este finde no voy a _____________ al fútbol.

g. Luego no voy a _____ ___ un concierto.

h. ¿Qué ___________ a hacer este fin de semana?

i. ¿Qué te _____________ beber?

j. Normalmente suelo _____________ café.

k. _____________ domingo, voy a tocar el piano.

l. No será _____________ aburrido.

m. Después voy a comer _________ magdalena.

3. Slalom translation (left to right) *e.g. This weekend I am going to go shopping.*

a. This Saturday we are going to watch a film.

b. I think it will be very exciting.

c. For breakfast I like to eat cheese.

d. For lunch I tend to have fruit.

e. This Sunday I am not going to play the guitar.

f. Next Sunday we are not going to do sports.

g. Are you going to eat cereal for breakfast?

h. What do you tend to do on Saturdays?

Este fin de semana	me gusta	ir	la guitarra.
Para el almuerzo	voy a	hacer	una película.
Este sábado	comer	tomar	para el desayuno?
El domingo que viene	será	ver	de compras.
Para el desayuno	suelo	hacer	fruta.
Creo que	no voy a	comer	deporte.
Este domingo	vamos a	muy	los sábados?
¿Vas a	sueles	cereales	queso.
¿Qué	no vamos a	tocar	emocionante.

UNIT 5. My weekend plans – food & leisure: WRITING & TRANSLATION

4. Gapped translation

a. *This Saturday, I am going to watch a match.* E _ _ _ s _ b _ d _ v _ _ a v _ _ un partid _ .

b. *I think it will be quite exciting.* Cr _ _ q _ _ ser _ b _ _ _ _ nte em _ cion _ _ _ _ .

c. *For dinner, I like to eat roast chicken.* P _ _ _ la cen _ me gusta com _ _ po _ _ o asad _ .

d. *This Sunday, we are going to go to a concert.* Este d _ _ _ _ _ _ v _ _ _ _ a _ _ a un conciert _ .

e. *I think it won't be fun at all.* C _ _ _ que n _ s _ _ _ n _ _ _ di _ _ _ _ ido.

f. *For lunch, I am not going to eat fish.* Para e _ a _ _ _ _ _ _ _ no voy a comer pescad _ .

g. *Next Saturday, I am going to go shopping.* E _ sábado q _ _ v _ _ _ _ v _ _ a _ _ de compras.

5. Write the questions for the answers below

a. Este fin de semana, voy a jugar al fútbol.

b. El sábado que viene voy a tocar el piano.

c. No, este domingo no voy a ir de compras.

d. Creo que será muy divertido.

e. Para el desayuno voy a comer fruta y miel.

f. Sí, suelo comer pescado para el almuerzo.

g. Para la cena me gusta comer una ensalada.

6. Translate into Spanish

a. This weekend I am going to play videogames.

b. Next Saturday I am going to go shopping.

c. This Sunday my family and I are going to watch a match.

d. I think it will be quite fun and interesting.

e. For breakfast, I usually have a cupcake.

f. For lunch, I like to eat a salad.

g. For dinner, I am going to eat roast chicken and drink orange juice.

7. Guided writing: write 3 short paragraphs in the first person (I) using the details below

	Person	Activities	Opinions	Food	Drink
a.	Iván	Homework Football	Fun A bit boring	Sandwich Fish	Water Orange juice
b.	Fátima	Guitar Shopping	Very exciting	A cupcake Roast chicken	Coffee Water
c.	Pilar	Concert Restaurant	Quite fun Not boring	Fruit and honey Toast	Tea A glass of milk

1. Buenos días. Soy Ana y tengo quince años. Soy de Barcelona pero vivo en Llastres, un pueblo en Asturias, en el norte de España. Vivo en una casa pequeña con mis padres, mi hermana mayor, Irene, y mi hermano menor. Mi hermano se llama Sergio y me llevo bien con él porque es muy cariñoso. A veces me llevo mal con Irene porque es terca.

2. Entre semana me acuesto bastante pronto a las nueve y media. Todos los días me levanto a las seis. Me ducho, me peino, desayuno y me lavo los dientes. Después salgo de casa a las siete y media y vuelvo a casa a las cuatro y media. Por la tarde tengo que hacer mis deberes y ayudar en casa. Luego puedo salir con mis amigos.

3. Voy a un colegio privado, así que tengo que llevar uniforme. En mi opinión, el uniforme es bonito. Cuando hace calor llevo una falda negra, una camisa blanca, una corbata roja y unos zapatos negros. Cuando hace frío también puedo llevar un jersey o un abrigo. Mi hermano está en primaria así que él no tiene que llevar uniforme, ¡qué suerte! *(how lucky!)*

4. Cuando tengo tiempo salgo de casa con mis amigos al parque o al polideportivo a jugar al ping-pong. Cuando hago deporte siempre llevo una camiseta sin mangas *(sleeveless)* verde y pantalones cortos blancos. Cuando hace frío llevo una chaqueta deportiva blanca también. Cuando llueve me quedo en casa y veo una película en el salón con Sergio.

5. Este fin de semana voy a ir a un concierto de Rosalía con mi hermana en el centro de la ciudad. Creo que será muy divertido y emocionante. El domingo mi familia y yo vamos a ir a un restaurante caro a las nueve para el cumpleaños de Sergio. Para la cena voy a comer pollo asado y tomar agua.

6. Como es su cumple, también vamos a preparar un desayuno especial. Para el desayuno vamos a comer churros con chocolate y vamos a tomar zumo de naranja. También le gusta la fruta así que voy a comprar una sandía *(watermelon)* y unas naranjas.

Ana, 15 años. Llastres, España

1. Answer the following questions in English

a. Where is Ana originally from?

b. Where is Llastres?

c. When does Ana wake up during the week?

d. What does she have to do in the afternoon?

e. What does Ana think of her uniform?

f. What does Ana do in her free time?

g. What does she do when it rains?

h. What is Ana doing this weekend?

i. What is special about this weekend?

j. What is Ana going to eat for breakfast on Sunday?

2. Find the Spanish equivalent in Ana's text

a. Very caring (1)

b. She is stubborn (1)

c. I brush my hair (2)

d. I can go out (2)

e. A black skirt (3)

f. He doesn't have to (3)

g. When I do sport (4)

h. When it's cold (4)

i. I'm going to watch (5)

j. For dinner (5)

k. A special breakfast (6)

l. He likes (6)

m. I'm going to buy (6)

3. Complete the translation of paragraph 5

This ________________, I am going to ________ ________ a Rosalía _______________ with my _______________ in the _______________ centre. I think it will be ____________ fun and _______________. On _______________, my family and I are going to an _______________ restaurant at ________ for Sergio's _______________. For _______________, I am going to eat ____________ _______________ and drink _______________.

Beatriz y Carmen están hablando de sus planes para el fin de semana.	
Beatriz	Carmen, ¿tienes planes para este fin de semana? ¿Qué vas a hacer?
Carmen	Este fin de semana tengo muchos planes. El viernes por la noche voy a ir de compras con mis padres en el centro comercial. ¿Y tú?
Beatriz	El viernes no tengo planes, pero el sábado por la mañana mi familia y yo vamos a ver el partido de mi hermano.
Carmen	¡Qué guay! ¿Cómo crees que será?
Beatriz	Sinceramente creo que será bastante aburrido ya que no me gusta mucho el fútbol. Además, el pobre *(the poor boy)* no va a ganar *(win)*.
Carmen	Ya veo *(I see)*, el pobre. ¿Y qué sueles hacer después de sus partidos?
Beatriz	Por lo general, mi familia y yo solemos ir al parque a dar una vuelta y tomar un granizado de limón *(lemon slushy)*. Pero bueno, ¿qué haces tú el sábado?
Carmen	¡Me encantan los granizados de limón! Este sábado voy a hacer una paella con mi padre en el jardín ya que es el cumpleaños de mi abuela.
Beatriz	¿Cuántos años va a cumplir tu abuela?
Carmen	¡Va a cumplir noventa y tres años! Para el desayuno vamos a tomar una magdalena y un café como siempre. ¿A ti qué te gusta tomar para el desayuno?
Beatriz	A mí me gusta tomar unas tostadas con miel y un vaso de leche. Sin embargo, este domingo voy a tomar fruta y miel.

4. True (T), False (F) or Not Mentioned (NM)?

Carmen has a lot of plans this weekend.	
Carmen is going shopping on Saturday.	
Carmen is going to the mall with her parents.	
Beatriz has plans on Friday.	
Beatriz is going to play the piano on Saturday.	
Beatriz thinks her brother's match will be boring.	
Beatriz is confident in her brother's chances of winning.	
After matches, Beatriz's family tend to go to the park.	
Carmen does not like lemon slushies.	
Carmen is making a paella with her mum.	
Carmen's grandmother is 93 years old.	
Carmen always has a coffee for breakfast.	
Beatriz likes to drink milk for breakfast.	

5. Complete the statements

a. Carmen is going _______________ with her _______________ on Friday night.

b. _______________ does not have plans on Friday.

c. Beatriz doesn't like _______________ very much.

d. Beatriz's family often go for a _______________ in the _______________.

e. Beatriz is going to eat _______________ and _______________ this weekend.

1. Fill in the missing words

a. ¿Qué _ _ _ _ _ en _ _ tiempo libre?

b. ¿Qué _ _ _ _ tu amigo en su tiempo libre?

c. ¿Adónde _ _ _ los fines de _ _ _ _ _ _ ?

d. ¿A qué _ _ _ _ te levantas entre semana?

e. ¿Qué haces _ _ _ _ _ _ _ _ del colegio?

f. ¿Qué haces para _ _ _ _ _ _ _ en _ _ _ _ ?

g. ¿Qué haces en tu _ _ _ _ _ _ _ _ _ _ _ ?

h. ¿Qué ropa _ _ _ _ _ _ _ en _ _ _ _ ?

i. ¿Qué ropa llevas cuando hace _ _ _ _ ?

j. ¿ _ _ _ _ _ es tu _ _ _ _ _ _ _ _ _ escolar?

k. ¿Qué _ _ _ a hacer este fin de semana?

l. ¿Qué vas _ _ _ _ _ _ para el desayuno?

m. ¿Qué _ _ _ _ _ _ _ comer para la _ _ _ _ ?

n. ¿Qué _ _ gusta _ _ _ _ _ _ ?

2. Choose the option that you hear

a. Me gusta hacer **equitación / natación**.

b. En su tiempo libre, juega al **rugby / fútbol**.

c. Los fines de semana, voy al **colegio / parque**.

d. Me levanto a las **seis / siete y media / siete**.

e. Hago **muchas cosas / mis deberes / mis tareas**.

f. **Siempre / Nunca** hago las tareas domésticas.

g. Juego **al ajedrez / a videojuegos / a la Play**.

h. Llevo **un chándal / una chaqueta deportiva**.

i. Llevo **una bufanda / una corbata / un abrigo**.

j. Mi uniforme es negro y **azul / feo / bonito**

k. Voy a ir **al parque / de compras / a casa**.

l. Voy a tomar **tostadas / fruta / cereales**.

m. Suelo comer **un bocadillo / pollo / queso**.

n. Me gusta beber **té / zumo de naranja / café**.

3. Listen and write in the missing information

a. En _______ tiempo libre, ___________ al fútbol con mis amigos en el _____________________.

b. En _______ tiempo libre, mi amiga María ___________ footing en el _______________.

c. Los fines de semana, _________ a casa de mi ___________ a ver una película en su ___________.

d. Entre semana, me ___________ a las ___________ porque ___________ que ir al colegio.

e. Antes del colegio, ______ ducho, me visto, _______________ mi mochila y _________ al colegio.

f. En casa, ___________ hacer las tareas _______________ todos los _______________ con mi padre.

g. Todos los ___________, _______________ música en mi _______________ y juego a la Play.

h. En casa, me gusta ___________ un jersey _______________ y pantalones ___________ negros.

i. Cuando hace ___________, llevo una _______________ sin mangas blanca y _______________.

j. Mi uniforme ___________ es muy feo; tengo que llevar una _______________ _______________.

k. Este fin de _______________, voy a ___________ el piano en casa y _________ una serie en Netflix.

l. Para el _______________, voy a _______________ fruta, _______________ y un chocolate caliente.

m. Para el _______________, suelo comer un _______________ de jamón y ___________ y fruta.

n. Para _______________, me gusta tomar _______________ de naranja pero ___________ beber agua.

THE LANGUAGE GYM
SPANISH TRILOGY II

4. Fill in the grid with your personal information

Question	Answer
a. ¿Qué haces en tu tiempo libre?	
b. ¿Adónde vas este fin de semana?	
c. ¿A qué hora te levantas entre semana?	
d. ¿Qué haces antes del colegio?	
e. ¿Qué haces para ayudar en casa?	
f. ¿Qué haces en tu dormitorio?	
g. ¿Qué ropa llevas en casa?	
h. ¿Qué ropa llevas cuando hace frío?	
i. Describe tu uniforme escolar.	
j. ¿Qué vas a tomar para el desayuno?	
k. ¿Qué sueles comer para el almuerzo?	
l. ¿Qué te gusta beber?	

5. Survey two of your classmates using the same questions as above and write down the main information you hear in Spanish

Q.	Person 1	Person 2
a.		
b.		
c.		
d.		
e.		
f.		
g.		
h.		
i.		
j.		
k.		
l.		

One Pen One Dice

Play in pairs. You only have 1 pen and 1 dice.

One person has the pen and starts translating the sentence into **English.** The other person rolls the dice until they roll a 6, they swap the pen and translate. The winner is the person who finishes translating all the sentences first.

1. ¿Qué haces en tu tiempo libre?	
2. A veces juego al baloncesto.	
3. Cuando hace frío voy al polideportivo.	
4. Cuando tiene tiempo, mi amigo Lionel hace ciclismo en el parque.	
5. Entre semana me ducho a las siete y media.	
6. Sin embargo, esta tarde no quiero hacer mis deberes.	
7. A eso de las seis de la mañana escucho música en mi dormitorio.	
8. Todos los días juego a la Play en el salón.	
9. Cuando hace calor llevo pantalones cortos y una camiseta blanca.	
10. Este fin de semana voy a tocar la guitarra con mi amigo.	

One Pen One Dice

Play in pairs. You only have 1 pen and 1 dice.
One person has the pen and starts translating the sentence into **Spanish.** The other person rolls the dice until they roll a 6, they swap the pen and translate. The winner is the person who finishes translating all the sentences first.

1. What do you do in your free time?	
2. Sometimes I play basketball.	
3. When it's cold I go to the sports centre.	
4. When he has time, my friend Lionel does cycling in the park.	
5. During the week I shower at 7:30.	
6. However, this afternoon I don't want to do my homework.	
7. At around 6:00 in the morning, I listen to music in my bedroom.	
8. Every day I play on the PlayStation in the living room.	
9. When it's hot I wear shorts and a white t-shirt.	
10. This weekend I am going to play guitar with my friend.	

No Snakes No Ladders

	1	2	3	4	5	6	7
 START	During the week	When the weather is good	When it's cold I play cards	When it's hot I play football	When it rains I stay at home	When it's foggy my friend goes to the park	During the week
15 Every day I watch television in my bedroom	14 Often I ride my bike in the garden	13 At around 6:00 in the morning I chat with my mum	12 What is your daily routine like during the week?	11 However, today I don't want to do my homework	10 At night I go to bed at 11:00	9 In the morning I have breakfast at 7:15	8 Before school I get up at 6:30
16 I never upload pictures to Instagram	17 When I have time I read comics on the terrace	18 Twice a week I do my homework in the kitchen	19 When it's hot I wear a baseball cap	20 When it rains I wear a yellow coat	21 At the beach I wear sandals	22 When I go out with my friends I wear a tracksuit	23 When I go out with my parents I wear jeans
 FINISH	30 For dinner I am going to eat chicken and rice	29 For lunch I tend to eat a sandwich	28 For breakfast I like to eat cereal	27 I think it will be very fun	26 This Saturday my family and I are going to go shopping	25 This weekend I am going to do homework	24 I never wear a suit

No Snakes No Ladders

SALIDA

1 — Entre semana

2 — Cuando hace buen tiempo

3 — Cuando hace frío juego a las cartas

4 — Cuando hace calor juego al fútbol

5 — Cuando llueve me quedo en casa

6 — Cuando está nublado mi amigo va al parque

7 — Durante la semana

8 — Antes del colegio me levanto a las seis y media

9 — Por la mañana desayuno a las siete y cuarto

10 — Por la noche me acuesto a las once

11 — Sin embargo, hoy no quiero hacer mis deberes

12 — ¿Cómo es tu rutina diaria entre semana?

13 — A eso de las seis de la mañana charlo con mi madre

14 — A menudo monto en bici en el jardín

15 — Todos los días veo la tele en mi dormitorio

16 — Nunca subo fotos a Instagram

17 — Cuando tengo tiempo leo tebeos en la terraza

18 — Dos veces a la semana hago mis deberes en la cocina

19 — Cuando hace calor llevo una gorra

20 — Cuando llueve llevo un abrigo amarillo

21 — En la playa llevo sandalias

22 — Cuando salgo con mis amigos llevo un chándal

23 — Cuando salgo con mis padres llevo vaqueros

24 — Nunca llevo traje

25 — Este fin de semana voy a hacer mis deberes

26 — Este sábado mi familia y yo vamos a ir de compras

27 — Creo que será muy divertido

28 — Para el desayuno me gusta comer cereales

29 — Para el almuerzo suelo comer un bocadillo

30 — Para la cena voy a comer pollo y arroz

LLEGADA

TERM 2 – OVERVIEW

This term you will learn:

Unit 6 – Saying where I live
- To describe where you live
- To say what is in your town and neighbourhood
- To say what you like to do in your neighbourhood

Unit 7 – Saying what I can do in my neighbourhood
- To say what there is to do in your neighbourhood
- To say what you like to or usually do in your neighbourhood
- To say where you do the activity

Unit 8 – Describing my street
- To say what there is on your street
- To describe where things are located in relation to one another
- To describe where your house is
- To say what you don't have on your street

Unit 9 – Describing my home & furniture
- To describe where your house is located
- To say what rooms there are in your house
- To describe why you like your house
- To say what there is in each room of the house

KEY QUESTIONS

¿Dónde vives?	*Where do you live?*
¿Qué hay en tu ciudad?	*What is there in your city?*
¿Te gusta tu barrio? ¿Por qué?	*Do you like your neighbourhood? Why?*
¿Qué se puede hacer en tu barrio?	*What can one do in your neighbourhood?*
¿Adónde se puede ir?	*Where can one go?*
¿Qué se puede ver y visitar?	*What can one see and visit?*
¿Qué hay en tu calle?	*What is there on your street?*
¿Dónde está tu casa?	*Where is your house?*
¿Qué sitios hay en tu barrio?	*What places are there in your neighbourhood?*
¿Cuántas habitaciones hay en tu casa?	*How many rooms are there in your house?*
¿Te gusta tu casa? ¿Por qué?	*Do you like your house? Why?*
¿Qué hay en la cocina / el salón?	*What is there in the kitchen / living room?*

UNIT 6
Saying where I live

In this unit you will learn:
- To describe where you live
- To say what is in your town and neighbourhood
- To say what you like to do in your neighbourhood

You will revisit:
- Locations and where you live
- Places in town
- Adjectival agreement

UNIT 6. Saying where I live

¿Dónde vives?			Where do you live?	
¿Qué hay en tu ciudad?			What is there in your city?	
¿Te gusta tu barrio? ¿Por qué?			Do you like your neighbourhood? Why?	

	Berlín		el centro de	Alemania
Vivo en	**Cardiff**		**el centro de**	**Canadá**
I live in	**Dublín**		**el norte de**	**Escocia**
	Edimburgo	**Está en**	**el este de**	**España**
	Londres	*It is in*	**el sur de**	**Francia**
Vivimos en	**Madrid**		**el oeste de**	**Gales**
We live in	**Niza**		**el noroeste de**	**Inglaterra**
	París		**el sureste de**	**Irlanda**
	Roma			**Italia**

		cafeterías *cafés*	**un acuario**	*an aquarium*
Cerca de mi casa *Near my house*	**hay** *there is/are*		**un centro comercial**	*a shopping mall*
			un cine	*a cinema*
		restaurantes *restaurants*	**un club juvenil**	*a youth club*
			un parque	*a park*
En el centro *In the centre*	**no hay** *there isn't / aren't*	**una calle peatonal** *a pedestrian street*	**una pista de patinaje**	*a skating rink*
			un polideportivo	*a sports centre*
			un jardín botánico	*a botanical garden*
En mi barrio *In my neighbourhood*		**muchas cosas que hacer**	*many things to do*	
		muchas cosas que ver	*many things to see*	
		mucho que hacer para los jóvenes	*a lot to do for young people*	
		muchos jóvenes	*lots of young people*	
En mi calle *On my street*	**tenemos** *we have*	**muchas** *many (f – pl.)*	**áreas verdes**	*green areas*
			calles bonitas	*beautiful streets*
			instalaciones deportivas	*sports facilities*
			tiendas	*shops*
En mi ciudad *In my city*	**no tenemos** *we do not have*	**muchos** *many (m – pl.)*	**edificios antiguos**	*old buildings*
			restaurantes	*restaurants*

	***es** *it is*	**peligroso**	*dangerous*
		seguro	*safe*
(No) Me gusta mi barrio porque	**está** *it is*	**bien/mal cuidado**	*well/badly looked after*
		limpio	*clean*
		sucio	*dirty*
I (don't) like my neighbourhood because	**(no) hay** *there is (not)*	**mucha contaminación**	*a lot of pollution*
		mucho ruido	*a lot of noise*
		mucho tráfico	*a lot of traffic*
	(no) se puede *one can (not)*	**comer bien**	*eat well*
		hacer deporte	*do sport*
		pasear	*go for a walk*

***Author's note:** "es" and "está" are used for different things. "Es" comes from **SER** and refers to <u>physical</u> and <u>character descriptions</u>. "Está" comes from **ESTAR** and is used to describe <u>states</u> and <u>conditions</u>. You will practice them in context in this unit. For a full explanation and practice exercises check out the matching unit in our **Spanish Verb Pivots** grammar book.

1. Listen and fill in the gaps

a. Vivo en Berlín. Está en el __________ de Alemania.

b. Vivimos en Madrid. Está en el __________ de España.

c. Vivo en Londres. Está en el __________ de Inglaterra.

d. __________ en Edimburgo, en el sureste de Escocia.

e. __________ en Roma. Está en el centro de Italia.

f. __________ en Cardiff. Está en el sureste de Gales.

g. Vivo en __________. Está en el centro de Francia.

h. Vivo en __________. Está en el noroeste de Inglaterra.

i. Vivimos en __________. Está en el ______ de __________.

2. Multiple choice: tick the place you hear

e.g.	A cinema ✔	A park
a.	Shops	Restaurants
b.	A pedestrian street	A shopping mall
c.	A park	A skating rink
d.	A youth club	Cafés
e.	A pedestrian street	A skating rink
f.	A botanical garden	An aquarium
g.	A shopping mall	A sports centre

3. Fill in the blanks

a. ¿Dónde vivo? Vivo en Berlín, la __________ de Alemania. Berlín es una __________ muy grande así que hay __________ cosas que hacer. __________ de mi casa, hay un __________ comercial y muchas calles __________. Además, hay mucho que __________ para los __________ ya que hay un __________ grande, una pista de __________ y un jardín botánico.

b. En mi calle, __________ algunas __________ antiguas y varios restaurantes baratos. Me __________ mi barrio porque es __________ y nunca está __________. Lo mejor es que se puede __________ por las __________ bonitas y también se puede __________ bien en los __________. Sin embargo, no se puede hacer __________ ya que no hay __________.

4. Faulty translation: listen and correct the errors

e.g.	Near my house	there is	~~a sports centre~~ *a youth club*
a.	Near my house	there is	a pedestrian street.
b.	In my city	there is	a youth club.
c.	In the centre	there are	lots of pretty streets.
d.	On my street	there are	cafés.
e.	In my neighbourhood	we don't have	many restaurants.
f.	Near my house	there is	a pedestrian street.
g.	In the centre	we have	a sports centre.
h.	On my street	there isn't	a big park.

5. Why do they like/dislike their neighbourhood?

	Opinion	Reason
a.	**I like my neigbourhood**	
b.	**I don't like my neigbourhood**	
c.	**I don't like my neigbourhood**	
d.	**I love my neighbourhood**	
e.	**I like my neighbourhood**	
f.	**I like my neighbourhood**	
g.	**I love my neighbourhood**	
h.	**I don't like my neighbourhood**	

6. Listen, spot and correct the grammar and spelling errors

a. Hola, mi llamo Joaquín. Soy español y vivir con mi padre en Alicante. Alicante es en el sureste de España. Vivimos en un piso en el centro de la ciudad. Cerca de mi casa hay muchos cafeterías y muchos restaurantes. También hay una centro comercial y un parque grande pero no hay un juvenil club.

b. En mi bario hay muchas cosas que hacer. Por ejemplo, hay muchas tiendas y también tenemos un polideportivo moderno con instalaciones deportivas bueno. Me gusta mi barrio porque es no peligroso y porque está bien cuidado. Además, no hay mucha contaminación aunque sí que hay bastante tráfico.

7. Listen to Ana del Casar and answer the questions in English

a. Where is she from?

b. Where does she live? (2 details)

c. What is there near her house? (3 details)

d. How does she describe her neighbourhood? (3 details)

e. What is her overall impression of her neighbourhood?

UNIT 6. Saying where I live: VOCABULARY BUILDING 1

1. Match

Hay muchos jóvenes	There are many green spaces
Hay muchas calles peatonales	There are many shopping malls
Hay muchos edificios antiguos	There are many good restaurants
Hay muchas tiendas	There is a lot to see
Hay mucho ruido	There are many shops
Hay muchos centros comerciales	There are many modern buildings
Hay muchas instalaciones deportivas	There are many pedestrian streets
Hay muchos restaurantes buenos	There are many sports facilities
Hay muchas áreas verdes	There is a lot of noise
Hay muchos edificios modernos	There are many things to do
Hay muchas cosas que hacer	There are many old buildings
Hay mucho que ver	There are many young people

2. Break the flow

a. MiciudadestáenelcentrodeInglaterra

b. MiciudadestáeneloestedeFrancia

c. Enmiciudadhaymuchosbaresydiscotecas

d. Enmibarriohaymuchoquehaceryver

e. Enmibarrionohaymuchacontaminación

f. Enmibarriohaymuchasáreasverdes

g. Enmibarriohaymuchoscentroscomerciales

h. Enmibarriohaymuchastiendasquemegustan

3. Missing letters

a. Ha__ muchas cal__es pea__onales.

b. H__y mucho__ edi__icios anti__uos.

c. __ay muchas __reas ver__es.

d. No ha__ much__ rui__o.

e. Ha__ much__s jó__enes.

f. No h__y much__ contaminaci__n.

g. Ha__ much__s instala__iones deporti__as.

4. Translate into English

a. Mucha contaminación

b. Muchas cosas que hacer

c. Muchas tiendas que me gustan

d. Muchas calles peatonales

e. Mucho ruido

f. Muchas áreas verdes

g. Muchos edificios antiguos

h. Hay mucho que ver

i. Hay muchas instalaciones deportivas

5. Complete

a. Hay muchas cosas que h____________.

b. Hay muchas instalaciones d______________.

c. Hay muchas á________ verdes.

d. Hay muchos edificios a______________.

e. Hay muchas t____________.

f. Hay mucho r__________.

g. Hay muchas calles p______________.

h. Hay muchos j______________.

i. No hay mucho t______________.

j. No hay mucha c______________________.

6. Faulty translation: correct the English
(Please note - not all the translations are wrong)

a. Mi ciudad está en el oeste de Alemania.
My town is in the east of Scotland.

b. Vivo en una casa grande en la costa.
I live in a small house on the coast.

c. Mi barrio está en las afueras.
My neighbourhood is on the outskirts.

d. Mi barrio es muy grande y moderno.
My town is very big and modern.

e. En mi barrio hay mucho que hacer para los jóvenes.
In my neighbourhood there is a lot to do for young people.

f. Me encanta mi barrio porque no hay crimen.
I like my neighbourhood because there is no crime.

g. En mi barrio hay muchas tiendas buenas.
In my neighbourhood there are many cheap shops.

h. En mi barrio se puede hacer muchas cosas.
In my neighbourhood one can do many things.

7. Complete the table

English	Español
Old buildings	
Neighbourhood	
	Mucho que hacer
	No hay ruido
It is in the north	
	Está en el sureste
	Edificios modernos

8. Complete the table

English	Español
	Hay contaminación
A lot to do	
	Muchas cosas
Many good shops	
	Muy limpio
	En mi ciudad
In my neighbourhood	

9. Complete the translation

a. Hay muchas tiendas que me gustan.
There are many _____________ that I like.

b. Hay mucho que hacer para los jóvenes.
There is a lot to do for _____________ _____________.

c. Hay muchas áreas verdes.
There are a lot of _____________ _____________.

d. Se puede comer bien.
One can _____________ well.

e. Es un barrio seguro.
It is a _____________ neighbourhood.

f. Hay mucha contaminación.
There is a lot of _____________.

g. No hay mucho ruido.
There isn't much _____________.

UNIT 6. Saying where I live: VOCABULARY BUILDING 2

1. Translate into English

a. En mi ciudad hay mucho que hacer para los jóvenes.

b. En mi barrio hay muchos bares y restaurantes buenos.

c. Me encanta mi barrio porque hay muchas instalaciones deportivas.

d. Lo mejor *(the best thing)* de mi barrio es que es seguro.

e. Lo mejor de mi barrio es que está muy limpio y es tranquilo.

f. En mi barrio hay muchos centros comerciales con muchas tiendas buenas.

g. En mi barrio hay mucho que hacer para los niños *(children)*.

h. Lo peor *(the worst thing)* de mi ciudad es la contaminación.

2. Correct the grammar and spelling errors

a. Muchos edificios antiguo.

b. Hay mucho hacer.

c. Mi encanta mi barrio.

d. Hay mucha tiendas buenos.

e. Esta en el norte de Alemania.

f. Hay mucho jovenos.

g. Hay mucho contaminacion.

h. Hay mucho que hacer para los jovenes y los ninos.

3. Sentence puzzle: rewrite the sentences in the correct order

a. barrio En hay mi hacer que mucho — *In my neighbourhood there is a lot to do.*

b. ciudad Mi norte en de el Inglaterra está — *My city is in the north of England.*

c. buenas mi calle En hay tiendas muchas — *On my street there are many good shops.*

d. en Vivo barrio un y muy moderno grande — *I live in a very big and modern neighbourhood.*

e. sur ciudad Mi en el España de está — *My city is in the south of Spain.*

f. mi En calle muchos hay edificios históricos — *On my street there are many historic buildings.*

4. Match

Antiguo	Dangerous
Moderno	Beautiful
Limpio	Safe
Sucio	Quiet
Feo	Clean
Bonito	Ugly
Tranquilo	Noisy
Ruidoso	Dirty
Seguro	Modern
Peligroso	Old

5. Multiple choice: choose the grammatically correct answer

1	2	3
Tiendas buenas	Tiendas buena	Tienda buenas
Edificios antiguo	Edificio antiguos	Edificios antiguos
Mucho de hacer	Mucho hacer	Mucho que hacer
Mucho de ver	Mucho que ver	Mucho ver
Una calle sucio	Una calle sucia	Una sucia calle
Una ciudad fea	Una fea ciudad	Un ciudad feo
Hay muchas cosa	Hay mucha cosas	Hay muchas cosas
Tiendas cara	Cara tiendas	Tiendas caras
Está en el sur	Está en sur	Esta en el sur

6. Complete with the correct option

a. En mi ciudad _______ mucho que ver y hacer.

b. Mi ciudad ________ en el norte.

c. En mi _________ hay muchos edificios antiguos.

d. En mi barrio hay muchas ___________ bonitas.

e. Me ____________ mi barrio porque no hay ruido.

f. Me gusta mucho la __________ de mi barrio.

g. Mi barrio es un __________ seguro.

h. En mi ciudad hay mucho que hacer para los

____________.

tiendas	gente	está	encanta
lugar	hay	calle	jóvenes

7. Match

Mucho que hacer	Old buildings
En mi barrio	Many things
En mi ciudad	Many shops
Edificios antiguos	For young people
En el norte	A lot to do
La gente	In my neighbourhood
Para los jóvenes	Green spaces
Muchas tiendas	On my street
Áreas verdes	In my city
En mi calle	The people
Muchas cosas	In the north

8. Spot the intruders: cross out the unnecessary Spanish word(s)

a. Me gusta mucho la gente de mi barrio.
I like the people of my neighbourhood.

b. En mi calle hay muchas tiendas buenas.
On my street there are a lot of shops.

c. Mi ciudad está en el norte del país.
My city is in the north.

d. Lo peor de mi barrio es la contaminación del aire.
The worst thing about my neighbourhood is the pollution.

e. En mi barrio siempre se puede hacer muchos deportes al aire libre.
In my neighbourhood one can do a lot of outdoor sports.

f. En mi barrio no hay mucho que hacer para los jóvenes.
In my neighbourhood there is a lot to do for young people.

g. Mi barrio está en las afueras de la ciudad.
My neighbourhood is on the outskirts.

h. Me encanta mi barrio porque hay muchos edificios históricos muy bonitos.
I love my neighbourhood because there are many historical buildings.

i. Mi barrio es demasiado ruidoso.
My neighbourhood is noisy.

Me llamo Marta. Vivo en Barcelona, pero soy de Alcalá de Henares. Barcelona está situada en el noreste de España. Vivo en un barrio muy bonito, en el centro de la ciudad. Es la parte más antigua de la ciudad.

En mi barrio hay muchos edificios históricos, pero no hay muchas instalaciones deportivas. Sin embargo, hay mucho que hacer para los jóvenes. ¡Mi barrio es el más animado! Hay muchos bares y restaurantes. También hay muchas tiendas buenas.

Por lo general, la gente de mi barrio es muy simpática. Lo que no me gusta es que hay demasiados turistas, así que (*therefore*) hay mucho ruido.

Marta, 14 años. Alcalá de Henares, España

Me llamo Ian. Tengo dieciséis años. Vivo en Valencia, pero soy de Reading, en Inglaterra. Valencia está situada en el este de España, en la costa. Vivo en un barrio residencial muy feo en las afueras de la ciudad.

En mi barrio hay muchísimos edificios sucios y feos. No hay muchas instalaciones deportivas ni tiendas. Tampoco hay cosas para los jóvenes. También hay mucho crimen, así que no salgo a menudo. Además, cerca de mi barrio hay muchas fábricas (*factories*), así que hay bastante contaminación.

Mi edificio está situado muy cerca del aeropuerto, así que hay mucho ruido. Eso es lo peor de todo.

Ian, 16 años. Reading, Inglaterra

1. Find in the text

a. I am from

b. Is located

c. A very beautiful neighbourhood

d. Many buildings

e. Sports facilities

f. There is a lot to do

g. The liveliest neighbourhood

h. Many good shops

i. What I don't like

j. A lot of noise

2. Complete the translation of Ian's text

My name is Ian. I am sixteen years old. I live in Valencia, but I am from Reading in England. Valencia is located in the _______ of Spain, on the _______. I live in a very _________ residential neighbourhood on the ___________ of the city.

In my neighbourhood there are many ________ and ugly buildings. There are not many __________ _________ nor _______. There are not things for _________ ________ either. Also, there is a lot of __________, therefore I don't ____ ______ often. _________, near my neighbourhood there are many _________, therefore there is quite a bit of ______________.

My building is located very _______ the airport, therefore there is a lot of _________. This is the _________ of all.

3. Answer the questions about Ian (in Spanish)

a. ¿Cuántos años tiene Ian?
b. ¿Dónde vive?
c. ¿De dónde es?
d. ¿Dónde está el barrio de Ian?
e. ¿Cómo son los edificios de su barrio?

f. ¿Hay muchas cosas para los jóvenes?
g. ¿Es un barrio seguro? ¿Por qué?
h. ¿Por qué hay bastante contaminación?
i. ¿Por qué hay mucho ruido?
j. ¿Qué es lo peor de todo?

UNIT 6. Saying where I live: READING 2

Me llamo Alejandro. Soy de Buenos Aires, en Argentina, pero vivo en Madrid por el trabajo de mi padre. Madrid está situada en el centro de España. Vivo en un barrio histórico muy bonito en el centro de la ciudad. Es un barrio muy turístico, así que hay mucha gente, tráfico y ruido. Siempre hay atascos *(traffic jams)*. Eso es lo peor de todo.

En mi barrio hay mucho que hacer para los jóvenes. ¡Es muy animado! Hay muchas calles peatonales con muchos bares y restaurantes al aire libre. También hay muchas discotecas que están abiertas *(open)* hasta las seis de la mañana. Además hay muchas tiendas bonitas.

Por lo general, la gente de mi barrio es muy simpática y tranquila. Lo que no me gusta es que hay demasiados turistas, así que hay mucho ruido. Lo mejor es que es bastante seguro porque no hay mucho crimen y hay muchos policías en las calles.

Alejandro, 13 años. Buenos Aires, Argentina

Me llamo Gabriela. Soy de Santiago, en Chile, pero vivo en Sevilla, en España. Vivo en un barrio en las afueras de la ciudad. Me gusta mucho mi barrio porque hay muchas instalaciones deportivas, como piscinas y polideportivos, y un centro comercial enorme donde hay un cine, una bolera *(bowling alley)*, una pista de patinaje y muchas tiendas buenas. No hay ni contaminación ni ruido.

Cerca de mi casa hay un jardín botánico, un museo, una piscina, un centro comercial enorme y un parque donde hago footing, monto en bici y paseo a mi perro.

Por lo general, la gente de mi barrio es educada, tranquila y servicial *(helpful)*. Es un barrio seguro y muy bonito. Lo mejor de todo es que hay muchas áreas verdes. Hay parques con árboles muy grandes y viejos. ¡A mí me encanta la naturaleza!

Gabriela, 11 años. Santiago, Chile

1. Find in the text

a. Because of my father's job

b. Is located

c. Beautiful

d. Therefore there are

e. Noise

f. There are always traffic jams

g. This is the worst of all

h. For young people

i. It is very lively

j. Pedestrian streets

k. Outdoor

l. Which are open until 6.00 a.m.

m. Many beautiful shops

n. The people of my neighbourhood

o. Too many tourists

p. It is quite safe

q. In the streets

2. Comprehension questions

a. In which part of Sevilla does she live?

b. What sports facilities does Gabriela mention?

c. What can be found in the shopping mall? (4 details)

d. What does she say about pollution and noise?

e. What is there near her house? (5 details)

f. What does she do at the park? (3 details)

g. How does she describe the people in her neighbourhood?

h. What is Gabriela's favourite thing about her area? Why?

UNIT 6. Saying where I live: WRITING 1

1. Complete the sentences with the missing words

a. La _ _ _ _ _ de mi barrio es _ _ _ _ _ _ _ _ _ .

The people of my neighbourhood are nice.

b. En mi _ _ _ _ _ _ hay mucha _ _ _ _ _ _ _ _ _ _ _ _ _ .

In my neighbourhood there is a lot of pollution.

c. En mi ciudad _ _ _ muchas _ _ _ _ _ _ _ _ .

In my city there are a lot of factories.

d. Hay _ _ _ _ _ _ turistas, así que hay mucho _ _ _ _ _ _ .

There are a lot of tourists, so there is a lot of noise.

e. Me encanta mi _ _ _ _ _ _ porque hay muchas _ _ _ _ _ _   _ _ _ _ _ _ .

I love my city because there are many green areas.

f. En mi _ _ _ _ _ hay muchas _ _ _ _ _ _ _ buenas.

On my street there are many good shops.

g. _ _ ciudad es un _ _ _ _ _ muy _ _ _ _ _ _ _ .

My city is a very safe place.

h. Cerca de mi _ _ _ _ hay un _ _ _ _ _ _ donde monto en _ _ _ _ _ y paseo a mi _ _ _ _ _ _ .

Near my house there is a park where I ride my bike and walk my dog.

2. Translate into English

a. Fábricas	e. Ciudad	i. Calle
b. Hay	f. Se puede	j. Parque
c. Tiendas	g. Instalaciones	k. Cerca
d. Barrio	h. Además	l. Es seguro

3. Find in the wordsearch the Spanish translation of the phrases below, then write it next to each of them as shown in the example

W	G	S	E	P	U	E	D	E	V	I	V	I	R	H	S	V	Y	W	Y
E	F	F	L	U	L	N	L	I	K	L	J	O	V	M	N	E	C	N	J
B	P	M	Y	R	X	L	C	Z	K	E	R	V	Q	F	Q	I	D	T	Y
B	N	Ó	I	C	A	N	I	M	A	T	N	O	C	Y	A	H	P	M	T
M	I	U	G	C	B	H	N	Q	O	A	U	R	E	R	H	Y	D	J	C
H	M	A	I	M	F	Z	U	O	T	Z	E	V	O	P	P	Y	R	C	Z
M	W	M	V	G	I	E	I	A	I	E	Y	G	M	J	O	F	P	G	N
R	N	S	A	N	E	U	B	S	A	D	N	E	I	T	E	L	M	B	R
E	C	E	R	C	A	D	E	M	I	C	A	S	A	T	M	M	H	R	N
I	C	W	T	L	R	H	L	Q	X	D	C	X	Y	T	X	L	O	H	F
L	A	G	E	N	T	E	E	N	M	I	B	A	R	R	I	O	F	L	W
E	B	B	X	U	E	X	V	Y	R	W	H	D	L	C	N	P	A	U	X

e.g. Se puede vivir
One can live

a. Good shops

b. Near my house

c. There are

d. There is pollution

e. The best thing

f. The people

g. On my street

h. The worst thing

i. In my neighbourhood

UNIT 6. Saying where I live: WRITING & TRANSLATION

1. Complete with a suitable word

a. Vivo en una _______ en el norte de __________.

b. Mi barrio está en las __________ de la ciudad.

c. No me gusta mi barrio porque es __________.

d. No ________ muchas tiendas ______________.

e. Hay __________ crimen también, así que no

   es un lugar ______________.

f. Lo peor es que hay muchas fábricas cerca de

   mi barrio, así que hay mucha ______________.

g. En mi calle hay solo una ____________.

h. Vivo en un edificio ____________ y antiguo.
   No me ____________.

2. Match

Vivo en el	tráfico.
Hay un	mucho mi barrio.
La gente	buenas.
Mi ciudad está	feo y está mal cuidado.
Me gusta	contaminación.
Hay tiendas	hay muchas fábricas.
Lo peor de mi barrio es el	es muy simpática y graciosa.
En mi barrio	polideportivo grande.
Mi edificio es	sur de España.
En mi ciudad hay mucha	en el norte de España.

3. Guided translation

a. E_ m_ b________ h______ m________ t__________.
In my neighbourhood there is a lot of traffic.

b. N_ m_ g________ m_ b________ p________ e____ s_____ y e_ p________.
I don't like my neighbourhood because it is dirty and dangerous.

c. E_ m_ c________ h______ m__________ t________ b________.
On my street there are many good shops.

d. M_ c________ e______ e_ e_ n______ d_ I__________.
My city is in the north of England.

e. L_ p_____ d_ m_ b________ e_ l_ c______________.
The worst thing about my neighbourhood is the pollution.

f. E_ m_ c________ h___ m______ q___ h______ p___ l__ j________.
In my city there is a lot to do for young people.

g. C________ d_ m_ c______ h__ u_ p________ y u__ p__________.
Near my house there is a park and a swimming pool.

h. L_ m________ d_ m_ b________ e_ q__ e_ s________.
The best thing about my neighbourhood is that it is safe.

i. P_ l_ g__________, l_ g______ d_ m_ b________ e_ m___ e__________.
In general, the people in my neighbourhood are very polite.

j. C______ d_ m_ c______ h___ u_ j__________ b____________.
Near my house there is a botanical garden.

---

4. Spot the missing word: there is a missing word in each line, spot it and add it in

a. En barrio hay mucha contaminación.

b. En mi ciudad muchas áreas verdes.

c. Por lo general, en mi barrio la gente muy simpática.

d. En mi calle muchas tiendas buenas.

e. Vivo en edificio muy antiguo y feo.

f. Vivo en barrio histórico.

g. Lo peor mi barrio es el ruido.

h. Vivo muy cerca aeropuerto.

i. Cerca de mi casa hay un parque muy bonito donde monto bici.

j. Mi barrio muy feo.

---

5. Tangled translation: rewrite in Spanish

a. Mi ciudad **is in** el sur **of Spain.**

b. Vivo **in a** ciudad en el **north** de **France.**

c. Mi **city** se llama Niza. Está **near** de Italia.

d. Me encanta **my** ciudad **because** es **very** bonita.

e. Cerca de mi **house** hay un **shopping mall.**

f. Mi **neighbourhood** está en las **outskirts of** Cádiz.

g. Mi barrio **is** muy **big** y **modern.**

h. Hay muchos **spaces** verdes e instalaciones deportivas como **swimming pools** y un **gym.**

i. No **there are** muchas tiendas **but** hay un centro comercial no muy **far** de mi **house.**

j. En mi **street** hay un parque muy **big** donde monto en **bike** y paseo al **dog.**

k. Lo **best of** mi barrio es **that** la gente **is** simpática.

---

6. Translate into Spanish

a. I live in a town

b. My neighbourhood is

c. Near my house

d. Green spaces

e. There is a shopping mall

f. On my street

g. Not far from

h. I walk the dog

i. I ride a bike

j. In the North of Spain

k. On the outskirts

l. I love my neighbourhood

m. The best thing

n. A lot to do for young people

---

7. Translate into Spanish

I live in a city in the north of Spain. My neighbourhood is on the outskirts of the city. My neighbourhood is big and modern. There are many green spaces and sports facilities. There are not many shops but there is a shopping mall near my house. On my street there is a gym, a small supermarket and a bar. Near my house there is a big park where I ride my bike and walk my dog. The best thing about my neighbourhood is that the people are friendly and polite. The worst thing is that there is not much to do for young people.

UNIT 6. Saying where I live: WRITING 2

1. Complete the sentences creatively

a. Mi ciudad está en...

b. Mi barrio está en...

c. Cerca de mi casa hay...

d. Me encanta mi barrio porque...

e. Lo mejor de mi barrio es...

f. Lo peor de mi barrio es...

g. Cerca de mi barrio hay un parque donde...

h. En mi calle hay...

2. Write a sentence for each of the following words

a. Barrio

b. Peor

c. Calle

d. Fábricas

e. Ruido

f. Edificios

3. Spot and correct the grammar and spelling mistakes (including missing words)

a. Mi barrio esta en la afueras de la ciudad.

b. Cerca de mi casa es una tienda de deporte.

c. El peor de mi barrio es la contaminacion.

d. Lo major de mi barrio es ruido.

e. Donde esta tus barrio?

f. La gente de mi barrio simpatico.

g. Mi barrio muy grande y modern.

4. Write a paragraph in Spanish about Marta in the first person singular (I) and one about Roberto in the third (he)

	Marta	Roberto
Location of city	North of Spain	South of Argentina
Location of neigbourhood	City centre	Outskirts
Sports facilities	Two sports centres, a tennis club and three gyms	A swimming pool, a stadium and a sports centre
Green spaces	Two big parks	One small park
Environment	A lot of pollution	No pollution but a bit of noise
Amenities for young people	Many bars, nightclubs and concerts	A shopping mall and the park
Best thing	Safety	The stadium
Worst thing	Too many tourists; noise	Crime
People in their neighbourhood	Very friendly and polite	Unfriendly and rude

TERM 2 - BRINGING IT ALL TOGETHER – 6

1. Hola, me llamo Darwin. Soy de Artigas, una ciudad en el norte de Uruguay. Vivo en una casa pequeña en el este de la ciudad. Vivo con mi padre, mis dos hermanas menores y mi abuela. Me llevo bien con mi padre porque es muy inteligente y me ayuda. También me llevo bien con mi abuela porque es simpática.

2. Entre semana siempre me levanto a las siete y cuarto y me ducho. Después desayuno tostadas con mermelada de fresa y tomo un café con leche con mi padre. Mi padre también se toma un café, pero sin *(without)* leche. Después del colegio debo recoger *(pick up)* a mis hermanas del colegio. También tengo que preparar la cena para la familia.

3. Todos los días monto en bici después del colegio con mi amigo Luis. Vamos al parque a dar una vuelta y después tomamos un helado *(ice cream)*. Cuando monto en bici siempre llevo gafas de sol y un gorro negro. Luis siempre lleva una chaqueta deportiva roja. Todas los noches veo una película en el salón con mis hermanas.

4. Cerca de mi casa hay un centro comercial donde hay muchas cosas que hacer. En el centro comercial hay un cine, muchos restaurantes y muchas tiendas. Todos los sábados Luis y yo vamos de compras y después comemos en mi restaurante favorito. Cuando hace buen tiempo también me gusta ir al parque que hay en mi calle. Si llueve, mi padre dice que *(says that)* tengo que llevar un abrigo.

5. En el centro también hay un polideportivo muy moderno. Este fin de semana voy a jugar al fútbol con mis amigos, ya que hay varias pistas de fútbol. Creo que será muy divertido y no será nada aburrido. Después voy a cenar pescado y arroz en casa.

6. A mí me gusta mi barrio porque es muy seguro y siempre está limpio. No hay mucha contaminación y tampoco hay mucho tráfico. Además, se puede comer bien y también se puede hacer mucho deporte. Sin embargo, el centro está un poco mal cuidado.

Darwin, 11 años. Artigas, Uruguay

1. Answer the following questions in English

a. Where does Darwin live? (2 details)

b. Who does he live with?

c. What time does he usually wake up?

d. What must he do after school? (2 details)

e. Where does he go with Luis after school?

f. What does he wear when he rides his bike?

g. What is near his house?

h. What does he do when the weather is good?

i. What will he do this weekend?

j. What is his opinion about his neighbourhood?

2. Find the Spanish equivalent in Darwin's text

a. I get on well with (1)

b. He helps me (1)

c. I always get up (2)

d. He also has (2)

e. With my friend (3)

f. In the living room (3)

g. Many things to do (4)

h. We go shopping (4)

i. Football pitches (5)

j. Fish and rice (5)

k. Lots of pollution (6)

l. Furthermore (6)

m. One can (6)

3. Complete the translation of paragraph 5

In the ___________________, there is _______________

a very ________________ sports centre. This

__________________, I am going to _____________

football with my ______________ given that there are

________________ football ______________. I think it

will be ____________ fun and not at all

_______________. _________________, for dinner I am

_______________ to have _____________ and

_______________ at home.

TERM 2 - BRINGING IT ALL TOGETHER – 6

Marcos, un chico español, está de vacaciones en Argentina. Está hablando con Fran, un chico local.

Marcos	Hola, me llamo Marcos. ¿Cómo te llamas?
Fran	Hola, Marcos. Me llamo Fran. ¿De dónde eres?
Marcos	Soy de Madrid, la capital de España. ¿Y tú? ¿Eres de aquí *(here)*?
Fran	Sí, este es mi barrio. ¿Estás de vacaciones?
Marcos	Sí. ¿Qué hay en tu ciudad? ¿Qué se puede hacer?
Fran	Hay muchas cosas que hacer en mi ciudad. Cerca de mi casa hay un centro comercial donde se puede ir de compras o ver una película en el cine.
Marcos	¡Qué guay! ¿Hay restaurantes buenos en el centro comercial?
Fran	Sí, claro. Pero los mejores restaurantes están en el centro de la ciudad. En el centro también hay un acuario nuevo. ¿Qué hay en tu ciudad?
Marcos	Qué chulo *(cool)*. Pua *(gosh)*, en Madrid hay muchísimas cosas que hacer. Tenemos muchos edificios antiguos, muchos restaurantes y, bueno, mucho de todo.
Fran	¿Y a ti? ¿Te gusta tu ciudad?
Marcos	Me encanta Madrid porque siempre se puede comer bien y está bastante bien cuidada. ¿Qué opinas tú de tu barrio?
Fran	Me gusta mi barrio porque está bien cuidado y está bastante limpio. Sin embargo, hay mucho tráfico así que también hay mucha contaminación.

4. True (T), False (F) or Not Mentioned (NM)?

Marcos is Argentinian.	
Marcos is from Madrid.	
The boys are in Fran's neighbourhood.	
Fran is on holiday.	
There isn't much to do in Fran's city.	
There is a big park on Fran's street.	
The best restaurants are in the centre.	
There is an old aquarium in the centre.	
There is lots to do in Madrid.	
Marcos doesn't like his city.	
Madrid is quite well looked after.	
Fran likes his neighbourhood.	
Fran's neigbourhood has a lot of pollution.	

5. Complete the statements

a. ________________ is on holiday in ________________ .

b. Fran has a ____________ near his house.

c. There is a new ________________ in the city centre.

d. ____________ loves Madrid because you can always ____________ well.

e. There is a lot of ____________ and ________________ in Fran's neigbourhood.

UNIT 7
Saying what I can do in my neighbourhood

In this unit you will learn:
- To say what there is to do in your neighbourhood
- To say what you like to or usually do in your neighbourhood
- To say where you do the activity

You will revisit:
- The verbs 'hacer', 'jugar' and 'ir' in the present indicative
- Places in town
- Free-time activities

UNIT 7. Saying what I can do in my neighbourhood

¿Qué se puede hacer en tu barrio?	What can one do in your neighbourhood?
¿Adónde se puede ir?	Where can one go?
¿Qué se puede ver y visitar?	What can one see and visit?

En mi barrio se puede hacer muchas cosas	In my neighbourhood one can do many things

Por ejemplo, *For example,* **se puede** *one can* **me gusta** *I like to* **suelo** *I tend to*	**hacer** *to do*	**deporte** / *sport* **equitación** / *horse riding* **footing** / *jogging* **natación** / *swimming* **senderismo** / *hiking* **turismo** / *sightseeing*		**en el bosque** *in the woods* **en el campo de fútbol** *on the football pitch* **en el casco antiguo** *in the old town* **en el centro comercial** *in the shopping mall* **en el centro de la ciudad** *in the city centre* **en el cine de mi barrio** *in my neighbourhood cinema* **en el club de tenis** *at the tennis club* **en el estadio** *in the stadium* **en el parque** *in the park* **en el polideportivo** *at the sports centre* **en la calle peatonal** *on the pedestrian street* **en la piscina** *in the swimming pool* **en la plaza mayor** *in the town square* **en la zona comercial de la ciudad** *in the commercial part of the city* **en la zona turística de la ciudad** *in the touristy part of the city*

The table, read by verb group:

hacer *to do*:
- **deporte** — *sport*
- **equitación** — *horse riding*
- **footing** — *jogging*
- **natación** — *swimming*
- **senderismo** — *hiking*
- **turismo** — *sightseeing*

jugar *to play*:
- **al fútbol** — *football*
- **al golf** — *golf*
- **al rugby** — *rugby*

ir *to go*:
- **a conciertos** — *to concerts*
- **al mercado** — *to the market*
- **de compras** — *shopping*
- **de marcha** — *clubbing*
- **de paseo** — *for a walk*

ver *to see*:
- **películas** — *films*
- **un partido de fútbol** — *a football game*

visitar *to visit*:
- **castillos** — *castles*
- **galerías de arte** — *art galleries*
- **mercados** — *markets*
- **museos** — *museums*
- **palacios históricos** — *historic palaces*
- **ruinas romanas** — *Roman ruins*

Left column phrases: **Por ejemplo,** *For example,* · **se puede** *one can* · **me gusta** *I like to* · **suelo** *I tend to*

Right column places:
- **en el bosque** — *in the woods*
- **en el campo de fútbol** — *on the football pitch*
- **en el casco antiguo** — *in the old town*
- **en el centro comercial** — *in the shopping mall*
- **en el centro de la ciudad** — *in the city centre*
- **en el cine de mi barrio** — *in my neighbourhood cinema*
- **en el club de tenis** — *at the tennis club*
- **en el estadio** — *in the stadium*
- **en el parque** — *in the park*
- **en el polideportivo** — *at the sports centre*
- **en la calle peatonal** — *on the pedestrian street*
- **en la piscina** — *in the swimming pool*
- **en la plaza mayor** — *in the town square*
- **en la zona comercial de la ciudad** — *in the commercial part of the city*
- **en la zona turística de la ciudad** — *in the touristy part of the city*

***Author's note:** Watch out for expressions like **"hacer natación"** that are translated as *'to go'* swimming. The literal translation is actually *'to do'* swimming. The verbs **"hacer"** and **"ir"** often translate differently in Spanish and English, so watch out for them :)

1. Multiple choice: tick the activity you hear

e.g.	Play football ✔	Go for a walk	Visit castles
a.	Go to a concert	Watch films	Watch a football game
b.	Play rugby	Play golf	Play tennis
c.	Visit museums	Visit Roman ruins	Visit galleries
d.	Go shopping	Go for a walk	Go clubbing
e.	Buy new clothes	Go to a concert	Watch TV
f.	Do sport	Go sightseeing	Do swimming
g.	Do jogging	Go hiking	Do horse riding

2. Spot the intruders

Me Soy Julio y vivo en un una barrio grande pequeño en mi pueblo ciudad. En mi el barrio se puede hacer muchas muchos cosas. Por ejemplo, se puede ir hacer footing en el bosque y en el cine parque. También se puede comprar ropa nueva de en el centro comercial, o hacer natación en la piscina mayor o visitar ver museos en el polideportivo casco antiguo.

3. Fill in the blanks

a. Buenos _____________. Me llamo Paloma y _________ de San Roque, en el _______ de España. Vivo en un piso en un ___________ muy ___________. En mi barrio se ___________ hacer muchas ___________. Por ___________, se puede ___________ deporte en el ___________ o jugar al fútbol en el ___________ de fútbol ___________ de mi ___________.

b. También se puede ir de ___________ en el parque ___________ y visitar ___________ en el casco ___________. Me gusta ___________ partidos de fútbol en el ___________. Sin embargo, no suelo hacer ___________ en el ___________ de la ciudad.

4. Listen to the different speakers and fill in the grid below in English

Name	One can do…	One can play…	One can go…	One can watch…	One can visit…
a. Dario					
b. Aida					
c. Pedro					

5. Gapped translation: fill in the blanks

	Sentence starter	Activity	Location
a.	One can	play football	
b.		visit castles	in the old town.
c.	I don't like to		in the stadium.
d.	I tend to		
e.	One cannot		
f.			at the tennis club.
g.		do jogging	

6. Narrow listening: gapped translation

_____________, how are you? I _____________ Esther. I am French _____________ I live in Seville, a _____________ in the _____________ of Spain. I _____________ in a house in an old _____________. In my neighbourhood _____________ _____________ do everything; one can do _____________ at the sports centre, go _____________ in the shops, go for a _____________ in the _____________ or watch films in the _____________. I _____________ to go to _____________ football _____________ in the _____________ or simply go _____________ in the park.

7. Listen to David and answer the questions in English

PART 1 – a.

1. How old is David?

2. Where does he live? (two details)

3. What can one do in his neighbourhood? (two details)

PART 2 – b.

1. What is there to do in the shopping mall?

2. What doesn't he like to do?

UNIT 7. What I can do in my neighbourhood: VOCAB BUILDING

1. Match

Se puede hacer deporte.	One can go to the stadium.
Se puede ir de paseo.	One can go to the bowling alley.
Se puede ir al estadio.	One can do jogging.
Se puede ir a la piscina.	One can go clubbing.
Se puede ir al cine.	One can do sport.
Se puede ir de marcha.	One can go to the cinema.
Se puede hacer footing.	One can go to concerts.
Se puede ir a la bolera.	One can go for a walk.
Se puede ir de compras.	One can visit art galleries.
Se puede ir a conciertos.	One can go shopping.
Se puede ver partidos de fútbol.	One can watch football matches.
Se puede visitar galerías de arte.	One can go to the swimming pool.

2. Complete with *hacer, ir, ver* o *visitar*

a. Se puede __________ deporte.

b. Se puede ________ turismo.

c. Se puede __________ footing.

d. Se puede __________ al estadio.

e. Se puede __________ castillos.

f. No se puede ________ de marcha.

g. Se puede ________ de paseo.

h. Se puede ________ a conciertos

3. Break the flow

a. Sepuedevisitargaleríasdearteenelcascoantiguo

b. Sepuedeirdepaseoenlaplaya

c. Sepuedehacerfootingenelparque

d. Sepuedeiraconciertosenelestadio

e. Sepuedeverpartidosdefútbolenelestadio

f. Sepuedevisitarcastillosenelcascoantiguo

g. Sepuedecomprarropademarcaenlacallepeatonal

h. Sepuedehacerdeporteenelpolideportivo

4. Sentence puzzle: rewrite the Spanish

a. puede Se fútbol partidos ver de

One can watch football matches.

b. Se ir puede paseo en de parque el

One can go for a walk in the park.

c. puede de ir Se marcha en centro el

One can go clubbing in the town centre.

d. puede visitar castillo un en Se el antiguo casco

One can visit a castle in the historic part of town.

e. puede hacer Se deporte el en polideportivo

One can do sport at the sports centre.

5. Translate into English

a. Se puede ir de paseo.

b. Se puede ir de marcha.

c. Se puede ir a la piscina.

d. Se puede ir de compras.

e. Se puede comprar ropa de marca.

f. Se puede montar en bici.

g. Se puede ir a la pista de patinaje.

h. Se puede ver partidos.

i. Se puede hacer footing en el parque.

6. Match each of the actions on the left with the places on the right

Se puede ver partidos de fútbol	en el jardín botánico.
Se puede ver plantas y árboles	en la piscina.
Se puede comer bien	en el estadio.
Se puede hacer natación	en las tiendas del centro.
Se puede comprar ropa bonita	en el cine cerca de mi casa.
Se puede montar en bici	en el casco antiguo.
Se puede ver películas	en el restaurante.
Se puede ver edificios históricos y castillos	en el parque.

7. Split sentences: form logical sentences

Se puede ver	de fútbol.
Se puede visitar edificios	platos típicos.
Se puede hacer natación	películas.
Se puede ver partidos	deporte.
Se puede comer	en la piscina.
Se puede ir de	históricos.
Se puede hacer	en bici.
Se puede montar	compras.

8. Translate into English

a. Ir de compras

b. El casco antiguo

c. Ver partidos

d. Ver películas

e. Ir al estadio

f. Las tiendas

g. La calle peatonal

h. Ir en bici

i. Ir de marcha

j. Hacer turismo

k. La plaza mayor

9. Faulty translation
(Please note - not all translations are wrong)
a. El casco antiguo: *The industrial area*

b. Un espectáculo de flamenco: *A flamingo show*

c. Edificios antiguos: *Modern buildings*

d. Ir al estadio: *To go to the park*

e. Hacer natación: *To do horse riding*

f. Ir de compras: *To go shopping*

g. La calle peatonal: *The main square*

h. Ir en bici: *To go running*

i. Ver castillos: *To see monuments*

j. Ir de marcha: *To go sightseeing*

k. Hacer turismo: *To see tourists*

l. Ir a la playa: *To go to the beach*

10. Spot and correct the grammar and spelling mistakes

a. Se puede comprar ropas nuevas.

b. Se puede ver edificio históricos.

c. Se puede ir natación.

d. Se puede visitar una castillo.

e. Se puede montar bici.

f. Se puede ir footing.

g. Se puede visitar el antiguo casco.

h. Se puede ver partidos de furbo.

i. Se puede veo una película en el cine.

j. Se puede jugar al tenís.

UNIT 7. What I can do in my neighbourhood: VOCAB BUILDING

11. Match

Hacer deporte	Visit museums
Jugar al fútbol	In the shopping mall
Ir de marcha	Do swimming
Visitar museos	In the stadium
Hacer footing	Go clubbing
En la plaza mayor	Go to concerts
Por ejemplo	Do sport
En el centro comercial	In the old town
En el estadio	In the town square
Ir a conciertos	Play football
Hacer natación	For example
En el casco antiguo	Do jogging

12. Complete with the missing letters

a. Hacer d _ p _ rt _

b. Ir d _ pas _ o

c. V _ r pel _ cul _ s

d. H _ cer t _ r _ sm _

e. _ is _ tar c _ st _ l _ os

f. J _ g _ r a _ f _ tb _ l

g. _ acer eq _ ita _ i _ n

h. La pla _ a ma _ o _

i. El c _ sc _ an _ ig _ o

13. Translate into English

a. Suelo visitar castillos en el casco antiguo.

b. Me gusta ir de paseo en el parque.

c. Se puede ir al estadio para ver un partido de fútbol.

d. No se puede jugar al golf en la piscina.

e. Me encanta hacer natación en la piscina.

f. Suelo jugar al tenis en el club de tenis cerca del colegio.

g. No suelo ir al cine para ver películas.

h. Me gusta visitar palacios históricos en la zona turística.

i. Suelo ir de compras al centro comercial con mi madre.

j. En mi barrio no se puede hacer muchas cosas.

k. En mi barrio se puede visitar museos en el centro de la ciudad.

14. Spot and add in the missing words

a. Me gusta castillos.

b. Me gusta de compras con mi hermana.

c. En mi barrio no puede hacer muchas cosas.

d. Se puede jugar fútbol.

e. Me gusta turismo en el centro de Madrid.

f. Me encanta barrio porque se puede hacer muchas cosas.

g. Suelo ir paseo en el parque.

h. No me gusta películas en el cine.

i. Se puede visitar museos en plaza mayor.

15. Fill in the gaps

a. Ver _ _ _ película.

b. _ _ _ _ _ deporte.

c. _ _ _ _ _ al tenis.

d. _ _ de compras.

e. Hacer f _ _ _ _ _ g.

f. Ir de p _ _ _ _.

g. Ir al _ _ _ _ para ver una película.

h. Me gusta _ _ _ _ _ al fútbol con mis amigos.

i. Se puede ir al _ _ _ _ _ _ _ a ver un partido de fútbol.

j. No me gusta ir a c _ _ c _ _ _ _ _ s en el parque.

k. Se puede _ _ _ _ _ _ _ palacios históricos en el casco antiguo.

l. Por la mañana no se puede _ _ _ _ _ nada.

UNIT 7. What I can do in my neighbourhood: READING

Hola. Soy Sergio. Vivo en las afueras de la ciudad, cerca del campo. Mi barrio es muy feo. Hay muchos edificios antiguos y sucios. No hay mucho que hacer para los jóvenes. Sin embargo, hay algunas (*some*) instalaciones deportivas como canchas de baloncesto, un club de tenis y un gimnasio. También hay un parque pequeño. Por lo tanto, se puede hacer deporte; me gusta hacer mucho deporte en mi tiempo libre. En mi barrio, también se puede hacer natación en el polideportivo o hacer footing en el bosque. No suelo ir de paseo pero me encanta hacer footing.

Sergio, 13 años. Logroño, España

2. Find the Spanish equivalent in Mercedes' text

a. The old town

b. Near the port

c. Historic buildings

d. Very beautiful

e. Flea market

f. In the open air

g. There isn't a lot to do

h. One can play

i. This weekend I'm going to go shopping

j. I am going to buy

k. I am going to go sailing

l. It will be a lot of fun

m. I am going to go to the cinema

n. We are going to watch a romantic film

3. Read Mercedes' text and tick the words not mentioned

a. Piscina	g. Afueras
b. Vela	h. Mercadillo
c. Pasé	i. Instalaciones
d. Vida	j. Novio
e. Cositas	k. Hay
f. Supermercado	l. Por lo tanto

1. Find and correct the mistakes in the translation of Sergio's text

Hi. I'm Sergio. I live in the outskirts of the city, near the sea. My neighbourhood is very beautiful. There are many old and historic buildings. There is not much to do for young people. Fortunately, there are some sports facilities such as tennis courts, a table-tennis club and a gym. Also, there is a big park. Therefore, one can go shopping; I like to do a bit of sport in my free time. On my street, one can also do swimming in the pond or do jogging in the city. I don't tend to go for a walk and I hate to do jogging.

Hola, soy Mercedes. Vivo en el casco antiguo de mi ciudad, cerca del puerto. Mi barrio es muy bonito. Hay un castillo, un palacio medieval y muchos edificios históricos.

No hay centros comerciales, pero hay muchas tiendas pequeñas muy bonitas y un mercadillo (*flea market*). Por lo tanto, se puede comprar muchas cosas interesantes y ropa bonita. Además, hay muchos restaurantes y cafeterías al aire libre. La vida nocturna es muy buena.

Me encanta mi barrio, pero no hay mucho que hacer para los jóvenes. Por ejemplo, no hay muchas instalaciones deportivas cerca de mi casa.

Afortunadamente, hay un parque pequeño donde se puede jugar al frisbi, montar en bici e ir de paseo. También hay un club de tenis y un club de vela.

Este fin de semana voy a ir de tiendas con mi madre y voy a comprar un vestido rosa y unos zapatos blancos. Luego voy a hacer vela con mi padre. ¡Será muy divertido! Después voy a ir al cine con mi novio. Vamos a ver una película romántica. ¡Qué emoción!

Mercedes, 12 años. Marbella, España

UNIT 7. What I can do in my neighbourhood: READING 2

Hola. Soy Roberto. En mi ciudad hay mucho que hacer para los jóvenes. Por eso (*for this reason*) me encanta. Hay muchos bares y restaurantes, muchas tiendas bonitas, muchas instalaciones deportivas, áreas verdes, lugares históricos y en el verano hay muchos espectáculos en la plaza mayor y en el estadio. Me encanta ir a conciertos porque me encanta la música en directo.

Mi barrio está en las afueras de la ciudad, cerca de la playa. Hay mucho que hacer. Se puede ir en bici en el parque cerca de mi colegio, se puede ver partidos de fútbol en el estadio, se puede hacer natación en la piscina municipal, se puede ir de compras, y mucho más.

Mañana por la mañana voy a ir al polideportivo con mis amigos. Voy a nadar y luego voy a hacer pesas con ellos. Después voy a ir de compras con mi madre al centro comercial cerca de mi casa. Luego, voy a montar en monopatín en el parque con mis amigos. Finalmente, voy a ir a casa de mi amigo Felipe para ver un partido de fútbol.

Roberto, 15 años. Teruel, España

1. True, False or Not mentioned?

a. Roberto loves his town.

b. There is a big theatre.

c. He lives on the outskirts.

d. He lives far from the beach.

e. He goes to the stadium often.

f. Tomorrow he is going to lift weights.

g. He is going to watch a football match with his girlfriend.

2. Find the Spanish in Roberto's text

a. There is a lot to do

b. For young people

c. Many beautiful shops

d. Historic places

e. Near the beach

f. One can ride a bike

g. One can watch matches

h. One can go shopping

i. Much more

j. Tomorrow morning

k. I am going to swim

l. I am going to do weights

m. I am going to go shopping

n. I am going to go skateboarding

o. I am going to go to my friend's house

3. Do the tasks below

a. List in English all the places mentioned in the first paragraph.

b. List in English the 5 things one can do in Roberto's neighbourhood, mentioned in the second paragraph.

c. List in English the 5 things Roberto is going to do, mentioned in the third paragraph.

4. Read Roberto's text: translate the words you can find in the text and cross out the rest

a. Casco antiguo	h. Mañana	o. Partido
b. Voy a ir de compras	i. Por la mañana	p. Gente
c. Natación	j. Tarde	q. La plaza
d. Compras	k. Cerca	r. Los jóvenes
e. Enseguida	l. Lejos	s. Los ancianos
f. Por fin	m. Voy a hacer	t. Pesas
g. Luego	n. Ver	u. Con nosotros

Hola. Soy Fernando. Mi ciudad se llama Tarragona. Está situada en el noreste de España, en la costa, cerca de Barcelona. Es una ciudad histórica con un casco antiguo muy bonito.

Hay muchos turistas, así que hay mucho tráfico y ruido, pero hay mucho que hacer para los jóvenes. Lo que más me gusta es la playa. Mi casa está en la orilla del mar. ¡Me encanta pasear por la playa!

Mi barrio es bastante moderno. Hay muchas tiendas muy bonitas, bares y restaurantes, tres centros comerciales, dos cines y muchas instalaciones deportivas, como piscinas, gimnasios y polideportivos. Hay muchas áreas verdes también. La vida nocturna es fenomenal.

Por lo tanto, se puede hacer muchas cosas: se puede comer bien, se puede ir al parque, se puede correr y hacer deporte al aire libre, se puede ir de paseo en la playa y mucho más.

Mañana por la mañana voy a ir a la playa con mis amigos. Voy a nadar, tomar el sol y jugar al voleibol con ellos. Luego voy a ir de compras con mi madre en el centro comercial cerca de mi casa. Después, voy a montar en bici en el parque con mi amigo Paco hasta las cinco de la tarde. Finalmente, voy a ir a casa de mi amigo Felipe para jugar a videojuegos.

Este fin de semana voy a ver un documental muy curioso. Se trata de una colonia de pingüinos de Magallanes, que viven en Patagonia (en el sur de Argentina). Es mi animal favorito. ¡Me encanta su forma de andar!

Fernando, 12 años. Tarragona, España

2. Correct any wrong statements about Fernando's text

a. His town is on the coast, far from Barcelona.

b. He lives close to the sea.

c. He loves going for a walk in the park.

d. His neighbourhood has an average nightlife.

e. His neighbourhood has no green spaces.

f. Yesterday he went for a walk with his mother.

g. He played videogames with Paco.

h. He watched a documentary about lions.

1. Translate into Spanish

a. Old town

b. Noise

c. Young people

d. On the shore

e. To have a walk

f. Sports facilities

g. Green spaces

h. Therefore

i. Many things

j. One can eat well

k. One can go for a walk

l. Much more

m. Tomorrow morning

n. I'm going to sunbathe

o. I'm going to go shopping

p. To play videogames

3. Complete the sentences in Spanish based on Fernando's text

a. Se llama ____________.

b. Su ciudad se llama ____________.

c. El casco antiguo de su ciudad es muy ____________.

d. Lo malo de Tarragona es que hay ____________.

e. Su casa está en la ____________.

f. Las tiendas de su barrio son muy ____________.

g. En su barrio hay mucho que hacer para los ____________.

h. Mañana va a ir a casa de su amigo Felipe a ________ __ ____________.

i. Este fin de semana Fernando va a ver un programa de televisión sobre unos ________ que viven en ________.

UNIT 7. What I can do in my neighbourhood: WRITING & TRANSLATION

1. Complete with the missing letters

a. E _ m _ b _ _ _ _ _   *In my neighbourhood...*

b. S _ p _ _ _ _ h _ _ _ _ m _ _ _ _ _ c _ _ _ _   *One can do many things.*

c. S _ p _ _ _ _ c _ _ _ _ bien   *One can eat well.*

d. S _ p _ _ _ _ i _ d _ c _ _ _ _ _ _ _   *One can go shopping.*

e. S _ p _ _ _ _ h _ _ _ _ d _ _ _ _ _ _   *One can do sport.*

f. S _ p _ _ _ _ m _ _ _ _ _ e _ b _ _ _   *One can ride a bike.*

g. M _ _ _ _ _ p_ _ l _ m _ _ _ _ _   *Tomorrow morning...*

h. V _ _ a i _ a_ c _ _ _ _ _ c _ _ _ _ _ _ _ _ _   *I am going to go to the shopping mall.*

i. V _ _ a v _ _ u _ _ p _ _ _ _ _ _ _ _   *I am going to watch a film.*

2. Sentence puzzle: write the sentences below in the correct order

a. al a una película a ir cine Voy ver

b. por la bici Mañana montar en mañana voy a

c. se puede En hacer deporte mi barrio

d. ir al centro semana voy fin de comercial a Este

e. muchas barrio En hay mi bonitas tiendas

f. En se puede mi hacer barrio muchas cosas

g. puede al en frisbi Se el jugar parque

h. La semana al voy a ir que viene polideportivo

i. estadio Voy con a ir al ver para un partido de fútbol

4. Translate into Spanish

a. The park

b. My neighbourhood

c. Next weekend

d. Tomorrow

e. Next week

f. Tomorrow morning

g. Near my house

h. One can eat

i. A football match

j. In the open air

3. Complete with a suitable word

a. Mañana _______ _ ___ al cine para ______ una ___________ de acción.

b. Este fin de ________ voy a ir de ________con mi _________ en el ____________ _______________ cerca de mi casa.

c. En mi __________ se puede __________ muchísimas cosas.

d. La semana que _________ voy a _________ en bici en el __________ cerca de mi casa.

e. Vivo en el __________ antiguo, la parte histórica de mi ____________.

f. En mi barrio ______ una vida nocturna fenomenal. Se puede ir a _________ y restaurantes al aire ___________.

g. El fin de __________ que viene ______ a ___ al ___________________ cerca de mi casa para ___________ natación y __________ al bádminton con mis ____________.

h. Se puede _________ muchos museos, galerías de _______ y palacios _____________.

i. Este fin de semana ________ a ______ de paseo en el campo. Será________________.

UNIT 7. What I can do in my neighbourhood: WRITING & TRANSLATION

5. Spot and correct the grammar and spelling mistakes

a. En mi barrio puede hacer muchas cosas.

b. Se puede ver muchas monumentos.

c. Se puede visitar museos y palacios históricos.

d. Mi barrio es en las afueras.

e. Manana voy a ir al centro comercial cerca de mi casa.

f. Voy comprar ropa en una tienda en el centro.

g. Este fin de semana voy a hago pesas con mi mejor amigo.

h. Se puede ir el estadio.

i. Mañana por la banana voy a ir de paseo en la playa.

j. Voy a juger al tennis con mi amigo Paco.

8. Write two paragraphs in the first person singular (I) about Yolanda and Luke. NOTE: you cannot repeat the same information twice

Yolanda (12 years old from Spain)	**Luke** (17 years old from England)
• Say your name, age and nationality	• Say your name, age and nationality
• Describe your physique and personality (4 details)	• Describe your physique and personality (6 details)
• Say you live in the north-east of Spain, near Barcelona, on the coast	• Say you live in the south of England, near London, in the countryside
• Describe your neighbourhood, what is there to see and do (4 details minimum)	• Describe your town: size, what is there to see and do (4 details minimum)
• Say one thing you like and one that you dislike about your neighbourhood	• Say one thing you like and one that you dislike about your town
• Say 4 things that you are going to do next weekend in your neighbourhood	• Say 2 things that you can do in your neighbourhood and 4 things you are going to do next weekend

6. Complete

a. Voy a na _ _ _   *I am going to swim*

b. Voy a v _ _   *I am going to see*

c. Voy a _ _   *I am going to go*

d. Voy a h _ _ _ _   *I am going to do*

e. Voy a m _ _ _ _ _   *I am going to ride*

f. Voy a v _ _ _ _ _ _   *I am going to visit*

g. Voy a j _ _ _ _   *I am going to play*

7. Translate into Spanish

a. In my neighbourhood one can do many things.

b. In my town there are many shops and a flea market.

c. There is a big park near my house.

d. In the old town there are many historic buildings and a medieval palace.

e. The nightlife is excellent. There are many bars and restaurants.

f. One can do many sports because there is a big sports centre.

g. Tomorrow I am going to go sailing with my father.

h. I am going to ride a bike in the park with my best friend.

i. Next weekend I am going to go for a walk on the beach with my friend.

j. Next week I am going to go sightseeing in Madrid.

k. I am going to go to the sports centre and I am going to swim.

TERM 2 - BRINGING IT ALL TOGETHER – 7

1. Hola, soy Sebastián y vivo en Quito, la capital de Ecuador. Quito está en el centro-norte del país. Vivo en un piso moderno en el centro de la ciudad. Vivo con mi padre, mi madrastra *(stepmother)* y mi hermana. Mi hermana se llama Lupita y tiene catorce años. Me llevo bien con ella porque es muy deportista y muy amable.

2. Antes del colegio me levanto a las siete y desayuno cereales con leche. Cuando vuelvo a casa después del colegio tengo que hacer mis deberes si quiero salir con mis amigos. Cuando tengo tiempo también juego a la Play en mi dormitorio. Sin embargo, si hace buen tiempo, me gusta leer un libro en la terraza.

3. Cerca de mi casa hay un jardín botánico. Este fin de semana mi familia y yo vamos a ir al jardín y después vamos a ir a un restaurante chino a comer. Creo que será muy divertido porque me encanta la comida china. Voy a comer mucho y voy a beber agua con gas *(sparkling water)*.

4. A mí me gusta mi barrio porque no es peligroso y está muy bien cuidado. Nunca hay basura *(rubbish)* en la calle. Sin embargo, lo malo es que siempre hay mucho tráfico. Además, por la noche hay mucho ruido en mi barrio ya que hay muchos restaurantes cerca de mi casa.

5. En mi barrio hay un polideportivo grande y un parque muy bonito. También hay un centro comercial moderno muy cerca de mi piso. Los fines de semana me gusta ir al parque a jugar al golf con mis amigos o hacer footing con mi hermana. Cuando hago footing siempre llevo una camiseta sin mangas y pantalones cortos. Sin embargo, cuando llueve prefiero ver una película en el cine en la plaza mayor.

6. En mi ciudad también hay mucha cultura. Si te gusta el turismo, se puede visitar castillos, galerías de arte y museos. A mi hermana le gusta visitar las ruinas incas en las montañas porque es fanática de la historia. Cuando hace mal tiempo ella prefiere visitar museos o la galería en el centro de la ciudad.

Sebastián, 12 años. Quito, Ecuador

1. Answer the following questions in English

a. Where is Quito?

b. Who does Sebastián live with?

c. What does Sebastián eat for breakfast?

d. What does Sebastián do if the weather is good?

e. What is Sebastián doing this weekend? (2 details)

f. What will he have to drink at the restaurant?

g. What does Sebastián think of his neighbourhood?

h. What does Sebastián do on weekends? (2 details)

i. What does Sebastián wear when he goes jogging?

j. What does his sister like to do?

2. Find the Spanish equivalent in Sebastián's text

a. Of the city (1)

b. She is called (1)

c. When I return (2)

d. I like to read (2)

e. We are going (3)

f. To eat a lot (3)

g. It isn't dangerous (4)

h. There is always (4)

i. Very close (5)

j. The town square (5)

k. There is a lot (6)

l. Visit castles (6)

m. She prefers (6)

3. Complete the translation of paragraph 6

In my ___________, there is also a _________ of culture.

If you like _________________, one can visit _________________, art galleries and _____________.

My _______________ likes to _______________ the Inca ruins in the _________________ because _________ is a fan of ___________________. When the _______________ is ___________, she prefers _______ _______________ museums or the ___________________ in the _________________ _________________.

Rebeca está hablando por Whatsapp con su prima Gabriela. Viven en diferentes países y están hablando de sus barrios.

Rebeca	Hola, prima. ¿Qué tal? ¿Estás bien?
Gabriela	Sí, guapa, estoy muy bien. ¿Y tú? ¿Qué tal está tu familia?
Rebeca	Todos estamos muy bien. Este fin de semana tenemos muchos planes. Vamos a salir por el barrio.
Gabriela	Ah, ¿sí? ¿Qué se puede hacer en tu barrio?
Rebeca	Cerca de mi casa hay un polideportivo, así que se puede hacer mucho deporte. Todos los sábados mis hermanos y yo vamos a jugar al tenis. ¿Y tú?
Gabriela	En mi ciudad también hay mucho que hacer. Se puede ir de compras en el centro comercial nuevo y además, en el centro de la ciudad también hay un cine muy grande.
Rebeca	¡Qué guay! ¿Sueles ir al cine?
Gabriela	Sí. Cuando tengo tiempo me encanta ir al cine con mis amigos. También me gusta ver espectáculos en la plaza mayor. ¿En tu barrio hay cosas que visitar?
Rebeca	¡Claro! En mi barrio hay un castillo antiguo, dos galerías de arte y cuatro museos. Mi museo favorito es el de ciencia. ¿Te gustan los museos?
Gabriela	No, prefiero ir de compras o a dar una vuelta por el parque. ¿Se puede ir de compras en tu barrio?
Rebeca	En mi barrio no hay muchas tiendas ni restaurantes, pero en el centro de la ciudad sí hay. No suelo ir de compras mucho pero mi hermano sí que va de compras a menudo.
Gabriela	En mi barrio tampoco hay restaurantes. Solo hay una cafetería pequeña y no me llevo bien con el dueño *(the owner)* porque es muy antipático.

4. True (T), False (F) or Not Mentioned (NM)?

Rebeca and Gabriela are friends.	
Rebeca has many plans this weekend.	
There is a shopping mall near Rebeca's house.	
Every Monday, Rebeca does her homework.	
Every Saturday, Rebeca plays tennis.	
There is a very big cinema in Gabriela's city.	
Gabriela tends to go to the cinema.	
Rebeca loves the aquarium.	
Gabriela prefers to go shopping.	
Gabriela hates going to the park.	
There are not many restaurants near Rebeca.	
Rebeca's brother goes clubbing a lot.	
Gabriela loves the small café in her neigbourhood.	

5. Complete the statements

a. Rebeca and Gabriela are
______________.

b. Rebeca plays ______________ with her ______________.

c. ______________ likes to watch ______________ in the town square.

d. Rebeca's favourite museum is the ______________ museum.

e. ______________ does not get on with the ______________ of the local café.

TERM 2 – MIDPOINT – RETRIEVAL PRACTICE

1. Answer the following questions in Spanish

¿Dónde vives?	
¿Dónde está tu ciudad?	
¿Qué hay en tu barrio?	
¿Qué hay cerca de tu casa?	
¿Qué hay en tu calle?	
¿Te gusta tu barrio? ¿Por qué?	
¿Qué se puede hacer en tu barrio?	
¿Adónde se puede ir en tu barrio?	
¿Qué se puede ver en tu barrio?	
¿Qué se puede visitar en tu barrio?	
¿Qué sueles hacer en tu barrio los fines de semana?	

2. Write a paragraph in the first person singular (I) providing the following details

a. Your name is Ana. You are 14 and are from Madrid.

b. You live in a small house in the centre of Madrid.

c. In your family there are four people: your father, mother and your older brother, Pedro.

d. Near your house, there are many things to do.

e. For example, there are cafés, restaurants, a cinema and a big park.

f. In the city centre, there is a big sports centre, a botanical garden and an aquarium.

g. On your street, there are some small shops and a local pool.

h. You like your neighbourhood because it is very safe, it is always clean and there is lots to do.

i. For example, in your neighbourhood you can do swimming, jogging and you can play football.

j. You can also go shopping in the shopping mall or for a walk in the park.

k. You can also watch football matches, go to concerts and visit the old castle.

UNIT 8
Describing my street

In this unit you will learn:
- To say what there is on your street
- To describe where things are located in relation to one another
- To describe where your house is
- To say what you don't have on your street

You will revisit:
- Places in town
- Definite and indefinite articles
- Adjectival agreement

UNIT 8. Describing my street

¿Qué hay en tu calle?	What is there on your street?
¿Dónde está tu casa?	Where is your house?
¿Qué sitios hay en tu barrio?	What places are there in your neighbourhood?

	Masculine nouns		**Feminine nouns**	
En mi calle hay *On my street there is* **Cerca de mi casa hay** *Near my house there is*	un aparcamiento	*a car park*	una biblioteca	*a library*
	un campo de fútbol	*a football pitch*	una carnicería	*a butcher's*
	un centro comercial	*a shopping mall*	una estación de tren	*a train station*
	un edificio	*a building*	una iglesia	*a church*
	un polideportivo	*a sports centre*	una mezquita	*a mosque*
	un parque pequeño	*a small park*	una panadería	*a bakery*
	un restaurante chino	*a chinese restaurant*	una piscina municipal	*a local pool*
	un supermercado	*a supermarket*	una sinagoga	*a synagogue*
	un teatro	*a theatre*	una zapatería	*a shoe shop*
	una tienda de	*a ... shop*	deporte	*sport*
			música	*music*
			ropa	*clothes*

				Feminine nouns	
El cine *The cinema* **Mi casa** *My house* **Mi edificio** *My building* **Mi piso** *My flat*	**está** *is*	a la derecha	*to the right*	**de la** *of/from*	biblioteca
		a la izquierda	*to the left*		carnicería
		al lado	*next to*		panadería
		cerca	*near*		piscina
		delante	*in front*		tienda de música
		detrás	*behind*	**Masc. nouns**	
		enfrente	*opposite*	**del** *of/from*	campo de fútbol
		en la esquina	*on the corner*		centro comercial
		lejos	*far*		colegio
		a diez minutos a pie *a 10 minute walk away*			estadio
		a diez minutos en coche *a 10 minute car ride away*			museo
					parque
	al final de la calle *at the end of the street*				

Mi casa **Mi piso**	**está**	**entre** *between*	la carnicería el cine	**y**	el supermercado la piscina

No hay *There is not*	ningún *any (m – sg.)*	**polideportivo** *sports centre*	cerca de donde vivo *near where I live* en mi barrio *in my neighbourhood*
	ninguna *any (f – sg.)*	**tienda buena** *good shop*	por aquí *around here*

1. Multiple choice: tick the place you hear

e.g.	A mall ✓	A church	A theatre
a.	A theatre	A football pitch	A building
b.	A restaurant	A clothes shop	A mosque
c.	A shoe shop	A bakery	A park
d.	A train station	A synagogue	A supermarket
e.	A sports shop	A butcher's	A restaurant
f.	A music shop	A train station	A local pool
g.	A bakery	A mall	A sports centre

2. Spot the intruders

Me Mi llamo Paula y vivo en un una barrio bastante pequeño grande en el norte este de Chile. En mi calle no hay varias cosas; hay una iglesia, una un zapatería, una estación de tren y un campo de fútbol. Mi piso casa está al lado del la campo de fútbol y la iglesia. La zapatería está entre la iglesia y la el estación de tren. Hay cerca un cine a diez minutos en tren coche pero no hay ninguna tienda de música ropa.

3. Fill in the blanks

a. Buenos días. _______ Xabi, tengo _________ años y _________ en Tolosa, una _________ en el País Vasco. Vivo en un ________ en una calle muy _________ en el _________ de la ciudad. En mi calle hay un ___________, una biblioteca y una ___________ muy mona.

b. La panadería está a la __________ de mi casa. La __________ está a la __________ y el supermercado está al final de la ________, en la __________. Mi casa está ________ la panadería y ______ biblioteca. Desafortunadamente, no ________ ningún restaurante en mi __________ pero sí hay un __________ chino a diez __________ en coche.

4. Faulty translation: one column contains a mistake - listen and correct the errors

e.g.	The cinema is	*to the* ~~left~~ *right*	of the library.
a.	My house is	next to	the shoe shop.
b.	The sports centre is	behind	the stadium.
c.	My flat is	near	the school.
d.	The butcher's	is to the left	of the music shop.
e.	Is the church	near	the theatre?
f.	The mosque isn't	opposite	the bakery.
g.	The restaurant is	near	my house.
h.	My building is	in front	of the museum.

5. Listening slalom: follow the speaker from top to bottom and number the boxes accordingly

e.g.	a	b	c	d
On my street there is	On my street there is	Near my flat there is	Near my house there isn't	Near my building there is
an Indian restaurant,	a church,	a shopping mall,	**a local pool,**	a mosque,
a big park	a small park	**a bakery**	a music shop	but there is a shoe shop
and a Chinese restaurant.	or a theatre.	and a library.	and a theatre.	**and a supermarket.**
The bakery is	The mosque is	The park is	The shop is	The church is
very far from	**opposite**	near	next to	far from
your house.	the restaurant.	the school.	**a football pitch.**	my house.

6. Narrow listening: gapped translation

a. Hello, my ______________ is Emiliano. I am from Spain but I live in _________ _______, the ______________ of Argentina. I live in a modern ______________ on the outskirts of the ______________. On my ______________ there are various places: a big ______________, an old ______________, ___ _________ _________ and an Italian ______________.

b. My house is ______________ the park and the pool. ______________ my house is the ______________ and the restaurant is to the ______________ of the supermarket. There aren't any ______________ shops ______________ where I live.

7. Listen to Irene and answer the questions in English

a. Where is she from?

b. Where does she live? (two details)

c. Who does she live with?

d. What is there on her street?

e. What places are in the town centre? (3 details)

f. What kind of restaurant does her neighbourhood **not** have?

UNIT 8. Describing my street: VOCABULARY BUILDING

1. Match

A la derecha de	Near
A la izquierda de	Ten minutes away on foot
Detrás de	On my street
Enfrente de	Behind
Al lado de	Far from
Cerca de	Next to
Lejos de	My house is
En mi calle	To the left of
Mi casa está	100 metres away from
En mi barrio	Opposite to
Mi edificio está	Ten minutes away by car
A diez minutos en coche	In my neighbourhood
A cien metros de	To the right of
A diez minutos a pie	My building is

2. Complete the translations

a. En mi calle   *On my __________*

b. Lejos de   *__________ from*

c. A cien metros de   *_______ metres from*

d. En mi barrio   *In my __________*

e. Mi casa está   *My _________ is*

f. No lejos de   *Not ______ from*

g. Mi edificio   *My __________*

h. A diez minutos   *Ten _________ away*

i. ...en coche   *...by _______*

j. Al lado de   *_________ to*

k. Detrás del cine   *_________ the cinema*

3. Verdadero (true) o falso (false). Write V for *verdadero* or F for *falso* next to each statement below, based on the map

Club de golf			Parque			
Carnicería	La casa de Antonio	Biblioteca	Tienda de música	Panadería	Supermercado Mercadona	Tienda de ropa
Calle Paco de Lucía						
La casa de B. Alba	Gimnasio	Bar	Restaurante indio	Restaurante chino	Cine	Tienda de esquina
Quiosco Ryan	Piscina	Restaurante italiano	Jardín		Aparcamiento	

a. La casa de Antonio está al lado de la biblioteca.   ___

b. La panadería está enfrente del restaurante chino.   ___

c. La tienda de música está delante del parque.   ___

d. Hay un centro comercial en la calle.   ___

e. El cine está cerca de la casa de Bernarda Alba.   ___

f. Hay un supermercado en la calle.   ___

g. El club de golf está detrás de la casa de Antonio.   ___

h. La tienda de ropa está entre el cine y el supermercado.   ___

UNIT 8. Describing my street: VOCABULARY BUILDING

4. Faulty translation: spot the mistakes in the English translations and correct them.
Please note: not all the translations have a mistake.

a. En mi calle hay muchas tiendas. *On my street there are not many shops.*

b. Cerca de mi casa hay un gimnasio y una piscina. *Near my house there are a gym and a pool.*

c. El club de tenis está enfrente de la escuela. *The tennis club is behind the school.*

d. No hay tiendas de ropa en mi calle. *There are no clothes shops in my house.*

e. ¿Hay una biblioteca por aquí? *Is there a library around here?*

f. El parque está detrás de la estación de tren. *The park is behind the bus station.*

g. Hay un supermercado al lado del cine. *There's a supermarket next to the sports centre.*

h. El restaurante chino está a una hora en coche. *The Chinese restaurant is 1 hour away on foot.*

5. Break the flow

a. Enmicallenohaytiendasderopa.

b. Hayunrestauranteadiezminutosapie.

c. Lapanaderíaestáalladodelacarnicería.

d. ¿Dóndeestálabiblioteca?

e. Elrestaurantechinoestáenfrentedelaiglesia.

f. Hayuncampodefútboldetrásdemicolegio.

g. Enmicallehaymuchastiendasbonitas.

h. Hayunrestaurantemuybuenocercademicasa.

6. Complete with the missing letters

a. Hay una igle _ _ _ cerca de mi ca _ _ .

b. Al la _ _ del supermercado hay un ci _ _.

c. Hay un parque det _ _ _ del restaurante.

d. No hay tiendas de ro _ _ en mi calle.

e. ¿Dón _ _ está la bibliote _ _ ?

f. Mi casa es _ _ enfrente del par _ _ _ _ .

g. La tien _ _ está a la derec _ _ del cine.

h. No ha _ restaurantes por aq _ _ .

7. Multiple choice: choose the correct translation

		1	2	3
a.	Behind	Delante de	Detrás de	Dentro de
b.	Next to	En la esquina	Lejos de	Al lado de
c.	Opposite	Enfrente de	Cerca de	Debajo de
d.	In front of	Encima de	Delante de	Detrás de
e.	To the right of	A la derecha de	A la izquierda de	En la esquina
f.	To the left of	Detrás de	A la derecha de	A la izquierda de
g.	Where is?	¿Quién es?	¿Dónde está?	¿Está aquí?
h.	In between	Al lado de	Dentro	Entre
i.	On the corner	Enfrente de	En la esquina	En mi pueblo
j.	Far from	Lejos de	Cerca de	Detrás de
k.	There is	Ay	Hay	Ahí
l.	On my street	En mi barrio	En mi casa	En mi calle

8. Location puzzle: complete the street map with the 10 missing names of places below, using the words in BOLD in the text below

   a. La **casa de Paco** está enfrente de la casa de Marta.
   b. Entre la casa de Marta y la piscina municipal hay un **supermercado** pequeño.
   c. Entre la tienda de ropa y la peluquería hay una **biblioteca**.
   d. A la derecha del club de golf hay un **aparcamiento** muy grande.
   e. Detrás del cine hay una **carnicería**.
   f. Al lado del cine, a la izquierda, hay una **cancha de baloncesto**.
   g. A la izquierda del Bar del Pingüino hay un **restaurante italiano**.
   h. Detrás del Gran Café Viñales hay una **tienda de juguetes**.
   i. Detrás de la casa de Paco hay un **campo de fútbol**.
   j. A la derecha de la tienda de juguetes hay una **heladería**.

Club de golf					
La casa de Marta		**Piscina municipal**	**Tienda de ropa**		**Peluquería Paloma**
Calle Barbastro					
	Gran Café Viñales		**Bar del Pingüino**		**Cine Conti**
			Jardín		

9. Translate into English

a. La casa de Marcelo está enfrente de la estación de tren.

b. La piscina municipal está entre el polideportivo y el supermercado.

c. La biblioteca está al final de la calle.

d. A la derecha del club de golf hay una biblioteca enorme.

e. Detrás del cine hay una pista de atletismo.

f. Al lado del cine, a la izquierda, hay una parada de autobús.

g. A la izquierda de mi colegio hay un restaurante chino.

h. Detrás de la comisaría hay una tienda de juguetes.

i. Al lado de la casa de Rafa hay un campo de fútbol y una cancha de baloncesto.

j. Cerca de mi casa hay un polideportivo muy grande con una piscina olímpica.

k. El estadio está muy lejos de mi casa.

l. Me encanta mi calle porque hay muchas tiendas.

UNIT 8. Describing my street: READING 1

Me llamo Luisa, soy de Úbeda, pero vivo en Málaga. Me encanta mi barrio porque hay muchas cosas que hacer. Hay muchas instalaciones deportivas, así que se puede hacer mucho deporte. Por ejemplo, en mi calle hay un gimnasio, un parque con una pista de patinaje y un polideportivo con una piscina olímpica. Ayer hice pesas en el gimnasio. Fue muy agotador pero muy divertido.

En mi barrio también hay muchas tiendas. Cerca de mi casa, a cinco minutos a pie, hay un centro comercial enorme. Se puede comprar de todo. A cien metros de mi casa está mi tienda de ropa favorita y al final de la calle hay una tienda de deporte muy guay. Ayer compré un par de zapatillas Adidas muy chulas.

En mi barrio hay muchos restaurantes buenos donde se puede comer muy bien. Al lado de mi casa, a la izquierda, hay un restaurante chino y al otro lado, a la derecha, hay un restaurante indio. El sábado pasado comí en el restaurante chino. La comida estaba muy rica.

Luisa, 15 años. Úbeda, España

1. Find the Spanish equivalent in Luisa's text

a. But I live

b. There are a lot of things to do

c. Sports facilities

d. On my street there are

e. A skating rink

f. I did weights

g. It was very tiring

h. There are many shops

i. Five minutes away on foot

j. 100 metres from my house

k. At the end of the street

l. Very cool

m. I bought a pair of shoes

n. One can eat very well

o. Next to my house

p. On the right

q. I ate in the Chinese restaurant

---

2. Tick the items that you can find in Luisa's text and cross out the ones you can't

a. In my neighbourhood	f. Yesterday	k. Olympic swimming pool
b. A lot of sport	g. Tomorrow	l. Trainers
c. Music shop	h. Very funny	m. A skirt
d. On the left	i. To do jogging	n. Near
e. The food was very tasty	j. Clothes shop	o. My house

---

3. Answer the questions in English

a. Why does Luisa like her neighbourhood?	g. Where is the sports shop?
b. What four sports facilities does Luisa mention?	h. How does she describe the sports shop?
c. What was tiring but fun?	i. How does she describe the restaurants?
d. How far is the shopping mall from her house?	j. What is next to her house, on the left?
e. What can one buy there?	k. Where did she eat last Saturday?
f. Where is the clothes shop?	l. What was the food like?

UNIT 8. Describing my street: READING 2

Me llamo Marcelo. Soy de Cádiz, pero vivo en Granada, una ciudad muy bonita e histórica en el sur de España. Vivo en un barrio residencial en las afueras de la ciudad. No me gusta porque no hay muchas instalaciones deportivas, así que no se puede hacer mucho deporte. Hay un gimnasio muy viejo y mal equipado, un parque muy pequeño, feo y mal cuidado, y un polideportivo muy malo: no tiene ni piscina ni canchas de tenis. Tampoco hay ningún campo de fútbol en mi ciudad. Ayer hice footing en el parque y monté en bici en el bosque cerca de mi casa. Fue muy agotador, pero bastante divertido.

Afortunadamente, hay un centro comercial enorme no muy lejos de mi casa, a diez minutos en coche. Hay muchas tiendas bonitas y se puede comprar de todo. Mi tienda favorita es la tienda de videojuegos.

Lo que más me gusta de mi barrio es que aquí tengo muchos amigos. Mi mejor amigo, Sergio, vive a cinco minutos a pie de mi casa, así que nos vemos *(we see each other)* a menudo.

En mi barrio hay muchos restaurantes bonitos donde se puede comer muy bien. Al lado de mi casa, a la izquierda, hay un restaurante italiano y al otro lado, a la derecha, hay un restaurante mexicano. El sábado pasado comí en el restaurante mexicano. La comida estaba muy sabrosa y picante. ¡Comí muchísimo!

Marcelo, 16 años. Cádiz, España

1. Find the Spanish equivalent in Marcelo's text

a. I live in

b. A very beautiful town

c. On the outskirts

d. Sports facilities

e. Therefore

f. A very old gym

g. Small, ugly

h. It has neither a swimming pool

i. Yesterday I did jogging

j. The wood

k. Near my house

l. Not very far from my house

m. Ten minutes away by car

n. One can buy all sorts of things

o. I have many friends here

p. Where one can eat very well

q. Next to my house

r. On the left

s. On the right

2. Answer providing as many details as possible.

a. What does Marcelo say about Granada?

b. Why does he not like his neighbourhood?

c. What does he say about the gym, the park and the sports centre?

d. What did he do yesterday?

e. Where is the shopping mall?

f. What can you buy there?

g. What is his favourite shop?

h. What does he like the most about his neighbourhood?

i. What is there to the left of his house?

j. What is there to the right?

k. Where did he eat last Saturday?

l. How was the food?

3. Tick the items that you can find in Marcelo's text

a. A pie	h. Mejor
b. En bici	i. Raramente
c. A la derecha	j. Sabrosa
d. Cerca	k. Grasienta
e. Todo	l. Agotador
f. Poco	m. Se puede
g. Mucho	n. Canchas

UNIT 8. Describing my street: WRITING & TRANSLATION

1. Translate into English

a. A la derecha del colegio

b. Cerca de mi casa

c. Enfrente del cine

d. Delante del supermercado

e. Al final de la calle

f. No lejos de mi casa

g. Al lado de la piscina

h. A cinco minutos a pie

i. A cien metros de mi casa

2. Sentence puzzle: rewrite the sentences in the correct order

a. mi En hay muchas barrio tiendas
In my neighbourhood there are many shops.

b. al un mi lado de gimnasio Hay casa
There is a gym next to my house.

c. al está La final la piscina calle de
The swimming pool is at the end of the street.

d. lejos no de Mi colegio está casa mi
My school is not far from my house.

e. cine entre El está parque el y biblioteca la
The cinema is between the park and the library.

3. Find in the wordsearch the Spanish translation of the phrases below, then write it next to each of them, as shown in the example

e.g. En mi calle
  On my street

```
A  L  F  I  N  A  L  D  E  L  A  C  A  L  L  E  Q  I  I  A  C
S  A  W  X  M  K  L  V  K  O  A  R  I  X  N  Z  T  G  L  E  S
E  K  I  C  O  R  Y  D  I  Z  O  M  B  C  G  L  W  A  R  L  O
N  N  E  T  Q  O  T  R  H  Z  U  W  O  N  X  A  D  C  S  A  J
M  Q  U  L  R  M  R  C  D  B  G  C  U  C  W  E  A  X  E  T  E
I  V  B  D  A  A  K  Y  M  Y  H  H  R  M  R  D  H  I  G  I  L
C  X  J  X  B  D  X  K  N  E  T  P  H  E  E  Q  P  U  K  E  Á
A  L  A  I  Z  Q  U  I  E  R  D  A  C  M  Z  A  I  U  A  N  T
L  R  M  C  Z  V  R  T  M  B  J  H  I  W  H  E  O  V  R  D  S
L  N  B  W  U  E  B  N  K  Z  A  C  I  W  J  V  S  P  D  A  E
E  E  S  B  P  U  M  D  E  H  A  P  L  T  Q  P  C  D  D  W  O
Z  N  U  K  H  B  X  A  A  S  X  C  F  D  N  W  O  E  H  L  N
H  K  G  M  S  O  V  Y  A  W  H  J  A  C  R  E  C  Á  T  S  E
```

a. On the left

b. It is near

c. On foot

d. By car

e. On the right there is

f. Near my house

g. In my neighbourhood

h. It isn't far

i. The shop

j. At the end of the road

4. Tick the words below which are names of shops

a. Una carnicería

b. Un bosque

c. Un parque

d. Una panadería

e. Un supermercado

f. Una manzana

g. Una biblioteca

5. Complete with the missing letters

a. Una pana _ _ _ _ _   *A bakery*

b. Una _ _ _ nicer _ _   *A butcher's*

c. Un par _ _ _   *A park*

d. Una bi _ lio _ _ _ _   *A library*

e. Una tie _ _ _ de m _ sic _   *A music shop*

f. Un e _ _ _ _ _ _ o   *A building*

g. Una _ _ _ nda de _ _ porte   *A sports shop*

6. Complete with the missing words

a. En mi calle hay muchas _____________. *On my street there are many shops.*

b. La panadería está a cinco minutos a _______. *The bakery is five minutes away on foot.*

c. La biblioteca está al ___________ de mi colegio. *The library in next to my school.*

d. La _____________ está allí, a la _______________. *The butcher's is there, on the right.*

e. Mi coche está _____________ del supermercado. *The car is in front of the supermarket.*

f. El estadio está muy ___________ de mi casa. *The stadium is very far from my house.*

g. La piscina está al ___________ de la calle. *The swimming pool is at the end of the road.*

h. En mi __________ no hay muchas ___________. *On my street there aren't many shops.*

i. _____________ de mi edificio hay un parque. *Behind my building there is a park.*

7. Translate into Spanish

a. *Next to my house* A_ l______ d_ m_ c______

b. *Opposite my building* E__________ d_ m_ e___________

c. *Far from here* L________ d_ a________

d. *On the right* A l_ d_______________

e. *On the left* A l_ i_______________

f. *Near my house* C_________ d_ m_ c_______

g. *Behind the butcher's* D_________ d_ l_ c______________

h. *Next to the bakery* A_ l______ d_ l_ p_____________

8. Write a paragraph in which you:

1. Say where in Spain your town is located, and whether you like it or not (*aim for 20 words*)
2. Say where your neighbourhood is located, what shops and other places there are, what is there to do and how much you like it (*aim for 40 words*)
3. Describe the street below as if it were the street where you live (*aim for 40 words*)

Club de tenis			El parque		
Mi casa	Supermercado	Piscina municipal	Tienda de ropa	Biblioteca	Peluquería
Calle del Cielo Azul					
Mi colegio	Gran Café Euskadi	Tienda de música	Bar La Leche	Gimnasio	Cine Paraíso

1. Buenas tardes, me llamo Rafa y soy de Lloret de Mar, en Cataluña. Tengo diecisiete años y mi cumpleaños es el diecisiete de febrero. Vivo en una casa bastante grande y moderna y vivo con mis padres y mi abuela. Soy hijo único. Me llevo bien con mi padre porque es muy paciente e inteligente. No me llevo bien con mi madre porque me obliga a hacer tareas domésticas.

2. Tengo que hacer las tareas domésticas después del colegio. Vuelvo a casa a la una y media y limpio el baño y la cocina. Después tengo que hacer mis deberes. Siempre hago mis deberes en el salón porque después juego a la Play.

3. A mí me gusta mi barrio porque se puede hacer muchas cosas. Por ejemplo, se puede hacer footing o ir de paseo en el parque. También se puede ir de compras en el centro comercial. Además, hay tiendas buenas en la plaza mayor. Suelo ir a la plaza mayor con mis amigos los viernes por la noche. Lo mejor de mi barrio es que está muy bien cuidado y nunca está sucio.

4. En mi barrio, cuando hace calor, me gusta ir de paseo en el parque y tomar un helado o un granizado de horchata. Todos los días paseo al perro a las ocho de la mañana y a las nueve de la noche. A veces mi abuela también da una vuelta con el perro.

5. En mi calle hay un restaurante, un parque pequeño y una iglesia muy antigua. Mi casa está enfrente del restaurante. El parque está entre la iglesia y el restaurante. Al final de la calle también hay una estación de tren y una tienda pequeñita. Lo peor *(the worst)* es que el polideportivo está a diez minutos en autobús.

6. Este fin de semana tengo varias opciones. Si hace buen tiempo, voy a ir al polideportivo a jugar al pádel con mis amigos. El polideportivo está a la derecha de mi cafetería favorita. A la izquierda está el cine, así que, si llueve, voy a ir al cine a ver una película. Por la noche voy a ir al restaurante que está enfrente de mi casa. Me encanta comer allí.

Rafa, 17 años. Lloret de Mar, España

---

1. Answer the following questions in English

a. When is Rafa's birthday?

b. Who does Rafa get on with? Why?

c. What does Rafa have to do after school?

d. Why does he like his neighbourhood?

e. What is there in the town square?

f. What's the best thing about his neighbourhood?

g. When does he walk his dog?

h. What is opposite Rafa's house?

i. Where is the train station?

j. What will Rafa do this weekend if it rains?

---

2. Find the Spanish equivalent in Rafa's text

a. Only child (1)

b. She forces me (1)

c. I clean the bathroom (2)

d. In the living room (2)

e. I tend do (3)

f. At night (3)

g. To have an ice cream (4)

h. Every day (4)

i. Between the church (5)

j. Ten minutes away (5)

k. This weekend (6)

l. To the left (6)

m. If it rains (6)

---

3. Complete the translation of paragraph 5

On my ______________, there is a ________________,

a ______________ park and a very __________ church. My house is ______________ the restaurant.

The park is ________________ the ______________ and the restaurant. At the __________ of the street, there is also a ____________ __________________ and a small ________________. The worst thing is that the ________________ __________________ is a ten minute ____________ ride away.

Miguel y Facundo juegan en el mismo equipo de fútbol. Están hablando de sus barrios.

Miguel	¿Dónde vives, Facundo?
Facundo	Vivo en El Ravalet, tío *(slang: man)*. ¿Y tú? ¿Vives cerca de aquí?
Miguel	Vivo a diez minutos en coche de aquí. Mi barrio se llama Poble Nou. ¿Cómo es tu barrio?
Facundo	Pues a mí me gusta mi barrio porque es muy tranquilo y no hay mucho tráfico. Sin embargo, no hay mucho que hacer. ¿Y tú?
Miguel	No me gusta mi barrio porque hay mucho tráfico, aunque sí hay bastante que hacer. No me gusta el ruido.
Facundo	¿Y qué se puede hacer en tu barrio? ¿Qué hay en tu calle?
Miguel	En mi barrio se puede ir al cine o ir a un concierto en el estadio. En mi calle está el estadio nuevo, un supermercado grande y varias tiendas pequeñas. ¿Y tú?
Facundo	Mi casa está entre un restaurante chino y una biblioteca muy antigua. Al final de la calle hay una zapatería, pero no hay mucho más.
Miguel	¿Te gusta tu calle?
Facundo	Sí. Nunca hay mucho ruido y es bastante segura. Sin embargo, siempre quiero hacer deporte pero el polideportivo está lejos de mi calle. ¿Y a ti, te gusta tu calle?
Miguel	Sí, aparte del ruido me gusta mi calle porque siempre puedo ir de compras si quiero, aunque las tiendas buenas están en el centro comercial. ¿Tu casa está lejos del centro comercial?
Facundo	Sí, ¡está a cuarenta minutos en coche!

4. True (T), False (F) or Not Mentioned (NM)?

Miguel is Facundo's uncle.	
Miguel lives ten minutes away.	
Facundo lives in Poble Nou.	
Facundo's neighbourhood is calm.	
Miguel does not like tennis.	
Miguel does not like noise.	
Miguel lives close to a stadium.	
Facundo's house is next to a shoe shop.	
Facundo does not like his street.	
Facundo's neighbourhood is dangerous.	
Facundo loves to do sport.	
Miguel prefers shopping at the shopping mall.	
Facundo lives close to the shopping mall.	

5. Complete the statements

a. _________________ lives in El Ravalet.

b. There isn't much to do in _________________'s neighbourhood.

c. There is quite a lot to do in _________________'s neighbourhood.

d. There is a Chinese restaurant on _________________'s street.

e. _________________ can go shopping whenever he wants.

Unit 9
Describing my home & furniture

In this unit you will learn:
- To describe where your house is located
- To say what rooms there are in your house
- To describe why you like your house
- To say what there is in each room of the house

You will revisit:
- Locations
- Expressing opinions
- Adjectival agreement

UNIT 9. Describing my home & furniture

¿Cuántas habitaciones hay en tu casa?	*How many rooms are there in your house?*
¿Te gusta tu casa? ¿Por qué?	*Do you like your house? Why?*
¿Qué hay en la cocina / el salón?	*What is there in the kitchen / living room?*

Vivo en	**una casa**	*a house*	**en** *in*	**el campo**	*the countryside*
				el centro de la ciudad	*the city centre*
	un piso	*a flat*		**la costa**	*the coast*
				la montaña	*the mountains*
	un edificio	*a building*		**las afueras**	*the outskirts*

En mi casa *In my house*	**hay** *there are*	**cinco seis siete**	**habitaciones,** *rooms,*	**por ejemplo** *for example*	**el dormitorio de mis padres** *my parents' bedroom*
					mi dormitorio — *my bedroom*
				como *such as*	**una cocina** — *a kitchen*
En mi piso *In my flat*					**una sala de juegos** — *a playroom*
					un comedor — *a dining room*
					un cuarto de baño — *a bathroom*
					un salón — *a living room*

también hay *there is also*	**un desván**	*an attic*	**y**	**un garaje** — *a garage*
	un sótano	*a basement*		**un jardín** — *a garden*

Me gusta mi casa porque *I like my house because*	***es** *it is*	**acogedora** *cosy*	**espaciosa** *spacious*	
		antigua *old*	**grande** *big*	
		bonita *beautiful*	**luminosa** *well lit*	
		fea *ugly*	**pequeña** *small*	
No me gusta mi casa porque *I don't like my house because*	**está** *it is*	**bien amueblada** *well furnished*		
		limpia *clean*		
		sucia *dirty*		

Me gusta mi piso porque *I like my flat because*	**es**	**acogedor**	**espacioso**
		antiguo	**grande**
		bonito	**luminoso**
		feo	**pequeño**
No me gusta mi piso porque *I don't like my flat because*	**está**	**bien amueblado**	
		limpio	
		sucio	

En la cocina hay		En el salón hay		En mi dormitorio hay	
un horno	*an oven*	**un sillón** — *an armchair*		**un armario**	*a wardrobe*
un lavaplatos	*a dishwasher*	**un sofá**		**un escritorio**	*a desk*
				un espejo	*a mirror*
una despensa	*a pantry*	**una alfombra** — *a rug*		**un ordenador**	*a computer*
una mesa	*a table*	**una mesa** — *a table*			
una nevera	*a fridge*	**una mesita** — *a coffee table*		**una cama**	*a bed*
una silla	*a chair*	**una televisión**		**una estantería**	*a bookshelf*
				cortinas	*curtains*

***Author's note:** As mentioned earlier in the book, **"es"** (*it is*) and **"está"** (*it is*) are used for different purposes. You will see them used in context throughout this unit. For a full explanation or **ser & estar** and accompanying activities, please see the relevant sections in our Spanish Verb Pivots book ☺

1. Multiple choice: tick the correct description

e.g.	Old	Cosy ✔	Big
a.	Beautiful	Big	Clean
b.	Not well lit	Not clean	Not well furnished
c.	Modern	Spacious	Old
d.	Beautiful	Ugly	Dirty
e.	Clean	Small	Cosy
f.	Well furnished	Dirty	Spacious
g.	Big	Small	Well lit

2. Complete the words

a. Ed _ fi _ io   *Building*

b. M _ nta _ a   *Mountain*

c. _ abit _ ciones *Rooms*

d. _ ard _ n   *Garden*

e. Pe _ ue _ a   *Small*

f. A _ o _ edora   *Cosy*

g. E _ pa _ ioso   *Spacious*

h. La _ apla _ os *Dishwasher*

i. Es _ e _ o   *Mirror*

3. Fill in the blanks

a. Vivo en una ___________ en la _______________.

b. En mi casa ________ seis __________________.

c. Por ____________, hay una ____________ y un salón.

d. También hay un ____________ y un ___________.

e. En la __________ hay una ____________ y una mesa.

f. En el ___________ hay dos ____________ y un sofá.

g. En mi habitación hay una ________ y ____________.

4. Spot the intruders

Hola, soy Andrés. Mi Vivo en una piso casa en la costa. En mi la casa hay siete habitaciones, como mi dormitorio y una el sala de juegos. También hay tener un desván y un jardín. Me no gusta mi casa porque es no acogedora y o grande. Sin embargo, no mi piso casa es un poco fea feo. En la cocina baño hay un lavaplatos y en el salón hay una televisión. En mi habitación hay un una ordenador y una sillón cama.

5. Faulty translation: correct the translation errors

a. I live in a small house in the countryside. In my house there are seven rooms and three bathrooms.

b. I live in a house on the coast. In my flat there is a bedroom, a playroom and a bathroom.

c. I live in a house in the mountains. In my flat there is a dining room but there isn't a garden.

d. There is also a basement and a garden. I don't like my house because it is ugly and cosy. I like my house because it is clean.

e. I like your flat because it is big and beautiful. I don't like my house because it is well lit.

f. I like my flat because it is big and old. I like my house because it is well lit and small.

g. In my flat there is a beautiful kitchen. In the kitchen there is an oven, a fridge and a chair.

6. Listening slalom: follow the speaker from top to bottom and number the boxes

a.	b.	c.	d.
In my house	In my flat	In your house	In his flat
there are 7 rooms:	there are 6 rooms:	there are 8 rooms:	there are 5 rooms:
3 bedrooms,	2 bedrooms,	a kitchen,	a living room,
a dining room,	a bathroom,	a living room,	a kitchen,
a kitchen,	a playroom,	2 living rooms,	a living room,
a dining room,	an attic,	a kitchen,	a playroom,
and 2 bathrooms.	his bedroom.	and 2 playrooms.	and my bedroom.

7. Narrow listening: gapped translation

a. Hello, I _______ Aitana and I live in Bogotá, the ___________ of Colombia. I _________ in a house on the ____________ of the city. In my ________ there are _________ rooms: a living room, a __________, a ____________, my parents' bedroom and my ___________ . Well, there is also a ___________.

b. I like my house because it is ___________ and ____________, even though it is also _________. However, I don't like my house ___________ it isn't ___________. In the kitchen there is an ________ and a ________, and in the living room there is a new _________ and a _________ sofa. In my _________ there isn't much; there is only a __________ and a _____________.

8. Listen to Antonio and answer the questions in English

Part 1 – a.
1. How old is Antonio?
2. Where does he live? (4 details)
3. How many rooms are there in his flat?
4. What isn't there in his flat?

Part 2 – b.
1. Why does he like his flat? (2 details)
2. Why doesn't he like his flat? (2 details)
3. What is in his kitchen? (3 details)
4. What is in his living room? (2 details)
5. What is in his bedroom? (3 details)
6. What isn't there in his bedroom?

UNIT 9. Describing my home & furniture: VOCAB BUILDING

1. Translate into English

a. En el campo.

b. En las afueras.

c. En la cocina.

d. En el salón.

e. En la sala de juegos.

f. En el desván.

g. En el jardín.

h. En el garaje.

i. En mi dormitorio.

j. En el dormitorio de mis padres.

k. En el dormitorio de mi hermano.

l. En el sótano.

2. Match

Una despensa	An armchair
Una cama	A pantry
Una estantería	Some curtains
Una silla	A television
Un sillón	A desk
Un escritorio	A fridge
Una alfombra	A bed
Una televisión	An oven
Una nevera	A bookshelf
Un horno	A carpet
Unas cortinas	A chair

3. In Spanish, write in which rooms the following objects are most likely to be found

a. La silla	El salón, el comedor	i. La estantería	
b. El escritorio		j. Los juguetes	
c. La alfombra		k. La cama	
d. El sillón		l. La tele	
e. La ducha		m. El coche	
f. El lavabo		n. El árbol	
g. El horno		o. Las cortinas	
h. El armario		p. El espejo	

4. Complete with the missing letters

a. La du _ _ _   *The shower*

b. La me _ _   *The table*

c. La ca _ _   *The bed*

d. El escri _ _ _ _ _   *The desk*

e. El _ _ bol   *The tree*

f. La si _ _ _   *The chair*

g. Los jugu _ _ _ _   *The toys*

5. Write likely or unlikely next to the statements below, as in the example

e.g. En la cocina hay una ducha.   *Unlikely*

a. En el cuarto de baño hay un escritorio.   _______

b. En el salón hay un sofá.   _______

c. En mi dormitorio hay un horno.   _______

d. En el comedor hay un árbol.   _______

e. En el jardín hay un perro.   _______

UNIT 9. Describing my home & furniture: VOCAB BUILDING

6. Multiple choice: choose the correct translation

		1	2	3
a.	**Cupboard**	El armario	La puerta	La caja
b.	**Armchair**	La silla	La mesa	El sillón
c.	**Toys**	Los libros	Los juguetes	Las cosas
d.	**Oven**	El horno	El fuego	El armario
e.	**Tree**	El tres	El árbol	El estante
f.	**Rug**	El suelo	El techo	La alfombra
g.	**Table**	La mesa	El horno	La silla
h.	**Curtains**	La ventana	Las cortinas	La puerta
i.	**Desk**	El escritorio	La mesa	El armario
j.	**Chair**	El sillón	La silla	La mesa
k.	**Bookshelf**	El libro	La pared	La estantería

7. Faulty translation: correct the mistakes in the translations below
(Please note - not all translations are wrong)

a. En la cocina hay una mesa y cuatro sillas.   *In the kitchen there is a table and four armchairs.*

b. En mi dormitorio hay cortinas rojas.   *In my living room there are red curtains.*

c. En la cocina hay una televisión pequeña.   *In the kitchen there is a small television.*

d. En nuestro jardín no hay árboles.   *In our garden there are tall trees.*

e. En nuestro salón hay dos sillones.   *In our living room there are two armchairs.*

f. Al lado de mi cama hay una mesita.   *Beside my bed there is a mirror.*

g. El espejo está cerca de la puerta.   *The mirror is near the bookshelves.*

h. El armario está a la izquierda.   *The wardrobe is on the left.*

i. En la cocina hay un horno grande.   *In the kitchen there is a big table.*

8. Spot the hidden phrases, fill in the gaps and translate into English
HINT: the words are names of rooms or furniture + adjectives

a. Un d _ _ m _ t _ _ _ _ p _ q _ _ _ _ _ .

b. Una c _ _ a _ _ _ nd _ .

c. Un j _ _ d _ n ve _ _ e.

d. Una _ _ ci _ _ li _ _ _ a.

e. Un e _ _ _ _ torio m _ _ _ _ no.

f. Un c _ _ ed _ _ muy b _ _ _ t _ .

g. Un s _ _ ó _ b _ _ _ am _ _ _ _ ad _ .

9. Write Verdadero (true) or Falso (false) next to each statement below

a. Al lado de la cama hay una mesita de noche.   __________

b. La televisión está detrás de la cama.   __________

c. Entrando *(on entering)* a la derecha hay un espejo.   __________

d. El escritorio está cerca de la televisión.   __________

e. El armario está a la derecha de la cama.   __________

f. La televisión está entre el espejo y el escritorio.   __________

g. Hay una lámpara encima del escritorio.   __________

h. El gato está debajo de la cama.   __________

i. La puerta está entre la cama y el armario.   __________

j. La mesita de noche está entre el armario y la cama.   __________

k. Hay una silla cerca del escritorio.   __________

IZQUIERDA   **DERECHA**

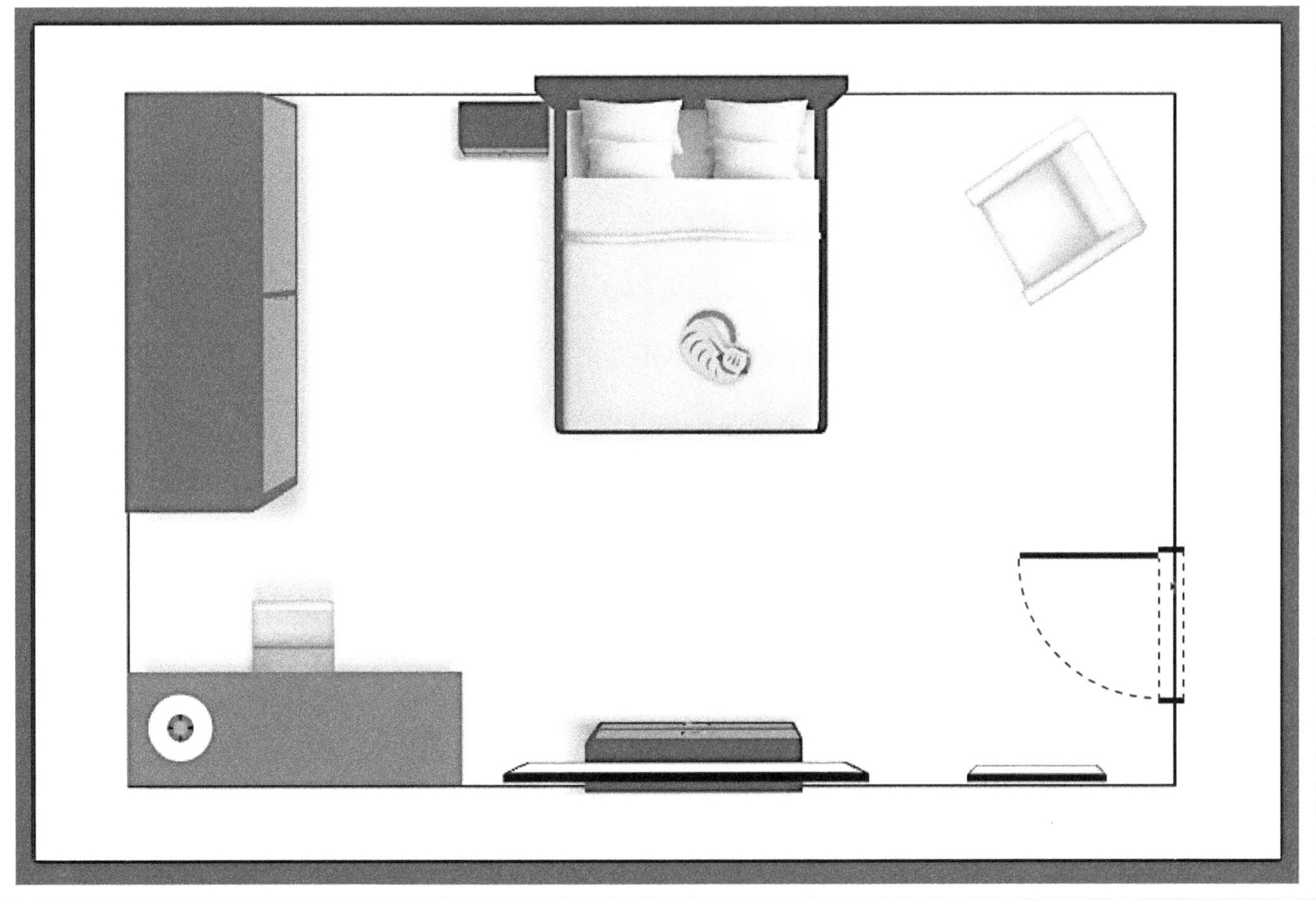

UNIT 9. Describing my home & furniture: READING 1

Me llamo Pedro y vivo en Cuenca. Vivo con mi familia en un piso moderno en las afueras de la ciudad. Vivo en un barrio residencial.

Me encanta mi barrio porque hay mucho que hacer para los jóvenes de mi edad. Hay un parque fenomenal cerca de mi casa donde hay un rocódromo *(a climbing wall)*, una pista de patinaje, un tobogán *(a slide)* y mucho espacio para jugar. Voy allí a menudo con mis amigos para jugar al frisbi, hacer footing y montar en bici. En mi barrio también hay un centro comercial enorme con muchas tiendas buenas e instalaciones deportivas. Por ejemplo, hay un gimnasio muy bueno al lado de mi casa y una piscina a cien metros a pie.

Vivo en un edificio moderno, en la séptima planta. En mi piso hay una cocina, un salón, dos cuartos de baño, una sala de juegos y tres dormitorios: mi dormitorio, el dormitorio de mi madre y el dormitorio de mi hermana mayor.

Mi habitación favorita es mi dormitorio porque es muy acogedor y está muy bien decorado. Hay una cama muy grande y cómoda. A la izquierda *(left)* de la cama hay un armario muy espacioso. A la derecha *(right)* hay una mesita de noche y un sillón. En la esquina, *(corner)* hay un escritorio. Al lado del escritorio, enfrente de la cama, hay una televisión. Es vieja *(old)*, pero todavía funciona. Detrás de la televisión hay una ventana muy grande y a la derecha de la ventana hay un espejo. Paso mucho tiempo en mi dormitorio escuchando música, leyendo libros y revistas y haciendo mis deberes.

Pedro, 14 años. Cuenca, España

3. Spot the FIVE words on the list below which are not contained in Pedro's text

a. Moto	f. Tiempo	k. Lejos
b. Decorado	g. Acogedor	l. Edificio
c. Cómoda	h. Sillón	m. Luminoso
d. Escritorio	i. Espejo	n. Espacioso
e. Esquina	j. Desván	o. Paseo

1. Answer the questions in English

a. In which part of Cuenca does Pedro live?

b. Name three things one can find in the park near his home.

c. How often does he go there with his friends?

d. What three activities does he like to do with his friends?

e. What two sports facilities can one find in his street?

f. On which floor does he live?

g. What rooms does Pedro list?

h. Why is his bedroom his favourite room in the house? (2 details)

i. What is there to the left of his bed?

j. What is there to the right of his bed?

k. What is there in the corner?

l. What is old but still functioning?

m. Name three things he does in his room.

2. Find the Spanish equivalent in Pedro's text

a. Near my house

b. A climbing wall

c. To ride a bike

d. 100 metres away on foot

e. On the 7th floor

f. A playroom

g. My older sister's bedroom

h. Is very cosy

i. Beside the desk

j. In the corner

k. Behind the television

l. To the right of the window

UNIT 9. Describing my home & furniture: READING 2

Me llamo Paco. Soy de Segovia pero vivo en Madrid. Vivo con mi familia en un edificio histórico en el centro de la ciudad. Vivo muy cerca del casco antiguo.

Me encanta mi barrio porque es muy bonito y hay mucho que ver y hacer. Hay dos parques muy bonitos cerca de mi casa donde hay mucho espacio para jugar. Voy allí a menudo con mis amigos. En mi barrio hay muchos monumentos, teatros, cines, restaurantes, bares al aire libre y muchas tiendas bonitas. También hay un gran acuario con delfines y tiburones.

Vivo en un edificio muy antiguo, en la primera planta, con una vista magnífica de la ciudad. En mi piso hay una cocina, un salón, un comedor, dos cuartos de baño, una sala de juegos y dos dormitorios: mi dormitorio y el de mis padres.

Mi habitación favorita es mi dormitorio, porque es muy acogedor y está muy bien amueblado y decorado. Hay una cama muy grande y cómoda. A la izquierda de la cama hay un escritorio muy espacioso. A la derecha hay una mesita de noche y un espejo. En la esquina, hay un armario enorme. Al lado del armario, enfrente de la cama, está mi ordenador y una televisión. La televisión es muy pequeña, pero es nueva. Detrás de la televisión hay una ventana muy grande. A la derecha de la ventana hay un sillón. Paso mucho tiempo en mi dormitorio escuchando música, jugando en mi ordenador, tocando la guitarra, leyendo y haciendo mis deberes.

Paco, 13 años. Segovia, España

1. Complete the sentences based on Paco's text, providing as many details as possible

a. He lives with his family in a…

b. In the parks there is…

c. In his neighbourhood… (3 details)

d. His building is….

e. In his flat there is… (3 details)

f. His favourite room is… because…

g. The bed is…

h. To the right of the bed there is…

i. There is a very big wardrobe in…

j. The television is… but…

k. Behind the television there is a…

2. Faulty translation: find the mistakes in the translation of the last paragraph of Paco's text

My favourite room is my bedroom because it is very spacious and is very well furnished and decorated. There is a very big and soft bed. To the left of the bed there is a very spacious wardrobe. To the right there is a coffee table and a television. In the skinner, there is a huge mirror. Next to the wardrobe, behind the bed, is my computer and a television. The television is very small, but good. Next to the television there is a very large window. To the right of the window there is an armchair. I spend a lot of time in my bedroom listening to music, playing the guitar, writing and doing my homework.

3. List as many words from Paco's text as possible, under the following headings

1. Adjectives

2. Furniture

3. Verbs

4. Locative adverbs/prepositions (*e.g. next to, behind, to the right, etc.*)

UNIT 9. Describing my home & furniture: WRITING & TRANSLATION

1. Arrange the words in each sentence in the correct order, based on the translation

a. una ordenador hay En un dormitorio no mi ni ni televisión
In my bedroom there is neither a television or a computer.

b. En hay una mesa, la y una despensa cocina dos una sillas, nevera, un horno
In the kitchen there is a table, two chairs, a fridge, an oven and a pantry.

c. el hay salón En dos sillones, un, una alfombra y sofá una televisión
In the living room there are two armchairs, a rug, a sofa and a television.

d. pero No hay hay un sillas sillón en mi dormitorio muy cómodo
There are no chairs in my bedroom but there is a very comfortable armchair.

e. puerta está El espejo de al la lado y detrás ventana del está la escritorio
The mirror is next to the door and the window is behind the desk.

---

2. Translate into Spanish

a. A beautiful chair   U____ s______ b__________

b. A bright kitchen   U____ c________ l________

c. A red carpet   U____ a__________ r______

d. Blue curtains   U____ c__________ a________

e. A spacious flat   U___ p_____ e__________

f. An old wardrobe   U___ a________ a________

g. A comfortable bed   U____ c______ c__________

h. A building   U____ e____________

i. A new television   U___ t__________ n______

3. Complete with a suitable word

a. En mi barrio hay muchas ______________

  ______________.

b. Mi habitación favorita es la ____________

  porque es ______________.

c. Al lado del armario hay una ____________.

d. El espejo ________ al lado de la

  ______________.

e. En mi casa __________ siete habitaciones.

f. Me encanta mi ____________ porque tengo

  una ______________ grande.

---

4. Insert *de la* o *del* as appropriate

a. El comedor está al lado ______ cocina.

b. La cocina está a la derecha ______ comedor.

c. El horno está cerca ______ nevera.

d. Mi casa está lejos ______ estadio.

e. Mi barrio está cerca ______ centro.

f. Mi edificio está al lado ______ colegio.

g. Mi escritorio está enfrente ______ cama.

h. El garaje está al lado ______ jardín.

5. Spot and add the missing words

a. La cocina al lado del comedor.

b. En mi casa siete habitaciones.

c. En el salón hay alfombra roja.

d. Vivo un edificio antiguo.

e. El espejo está lado de la puerta.

f. Me encanta cocina.

g. La televisión está enfrente mi cama.

h. El dormitorio de padres es muy grande.

6. Translate into Spanish

a. *In my flat there are six rooms.* E _ m _ p _ _ _ h _ _ s _ _ _ h _ _ _ _ _ _ _ _ _ _ _ .

b. *My favourite room is...* M _ h _ _ _ _ _ _ _ _ _ f _ _ _ _ _ _ _ e _ ...

c. *I also love my bedroom.* T _ _ _ _ _ _ m _ e _ _ _ _ _ _ m _ d _ _ _ _ _ _ _ _ _ .

d. *My bedroom is very cosy.* M _ d _ _ _ _ _ _ _ _ e _ m _ _ a _ _ _ _ _ _ _ .

e. *There is also a big desk.* T _ _ _ _ _ _ h _ _ u _ e _ _ _ _ _ _ _ _ g _ _ _ _ _ .

f. *There is a big and comfortable bed.* H _ _ u _ _ c _ _ _ g _ _ _ _ _ y c _ _ _ _ _ .

g. *I live in a modern building.* V _ _ _ e _ u _ e _ _ _ _ _ _ _ m _ _ _ _ _ _ .

h. *I don't like my living room.* N _ m _ g _ _ _ _ m _ s _ _ _ _ .

---

7. Spot and correct the grammar and spelling mistakes (including missing words)

a. En mi dormitorio es un escritorio muy grande.

b. En mi casa hay seis habitación.

c. En mi barrio hay muchas buenas tiendas.

d. Mi tienda favorita el salón. (2 errors)

e. Mi dormitorio es muy grande y acogedor.

f. Vivo in un edificio antiguo.

g. El salón es muy bien amueblado.

h. Al lado de cama hay una mesita noche. (2 errors)

i. Me encanta mi casa porque muy bonita.

9. Translate into Spanish

I live in a beautiful neighbourhood on the outskirts of Sevilla, a city in the south of Spain. I like my neighbourhood a lot because there are lot of things to do for people of my age. There are many good shops, two beautiful parks, three big shopping shopping malls and many sports facilities. There are also a lot of bars and restaurants.

I live in a big flat in a modern building. In my flat there are seven rooms. My favourite room is my bedroom because it is (*es*) spacious and it is (*está*) well furnished. Also, the bed is big and comfortable and there is a big desk with a new computer.

8. Complete each sentence with an appropriate verb

a. Mi ciudad se _________ Madrid.

b. Madrid _____ la capital de España.

c. Mi barrio _________ en las afueras de Madrid.

d. En mi barrio _________ muchas cosas que hacer para los jóvenes.

e. Por ejemplo, se _______ ir al parque, se puede _______ deporte y hay muchas tiendas buenas donde se puede __________ mucha ropa de calidad.

f. Me _________ mi dormitorio porque es muy acogedor.

g. El salón _______ bien amueblado.

h. P_____ mucho tiempo en mi dormitorio jugando a videojuegos.

i. Por lo general _______ mis deberes en el salón.

j. _______ con mi perro en el jardín.

k. _______ en bici en el parque cerca de mi casa.

l. No me _________ mi cocina porque es muy pequeña.

UNIT 9. Describing my home & furniture: WRITING

1. Write two 80-100 word paragraphs in the first person in which you say:

- You live in Bilbao.
- Your neigbourhood is in the centre of the city.
- You like your neighbourhood because there are many good shops and excellent sports facilities.
- There are many bars and restaurants.
- There is a beautiful park near your house.
- You live in a house with seven rooms.
- Your favourite room is your bedroom because it is spacious, bright and is well furnished.
- You hate the living room because it is badly furnished
- It is small and the sofa is old and ugly.

- Your house is big and modern.
- You love your living room because it is well furnished and bright.
- In the living room there is a big sofa. Next to the sofa there is a little table.
- Opposite the sofa there is a television.
- You also love your bedroom because it is cosy.
- In your bedroom there is a big and comfortable bed.
- Next to the bed there is a bedside table and next to the bedside table there is a huge wardrobe.
- Opposite the wardrobe there is a big desk with a computer.

2. Write a paragraph in Spanish in the first person in which you say:

a. You live in Buenos Aires, the capital of Argentina.

b. You live on the outskirts, in a residential neighbourhood.

c. You like your neighbourhood because one can do a lot of sport.

d. There are many sports facilities, such as gyms, a sports centre, two football pitches, some tennis and golf clubs, some swimming pools and a stadium.

e. Also, there is a huge shopping mall, a beautiful park and a river.

f. Last weekend you did a lot of sport. You went cycling in the park, you did weights in the gym, played football with your school friends and went to your favourite shopping mall with your boyfriend/girlfriend. You had a great time.

g. In your street there are many good shops and restaurants. For example, there is a good Italian restaurant next to your house.

h. In your house there are 7 rooms: a kitchen, two bathrooms, three bedrooms and a living room.

i. Your favourite room is the living room because it is big, well furnished and bright. There is also a very comfortable sofa and a new television.

j. The sofa is opposite the television. To the left of the sofa there is an armchair and to its right there is a big plant. In front of the sofa there is a small black table. Between the sofa and the television there is an old rug.

1. Hola, soy Benito y soy de Vega Baja, un pueblo en el centro-norte de Puerto Rico, una isla en el noreste del Caribe. Vivo en una casa antigua con mi familia. En mi familia somos mi padre, mi madre y mis dos hermanos menores. Mi madre es profesora y es muy trabajadora.

2. Mi pueblo es bastante pequeño pero siempre está bien cuidado. También me gusta mi barrio porque no es peligroso y hay mucho ambiente. Siempre hay gente tocando música en la calle. Cerca de mi casa hay mucho que hacer. Cuando hace calor me gusta ir al parque con mi familia o ir a la piscina municipal.

3. En mi calle hay un supermercado, un teatro, una iglesia y una tienda de música muy *chévere. Mi casa está entre la tienda de música y el supermercado. La iglesia está a la derecha del supermercado y el teatro está enfrente de la casa de mi mejor amigo Julián. No hay ningún polideportivo cerca de donde vivo.

4. Mi casa está en las afueras del pueblo, cerca de unas montañas. En mi casa hay seis habitaciones: un salón, una cocina, un cuarto de baño, el dormitorio de mis padres, el dormitorio de mis hermanos y mi dormitorio. Ah, también hay un jardín pequeñito y un garaje. Me gusta mi casa porque es acogedora, bonita y bastante luminosa. Sin embargo, no es muy espaciosa.

5. En la cocina hay un horno, una mesa, una nevera y unas sillas. No hay lavaplatos, así que tenemos que fregar *(wash)* los platos en el fregadero *(sink)*. En el salón hay un sofá verde, una alfombra grande y una televisión bastante moderna. Cuando llueve me quedo en casa a ver una película en el salón. En mi dormitorio tengo un ordenador, una cama y un armario.

6. Mi amigo Julián también vive en mi calle. Su casa es más grande que la mía y tiene más habitaciones. Sin embargo, no tiene garaje. A él le gusta su casa porque es muy moderna y bien amueblada. También tiene una sala de juegos donde jugamos a la Play después del colegio.

Benito, 14 años. Vega Baja, Puerto Rico

In Puerto Rico and a few other Latin American countries you will hear 'chévere' for 'cool' instead of 'chulo' or 'guay', which are more common in Spain.

1. Answer the following questions in English
a. Does Benito live in a city or a town?
b. What does his mum do for work?
c. Why does he like his neighbourhood?
d. What does he do when it's hot?
e. What is there next to his house?
f. What isn't there near his house?
g. How many bedrooms are in his house?
h. What doesn't he have in his kitchen?
i. What does he do when it rains?
j. What does he do at Julián's house?

2. Find the Spanish equivalent in Benito's text
a. We are (1)
b. Hardworking (1)
c. Near my house (2)
d. When it's hot (2)
e. Between (3)
f. Opposite (3)
g. On the outskirts (4)
h. There is also (4)
i. We have to (5)
j. I have a (5)
k. His house (6)
l. He doesn't have (6)
m. Where we play (6)

3. Complete the translation of paragraph 5

In the ____________, there is an _________, a table, a ___________ and __________ chairs. There isn't a __________________ therefore we have to wash the __________ in the sink. In the living room, there is a ___________ sofa, a big ________ and a __________ modern TV. When it _________, I ________ at home to _________ a _________ in the living room. In my bedroom, I ___________ a ____________, a bed and a __________________.

Esther quiere vender *(sell)* su casa. Está hablando de su casa con Pablo, un agente inmobilario *(estate agent)*.

Pablo	Hola, Esther. ¿Cómo te puedo ayudar?
Esther	Hola. Pues quiero vender mi casa. Vivo en una casa en las afueras de la ciudad pero quiero comprar un piso en el centro.
Pablo	Vale. ¿Cómo es tu casa? ¿Te gusta?
Esther	Me gusta mi casa porque es peque… no, es… acogedora y muy bonita. Es muy luminosa y está limpia.
Pablo	¿Y cuántas habitaciones hay en tu casa?
Esther	En mi casa hay cinco habitaciones. Hay un salón, una cocina, un cuarto de baño bastante grande y dos dormitorios.
Pablo	¿Hay un jardín o un garaje?
Esther	Sí. Hay un jardín muy espacioso pero no hay garaje. Sin embargo, sí que hay un desván.
Pablo	Gracias. Describe la cocina, por favor.
Esther	En la cocina hay un horno moderno, una mesa con cuatro sillas y una nevera. También hay una despensa muy bonita.
Pablo	¿Y el salón?
Esther	El salón es mi habitación favorita. Hay un sillón rosa, una alfombra y una televisión nueva. No hay una mesita.
Pablo	Dijiste *(you said)* que hay dos dormitorios. ¿Cómo son?
Esther	La verdad es que están bien amueblados. Tienen cama, unas estanterías, un armario y un espejo moderno. Mi dormitorio también tiene unas cortinas azules.
Pablo	Muchas gracias por tu tiempo, Esther.

4. True (T), False (F) or Not Mentioned (NM)?

Pablo wants to sell his house.	
Esther lives in the city centre.	
Esther likes her house.	
Esther's house is quite big.	
There are five bedrooms.	
There are two bedrooms.	
Esther's house is next to a church.	
The garden is very spacious.	
The kitchen has a coffee table.	
The kitchen is Esther's favourite room.	
Esther's armchair is pink.	
The bedrooms are well furnished.	
The curtains are green.	

5. Complete the statements

a. _______________ wants to move to the _____________ _______________ .

b. Esther's house is ___________ , very beautiful, ____________ and clean.

c. There is a spacious ___________ but there is not a _____________ .

d. The pantry is very _______________ .

e. ____________ thanks ___________ for ____________ time.

1. Fill in the missing words

a. ¿D _ _ _ _ viv _ _ ?

b. ¿Q _ _ hay en tu _ _ _ _ _ _ _ ?

c. ¿ _ _ gusta tu _ _ _ _ _ _ ? ¿Por qué?

d. ¿Q _ _ se puede _ _ _ _ _ en tu barrio?

e. ¿A _ _ _ _ _ se puede _ _ ?

f. ¿Q _ _ se puede _ _ _ y visitar ?

g. ¿Q _ _ h _ _ en _ _ calle?

h. ¿D _ _ _ _ e _ _ _ tu casa?

i. ¿Q _ _ sitios h _ _ en tu b _ _ _ _ _ ?

j. ¿Cu _ _ _ _ _ habitaciones hay en tu casa?

k. ¿ _ _ gusta _ _ casa? ¿ _ _ _ _ qué?

l. ¿Q _ _ h _ _ en _ _ cocin _ ?

m. ¿Q _ _ h _ _ en _ _ s _ _ _ _ ?

n. ¿Q _ _ t _ _ _ _ _ en _ _ dormitorio?

2. Choose the option that you hear

a. Vivo en el **sur / este / norte** de España.

b. Hay un **cine / acuario / club juvenil**.

c. Me gusta porque es **peligroso / seguro / grande**.

d. Se puede hacer **turismo / deporte / natación**.

e. Se puede ir al **centro / casco antiguo / estadio**.

f. Se puede visitar el **palacio / museo / castillo**.

g. Hay una **tienda / piscina / iglesia** en la esquina.

h. Está detrás del **colegio / museo / teatro**.

i. Hay un **polideportivo / mercado / parque**.

j. En mi casa hay **siete / seis / cinco** habitaciones.

k. No me gusta porque es **antigua / pequeña / fea**.

l. En la cocina hay un **horno / lavaplatos / espejo**.

m. En el salón hay una **silla / mesa / mesita**.

n. Tengo un **escritorio / ordenador / armario**.

3. Listen and write in the missing information

a. _____________ en Liverpool, una _______________ en el _______________ de Inglaterra.

b. En mi ciudad, _______________ muchas calles _______________ y varios _______________ grandes.

c. Me gusta mi _______________ porque no es _______________ y _______________ bien cuidado.

d. En mi barrio se _______________ hacer _______________ en el _______________ de la ciudad.

e. Se puede _________ de compras en el centro _______________________ _______________.

f. Se puede __________ un _______________ de fútbol en el _______________ o visitar museos.

g. En mi _______________ hay un _______________, un parque _______________ y una zapatería.

h. Mi casa _______________ a diez minutos a pie de la _______________ y la _______________.

i. En mi barrio _______ un mercado _______________ en la _____________ mayor y un centro comercial.

j. En mi casa hay _______________ habitaciones y también _________ un _______________.

k. Me _______________ mi casa porque está bien _______________ y es _________ bonita.

l. En la _______________ hay un _______________, un _______________, una nevera y una despensa.

m. En el salón hay un _______________ _______________ y una alfombra _______________.

n. En mi _______________ tengo unas _______________, una _______________ y un ordenador.

4. Fill in the grid with your personal information

Question	Answer
1. ¿Dónde vives?	
2. ¿Qué hay en tu ciudad?	
3. ¿Por qué te gusta tu barrio?	
4. ¿Qué se puede hacer en tu barrio?	
5. ¿Adónde se puede ir en tu barrio?	
6. ¿Qué se puede ver y visitar?	
7. ¿Qué hay en tu calle?	
8. ¿Dónde está tu casa?	
9. ¿Qué sitios hay en tu barrio?	
10. ¿Cuántas habitaciones hay en tu casa?	
11. ¿Te gusta tu casa? ¿Por qué?	
12. ¿Qué tienes en tu dormitorio?	

5. Survey two of your classmates using the same questions as above and write down the main information you hear in Spanish

Q.	Person 1	Person 2
a.		
b.		
c.		
d.		
e.		
f.		
g.		
h.		
i.		
j.		
k.		
l.		

No Snakes No Ladders

START

1. I live in
2. We live in
3. I live in London
4. It is in the centre
5. It is in the centre of England
6. We live in Edinburgh, the capital of Scotland
7. Near my house
8. In my city there is a shopping mall
9. In my neighbourhood there are many things to do
10. I like my neighbourhood because it is safe
11. I don't like my neighbourhood because it is very noisy
12. In my neighbourhood you can do many things
13. For example, you can do sport
14. I like to play football in the park
15. I tend to visit art galleries in the centre
16. I don't like to go for a walk in the woods
17. I don't tend to watch football matches in the stadium
18. What can you do in your neighbourhood?
19. On my street there is a sports centre
20. I like to play tennis at the sports centre
21. Near my house there is a supermarket
22. The cinema is to the right of the school
23. My flat is behind the library
24. My house is far from the pool
25. My house is between the butcher's and the supermarket
26. I live in a house in the countryside
27. In my house there are seven rooms
28. I like my house because it is pretty
29. I don't like my house because it is ugly
30. In the living room there is a sofa and a TV

FINISH

No Snakes No Ladders

SALIDA

1. Vivo en
2. Vivimos en
3. Vivo en Londres
4. Está en el centro
5. Está en el centro de Inglaterra
6. Vivimos en Edimburgo, la capital de Escocia
7. Cerca de mi casa
8. En mi ciudad hay un centro comercial
9. En mi barrio hay muchas cosas que hacer
10. Me gusta mi barrio porque es seguro
11. No me gusta mi barrio porque hay mucho ruido
12. En mi barrio se puede hacer muchas cosas
13. Por ejemplo, se puede hacer deporte
14. Me gusta jugar al fútbol en el parque
15. Suelo visitar galerías de arte en el centro
16. No me gusta ir de paseo en el bosque
17. No suelo ver partidos de fútbol en el estadio
18. ¿Qué se puede hacer en tu barrio?
19. En mi calle hay un polideportivo
20. Me gusta jugar al tenis en el polideportivo
21. Cerca de mi casa hay un supermercado
22. El cine está a la derecha del colegio
23. Mi piso está detrás de la biblioteca
24. Mi casa está lejos de la piscina
25. Mi casa está entre la carnicería y el supermercado
26. Vivo en una casa en el campo
27. En mi casa hay siete habitaciones
28. Me gusta mi casa porque es bonita
29. No me gusta mi casa porque es fea
30. En el salón hay un sofá y una televisión

LLEGADA

One Pen One Dice

Play in pairs. You only have 1 pen and 1 dice.
One person has the pen and starts translating the sentence into **English.** The other person rolls the dice until they roll a 6, they swap the pen and translate. The winner is the person who finishes translating all the sentences first.

1. ¿Dónde vives?	
2. Vivo en Madrid. Está en el centro de España.	
3. Cerca de mi casa hay muchas cosas que hacer.	
4. Por ejemplo, se puede hacer deporte en el polideportivo.	
5. También me gusta ir a conciertos en la plaza mayor.	
6. En mi calle hay un supermercado y una iglesia.	
7. Mi casa está a la derecha del colegio.	
8. Vivo en un piso moderno en las afueras de la ciudad.	
9. Me gusta mi casa porque es antigua y acogedora.	
10. En mi dormitorio hay una cama y un ordenador.	

One Pen One Dice

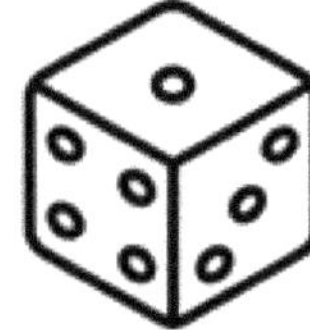

Play in pairs. You only have 1 pen and 1 dice.

One person has the pen and starts translating the sentence into **Spanish.** The other person rolls the dice until they roll a 6, they swap the pen and translate. The winner is the person who finishes translating all the sentences first.

1. Where do you live?	
2. I live in Madrid. It is in the centre of Spain.	
3. Near my house there are many things to do.	
4. For example, one can do sport at the sports centre.	
5. I also like to go to concerts in the town square.	
6. On my street there is a supermarket and a church.	
7. My house is to the right of the school.	
8. I live in a modern flat on the outskirts of the city.	
9. I like my house because it is old and cosy.	
10. In my bedroom there is a bed and a computer.	

TERM 3 – OVERVIEW

This term you will learn:

Unit 10 – Saying what I did in my neighbourhood
- To say what you did recently in your neighbourhood
- To say where you did the activity
- To say who you did the activity with

Unit 11 – Saying what I did & am going to do at the weekend
- To say what you did last weekend
- To give your opinion on the activities you did last weekend
- To describe what you are going to do next weekend
- To predict what your plans next weekend will be like

Unit 12 – Making after-school plans with a friend
- To make plans with other people
- To say what you would like to do today
- To accept or reject plans with reasons why
- To arrange when and where you will meet a friend

Unit 13 – A future trip to Cádiz
- To talk about an upcoming trip to Cádiz
- To describe events you will **and** would like to do on holiday
- To give future tense opinions

KEY QUESTIONS

¿Adónde fuiste el fin de semana pasado?	*Where did you go last weekend?*
¿Con quién fuiste?	*Who did you go with?*
¿Qué hiciste el sábado?	*What did you do on Saturday?*
¿Qué hiciste el fin de semana pasado?	*What did you do last weekend?*
¿Cómo fue?	*How was it?*
¿Qué vas a hacer el próximo fin de semana?	*What are you going to do next weekend?*
¿Qué va a hacer tu hermano/a?	*What is your brother/sister going to do?*
¿Qué quieres hacer esta mañana?	*What do you want to do this morning?*
¿Te gustaría ir al parque?	*Would you like to go to the park?*
¿A qué hora quedamos	*At what time shall we meet?*
¿Dónde quedamos?	*Where shall we meet?*
¿Adónde vas a ir este verano?	*Where are you going to go this summer?*
¿Cómo vas a viajar?	*How are you going to travel?*
¿Dónde vas a quedarte?	*Where are you going to stay?*
¿Qué vas a hacer?	*What are you going to do?*
¿Qué lugares vas a ver/visitar?	*What places are you going to see/visit?*

UNIT 10
Saying what I did in my neighbourhood

In this unit you will learn:
- To say what you did recently in your neighbourhood
- To say where you did the activity
- To say who you did the activity with

You will revisit:
- Time markers
- Free-time activities
- Places in town
- Friends and family members

UNIT 10. Saying what I did in my neighbourhood

¿Adónde fuiste el fin de semana pasado?		*Where did you go last weekend?*		
¿Con quién fuiste?		*Who did you go with?*		
¿Qué hiciste el sábado?		*What did you do on Saturday?*		

	compré *I bought*	**una camiseta de fútbol** — *a football shirt* **un videojuego** — *a videogame* **ropa nueva** — *new clothes*		
Anteayer *The day before yesterday*	**fui** *I went*	**a la pista de patinaje** — *to the skating rink* **a un concierto de Rosalía** — *to a Rosalía concert* **de paseo al parque** — *for a walk in the park* **de compras** — *shopping*		
Ayer *Yesterday* **Hace tres días** *Three days ago*	***hice** *I did*	**equitación** *horse riding* **footing** *jogging* **natación** *swimming*	**pesas** *weights* **senderismo** *hiking* **turismo** *sightseeing*	
	jugué *I played*	**al fútbol** **al golf**	**al rugby** **al tenis**	
El fin de semana pasado *Last weekend*	**toqué** *I played (an instrument)*	**el piano** **el violín**	**la batería** *drums* **la guitarra**	
El viernes pasado *Last Friday*	**vi** *I watched*	**un espectáculo de circo/danza/magia** — *a circus/dance/magic show* **un partido de fútbol** — *a football game* **una comedia** — *a comedy* **una película de acción/terror** — *an action/horror film*		
	visité *I visited*	**un castillo** *a castle* **una galería de arte** *a gallery* **un museo** *a museum*	**un palacio histórico** *a historic palace* **unas ruinas romanas** *some Roman ruins*	

en *in / at*	**el bosque** *the woods* **el campo de fútbol** *the football pitch* **el casco antiguo** *the old town* **el centro comercial** *the shopping mall* **el centro de la ciudad** *the city centre* **el cine** *the cinema* **el club de tenis** *the tennis club* **el estadio** *the stadium* **el polideportivo** *the sports centre* **la calle peatonal** *the pedestrian street* **la piscina (municipal)** *the (local) swimming pool* **la plaza mayor** *the town square*	**cerca de mi casa** *near my house* **de mi barrio** *in my neighbourhood*

con *with*	**mi hermano/a** *my brother/sister* **mi mejor amigo/a** *my best friend*	**mi novio/a** *my boyfriend/girlfriend* **mi primo/a** *my cousin*

***Author's note:** Watch out for expressions like **"hice natación"** that are translated as *'I went'* swimming. The literal translation is actually *'I did'* swimming. The verbs **"hacer"** and **"ir"** often translate differently in Spanish and English (so watch out for them).

1. Multiple choice: tick the location you hear

e.g.	The park ✓	The cinema	The old town
a.	The tennis club	The shopping mall	Near my house
b.	The sports centre	The city centre	The football pitch
c.	The pedestrian street	The park	The old town
d.	The town square	The sports centre	The woods
e.	In my town	In Madrid	In Málaga
f.	The cinema	The shopping mall	The city centre
g.	The woods	The bus stop	The park

2. Complete the words

a. Na _ a _ i _ n — *Swimming*

b. J _ g _ _ — *I played*

c. Eq _ it _ ció _ — *Horse riding*

d. Es _ ect _ cu _ o — *Show*

e. C _ sti _ _ o — *Castle*

f. M _ _ o _ — *Better/Best*

g. Pi _ ci _ _ — *Pool*

h. No _ _ _ — *Boyfriend*

i. El bos _ _ _ — *The woods*

3. Fill in the blanks with a suitable verb

a. Ayer ____________ un espectáculo de danza.

b. Hace tres días ____________ las ruinas romanas.

c. Anteayer ____________ deporte en el parque.

d. El viernes pasado ____________ la guitarra.

e. Esta mañana ____________ una película.

f. El jueves pasado ____________ senderismo.

g. Ayer no ____________ de paseo contigo.

h. Anteayer no ____________ el partido de fútbol.

4. Spot the intruders

¿Qué hice la el fin de semana pasado? Pues, hice muchos muchas cosas. El viernes, fui voy a un concierto de Rosalía. Después, jugué los a videojuegos en la casa. Hace tres dos días, hice deporte footing en la el bosque con mi hermana hermano y también hice equitación natación con en el polideportivo. Además, vi visité castillos en el casco antiguo.

5. Faulty translation: one column contains a mistake - listen and correct the errors

e.g.	~~Yesterday~~ *The day before yesterday*	**I went for a walk**	**with my friends.**
a.	Three days ago	I did tourism	at the shopping mall.
b.	The day before yesterday	I watched a concert	in the old town.
c.	Last weekend	I bought new clothes	with my best friend.
d.	Yesterday	I played rugby	with my cousins.
e.	Last weekend	I did horse riding	in the stadium.
f.	Last Friday	I visited art galleries	on the pedestrian street.
g.	Two days ago	I played tennis	at the sports centre.
h.	The day before yesterday	I went shopping	at the shopping mall.

6. Listening slalom: follow the speaker from top to bottom and number the boxes

a	b	c	d	e
Yesterday	Two days ago	Last weekend	Three days ago	Last Friday
I played	I watched	I went	I did	I visited
for a walk	museums	jogging	a film	football
at the cinema	in the woods	in the old town	in the park	in the stadium
near my house.	with my friend.	in my neighbourhood.	with my friends.	with my mother.

7. Narrow listening: gapped translation

What ____________ _____ ____________ last weekend? I did ______________ things. Last ________________ I

watched a ______________ at the __________________ in my neighbourhood ____________ my

________________ and I loved it. On ______________ I went for a walk in the ______________ with my

________________ at __________ o'clock in the morning. After, _______ went shopping at the

____________________ ______________ with ___________ parents. On Sunday morning I did

______________ in the __________________ ______________ with my sister _______ in the afternoon

________ ________________ my favourite ___________ __________________.

8. Listen to Juan and answer the questions in English

a. What country does Juan live in?

b. What did Juan do on Friday?

c. Where did this activity take place?

d. When did Juan visit museums?

e. Where did he visit museums?

f. Where did he watch the concert?

g. Who did he watch the concert with?

h. What two things did he do on Sunday?

UNIT 10. Saying what I did in my neighbourhood: VOCAB BUILDING

1. Match

Hice deporte	I went to the old town
Fui de paseo en el parque	I went to the skating rink
Fui al casco antiguo	I did jogging
Fui a la piscina municipal	I went clubbing
Fui al cine nuevo	I did sport
Fui de marcha	I went to the new cinema
Hice footing	I went to a concert
Fui a la pista de patinaje	I went for a walk in the park
Fui de compras	I visited some art galleries
Fui a un concierto	I went shopping
Vi un partido de rugby	I watched a rugby match
Visité unas galerías de arte	I went to the local swimming pool

2. Complete with the past tense of *hacer, ir, ver, visitar* or *comprar*

a. H_________ senderismo.

b. J_________ al golf.

c. H_________ natación.

d. F______ al estadio.

e. V_________ un castillo antiguo.

f. C_________ ropa nueva.

g. F______ de compras.

h. F______ a un concierto.

3. Break the flow

a. Visitéunagaleríadearteenlaplazamayor

b. Fuidepaseoporelcentro

c. Hicefootingenelparqueconminovio

d. Fuiaunconciertoenelestadio

e. Viunpartidodefútbolenelparque

f. Visitéunasruinasromanas

g. Compréropadeportivaenlacallepeatonal

h. Hicenataciónenelpolideportivo

4. Sentence puzzle: rewrite the Spanish

a. una Vi película con Luis en cine el

I saw a film at the cinema with Luis.

b. Fui paseo en de parque el

I went for a walk in the park.

c. de Fui a un concierto Rosalía

I went to a Rosalía concert.

d. castillo Visité un en el antiguo casco

I visited a castle in the old town.

e. deporte mis con Hice amigos

I did sport with my friends.

f. mi con al tenis Jugué hermano

I played tennis with my brother.

5. Translate into English

a. Fui de paseo en el bosque.

b. Fui de compras con mis amigos.

c. Fui a la piscina municipal.

d. Fui a la pista de patinaje con mi mejor amiga.

e. Compré ropa nueva en el centro comercial.

f. Hice equitación en la playa.

g. Visité un museo en el centro de la ciudad.

h. Vi un partido de fútbol en el estadio con Javier.

i. Hice footing en el polideportivo con mi primo.

6. Match each of the actions on the left with the places on the right

Vi un partido de fútbol	en la galería de arte.
Vi esculturas *(sculptures)*	en la piscina municipal.
Comí una paella deliciosa	en el estadio.
Hice natación	en el centro comercial.
Compré ropa nueva	en el cine de mi barrio.
Toqué la guitarra	en el casco antiguo.
Vi una comedia	en el restaurante.
Visité museos y castillos	en clase de música.

7. Split sentences: form logical sentences

Vi	de fútbol con Paco.
Visité un castillo	una camiseta de fútbol.
Hice natación	una película en el cine.
Vi un partido	en el polideportivo.
Compré	en la piscina.
Fui de	en el casco antiguo.
Hice deporte	tenis.
Jugué al	de magia.
Vi un espectáculo	compras con mi madre.

8. Translate into English

a. Fui de compras

b. Un espectáculo de danza

c. Vi un partido de fútbol

d. Vi una película

e. Fui al bosque

f. El centro comercial

g. El viernes pasado

h. Toqué la guitarra

i. Hice senderismo

j. Hice turismo

k. El cine de mi barrio

9. Faulty translation: correct the English (Please note - not all translations are wrong)

a. Ropa nueva: *New ropes*

b. Un espectáculo: *A pair of spectacles*

c. Edificios modernos: *Historic buildings*

d. Fui al cine: *I went to the park*

e. Hice equitación: *I did horse riding*

f. Fui al museo: *I went to see Muse*

g. La plaza mayor: *The major square*

h. Unas ruinas romanas: *A ruined Roman*

i. Vi un castillo: *I saw cattle*

j. Fui de paseo: *I went passing*

k. Con mi primo: *With my brother*

l. Compré una camiseta: *I sold a t-shirt*

10. Spot and correct the grammar and spelling mistakes

a. Ví un espectaculo de magía.

b. Vi edificio históricos.

c. Fui natación.

d. Visite una palacio histórico.

e. Compre un camiseta de futból.

f. Hicé turismo.

g. Visité una gallería de arte.

h. Vi un partidos de futbol.

i. Vie una película en el cine.

j. Jugé al tenise.

UNIT 10. Saying what I did in my neighbourhood: VOCAB BUILDING

11. Match

Visité un palacio histórico	Last weekend
Hice turismo	Three days ago
Fui a la playa	Who did you go with?
Toqué la guitarra	I visited an historic palace
Vi una película	Last Friday
El viernes pasado	I played the guitar
Anteayer	I went shopping
Hace tres días	I did sightseeing
¿Con quién fuiste?	The day before yesterday
El fin de semana pasado	I watched a film
Fui de compras	Where did you go?
¿Qué hiciste?	I went to the beach
¿Adónde fuiste?	What did you do?

12. Complete with the missing letters

a. Fui en b _ _ _

b. Hi _ _ deporte

c. A _ _ _ _

d. Hice tur _ _ _ _

e. Fui a la p _ _ _ _

f. Saq _ _ much _ _ fotos

g. El fin de semana pas _ _ _

h. Ante _ _ _ _

i. V _ una pel _ _ _ _ _ _

13. Translate into English

a. Anteayer visité un palacio histórico en el casco antiguo.

b. El viernes pasado fui al parque con mi familia.

c. Hace tres días fui al estadio para ver un partido de fútbol.

d. El sábado pasado toqué el violín en el parque.

e. El domingo pasado fui a la piscina.

f. Ayer jugué al tenis con mi primo y mis hermanas.

g. La semana pasada fui al cine con mi novia.

h. Ayer por la tarde vi una película de acción en la tele.

i. El fin de semana pasado fui de compras con mi madre.

j. Ayer por la mañana no hice nada.

k. Ayer hice pesas con mi tío en el gimnasio cerca de mi casa.

14. Spot and add in the missing words

a. Ayer visité castillo.

b. Anteayer fui compras con mi mejor amigo.

c. El domingo pasado hice nada.

d. El viernes pasado fui estadio.

e. Hace tres días turismo en el centro de Barcelona.

f. Ayer hice muchas cosas en barrio.

g. La semana pasada fui centro comercial.

h. Ayer por tarde vi una película.

i. Ayer toqué guitarra.

15. Fill in the gaps

a. Vi _ _ espectáculo.

b. _ _ _ _ turismo.

c. _ _ _ _ _ al baloncesto.

d. _ _ _ _ _ _ un videojuego.

e. Hice _ _ _ _ _ _ _ .

f. Fui de _ _ _ _ _ _ _ _ .

g. Fui al _ _ _ _ con mi padre para ver una película.

h. Ayer _ _ _ _ _ al baloncesto con mi hermano.

i. Anteayer fui al _ _ _ _ _ _ _ a ver un partido de fútbol.

j. Hace tres días toqué la _ _ _ _ _ _ _ _ en mi dormitorio.

k. Ayer _ _ _ _ _ _ unas ruinas romanas en el casco antiguo.

l. Ayer por la mañana no _ _ _ _ deporte con mis primos.

UNIT 10. Saying what I did in my neighbourhood: READING 1

Hola, soy Santi. Vivo en el centro de la ciudad, cerca del supermercado. Mi ciudad es muy ruidosa porque hay muchos edificios nuevos y grandes. En mi opinión hay mucho que hacer cerca de mi casa. Por ejemplo, la semana pasada fui al polideportivo e hice mucho deporte. Por la mañana jugué al baloncesto en la cancha de baloncesto con mis amigos e hice natación en la piscina municipal con mi mejor amigo Pablo. Por la tarde monté en bici en el parque con mi hermano y mi padre. Luego mi familia y yo vimos una película en el salón. Por la noche hice pesas en el gimnasio.

Santi, 15 años. Las Palmas, España

1. Find and correct the mistakes in the translation of Santi's text

Hi. I'm Santi. I live in the old town of the city, near the church. My neighbourhood is quite pretty because there are lots of new and modern buildings. In my opinion, there isn't a lot to do near my flat. For example, last week I went to the shopping mall and I did a bit of sport. In the morning, I played tennis on the basketball court with my cousins and I did skating in the local pool with my uncle Pablo. In the afternoon, I rode my bike in the woods with my sister and my mum. Later on, my family and I watched a football match in the living room. At night, I did weights in the kitchen.

2. Find the Spanish equivalent in Lucía's text

a. In a flat

b. Very pretty

c. A theatre

d. On my street

e. Where one can

f. I went shopping

g. A tracksuit

h. We went

i. I ate

j. He ate fish

k. Near my house

l. I played

m. Last Friday

n. An ice cream

Hola, soy Lucía. Vivo con mis padres en un piso en el centro de la ciudad. Vivo en un barrio muy pequeño pero muy bonito. Hay varios restaurantes, un teatro y un mercado en mi calle.

En mi ciudad hay un centro comercial muy grande donde se puede comprar muchas cosas interesantes. Ayer fui de compras con mi padre y compré un chándal negro y unas zapatillas blancas. Mi padre compró unos zapatos marrones y un abrigo. Después fuimos a un restaurante a comer. Yo comí pollo asado y mi padre comió pescado.

Cerca de mi casa, hay un polideportivo grande. Es muy antiguo pero está bien equipado. El fin de semana pasado fui al polideportivo y jugué al tenis con mi amiga. Después fuimos a su casa a jugar a las cartas. Luego volví a casa y vi una película en el salón.

El viernes pasado, fue mi cumpleaños. Por la mañana hice natación en la piscina municipal con mi amiga. Por la noche fui a dar un paseo por el parque con mis padres y tomamos un helado. ¡Lo pasé bomba!

Lucía, 14 años. Girona, España

3. Read Lucía's text and tick the words not mentioned

a. Barrio	g. Equipado
b. Mercado	h. Pasado
c. Cajas	i. Fútbol
d. Hermano	j. Jugamos
e. Marrones	k. Natación
f. Arroz	l. Perro

UNIT 10. Saying what I did in my neighbourhood: READING 2

Hola, soy Zara. Vivo en una casa pequeña en un barrio bastante tranquilo. El barrio está en el centro de la ciudad así que siempre hay mucho que hacer. Por ejemplo, el fin de semana pasado fui a un museo de arte que está muy cerca de mi casa. Luego a las ocho vi un partido de fútbol en el estadio con mi padre y mi hermano.

El domingo pasado fui a la playa e hice natación con mi hermano. Después fuimos al centro comercial para ir de compras y comer. Fuimos a un restaurante moderno y comimos tapas. También fuimos al cine y vimos una película nueva. Me gustó aunque fue muy caro. A mi hermano no le gustó nada la película.

Ayer por la mañana mis amigas y yo fuimos a la piscina municipal a hacer natación. Fue muy agotador pero también fue divertido. Después tomé un zumo de naranja. Luego fui al parque con mi hermano a dar una vuelta con el perro. Finalmente, descansé en mi dormitorio y vi una serie nueva.

Zara, 11 años. Roquetas del Mar, España

1. True, False or Not mentioned?

a. Zara lives in a small house.

b. Zara lives in the city centre.

c. Zara watched a concert with her dad.

d. Last Sunday, Zara went to the woods.

e. Zara did not eat tapas.

f. Zara's brother liked the film.

g. Zara went swimming yesterday.

h. Zara watched a new series at night.

2. Find the Spanish in Zara's text

a. A small house

b. The neighbourhood is

c. There is always

d. Very close to my house

e. In the stadium

f. I went to the beach

g. We went to the shopping mall

h. Even though it was

i. (He) Didn't like the film at all

j. The local swimming pool

k. It was very tiring

l. I had an orange juice

m. To go for a walk with the dog

n. I relaxed

o. I watched a new series

3. Do the tasks below

a. List in English all the places mentioned in the first paragraph.

b. List in English the things Zara did last weekend.

c. List in English the things that Zara did yesterday.

4. Translate the words you can find in Zara's text and cross out the rest

a. Casco antiguo	h. Cerca	o. Comimos
b. Pequeña	i. Luego	p. Película
c. Tranquilo	j. Concierto	q. Barato
d. Afueras	k. Primo	r. Ayer
e. Siempre	l. Domingo	s. Zumo
f. Ejemplo	m. Mar	t. Tarde
g. Galería	n. Fuimos	u. Nueva

Hola. Soy Miguel. Vivo en Milagro, una ciudad bastante grande en el centro-sur de la Región Costa de Ecuador. Vivo en un piso que está muy cerca de la playa. Vivo con mis padres, mi hermano mayor y mi hermana menor.

En mi ciudad hay mucho que hacer para los adultos, pero no hay mucho para los jóvenes. Sin embargo, el sábado pasado, fui a la playa con mis amigos. Nadamos, tomamos el sol y escuchamos música rock. Luego, fuimos a un restaurante a comer. Comí una hamburguesa de pollo pero mis amigos comieron marisco. A mí no me gusta el marisco.

Mi barrio es bastante antiguo pero está muy bien cuidado. En mi barrio hay un polideportivo bastante nuevo, unas tiendas, unos restaurantes y un parque muy grande y bonito. El domingo pasado, fui al polideportivo con mis amigos a jugar al fútbol en la pista de fútbol sala. Después, fuimos a casa de un amigo a ver una película. También jugamos a la Play.

Anteayer, fui de compras con mi hermano en las tiendas que hay cerca de mi casa. Fuimos a una tienda de deporte que me gusta muchísimo. Finalmente, fuimos a casa de mi primo a comer como todos los sábados. ¡Su padre cocina muy bien!

Ayer por la mañana, desayuné cereales con leche y tomé un café en la terraza. Después, fui al estadio con mis amigos a ver un partido de fútbol. Vimos el partido y después fuimos a la plaza mayor a tomar un refresco y almorzar. Pedí *(I ordered)* un bocadillo pero mis amigos pidieron una pizza.

Miguel, 15 años. Milagro, Ecuador

1. Translate the chunks from the text

a. A rather big city

b. I live in

c. A flat

d. Very close to the beach

e. There is a lot to do

f. Last Saturday

g. We sunbathed

h. I ate a chicken burger

i. They ate

j. I don't like seafood

k. In my neighbourhood

l. A very big and pretty park

m. We played

n. I went shopping

o. I ate for breakfast

p. They ordered

2. Correct any wrong statements about Miguel's text

a. His town is on the coast of Venezuela.

b. He lives quite far from the beach.

c. There is lots to do for young people.

d. His friends ate burgers.

e. His neighbourhood is very modern.

f. Last Saturday, he went to the sports centre.

g. His auntie is a very good cook.

h. He went to the park to watch a football match.

3. Complete the sentences in Spanish based on Miguel's text

a. Su ciudad se llama __________________.

b. Vive con sus __________________, su

__________________ y su __________________.

c. El sábado pasado, fue a la __________________.

d. Luego, comió una __________________ de

__________________.

e. Su barrio es bastante __________________.

f. El domingo pasado, fue al __________________.

g. Fue al polideportivo con sus __________________.

h. Fue de compras con su __________________.

i. Comieron en casa de su __________________.

UNIT 10. What I did in my neighbourhood: WRITING & TRANSLATION

1. Complete with the missing letters

a. E _ v _ _ _ _ _ _ pas _ _ _   *...Last Friday...*

b. A _ _ _ h _ _ _ much _ _ cos _ _ .   *Yesterday I did many things.*

c. A _ _ _ _ _ _ _ f _ _ de compr _ _ .   *The day before yesterday I went shopping.*

d. H _ _ _ tres d _ _ _ h _ _ _ deporte.   *Three days ago I did sport.*

e. Tamb _ _ n toq _ _ la guitarra en el parq _ _ _ .   *I also played the guitar in the park.*

f. A _ _ _ _ _ _ _ _ _ _ _ al centro comercial.   *The day before yesterday I went to the mall.*

g. H _ _ _ t _ _ _ días v _ u _ _ películ _ .   *Three days ago I watched a film.*

h. _ _ _ _ f _ _ a v _ _ u _ partid _ de fútbol.   *Yesterday I went to watch a football match.*

i. _ _ f _ _ de semana pasad _ jug _ _ al tenis.   *Last weekend I played tennis.*

2. Sentence puzzle: write the sentences below in the correct order

a. al a una película cine Ayer fui ver

b. la toqué en el Anteayer salón guitarra

c. hice el Ayer polideportivo deporte en

d. tres fui días al centro Hace comercial

e. viernes compras de El pasado fui

f. arte tres Hace visité de días una galería

g. jugué Ayer al el tenis en parque

h. La fui de circo pasada a un semana espectáculo

i. partido Fui con a mi hermano un de fútbol

4. Translate into Spanish

a. I played guitar

b. I played tennis

c. Three days ago

d. Yesterday

e. The day before yesterday

f. Last week

g. The skating rink

h. I played

i. A Rosalía concert

j. In the stadium

3. Complete with a suitable word

a. Ayer __________ al cine y ___________ una ___________________ de acción.

b. Anteayer ____________ de compras _________ mi padre en el ___________ _________________ de mi barrio.

c. Hace _________ días, ___________ footing en el bosque con ________ _______________ .

d. La semana pasada _____________ la batería en mi _________________________ .

e. Fui al _____________ antiguo y ______________ unas galerías de arte.

f. El _______________ pasado, ______________ senderismo en el ____________________ .

g. El fin de __________ pasado _____ al _____________________ cerca de mi casa.

h. _______ natación y __________ al tenis con mis ________________ .

i. La semana pasada ________ de paseo en el campo con _________ primos.

UNIT 10. What I did in my neighbourhood: WRITING & TRANSLATION

5. Spot and correct the grammar and spelling mistakes. Please note: not all sentences are incorrect

a. La semana pasada hice muchos cosas.

b. Ver muchos monumentos en el casco antiguo.

c. Visité museos y palacios históricas en el centro.

d. Hice footing en el bosque con mis amigos.

e. Ayer yo fue al centro comercial con mi abuela.

f. Anteayer fui de compras en la centro de la ciudad.

g. Hace tres días yo hacer turismo con mi mejor amigo.

h. Fui al estadio con mi abuelo.

i. Ayer por la mañana ir de paseo al parque.

j. Anteayer jugué al fútbol con mi amigas Nadia.

6. Complete

a. V _		*I saw*
b. F _ _		*I went*
c. H _ _ _		*I did*
d. M _ _ _ _		*I rode*
e. V _ _ _ _ _		*I visited*
f. J _ _ _ _		*I played*

7. Translate into Spanish

a. Last week I did many things.

b. Yesterday I went shopping in the town square.

c. Two days ago I went to the park with my friends.

d. I visited historic palaces and museums in the old town.

e. Last weekend I went to a Rosalía concert.

f. Last Friday I did a lot of sport at the sports centre.

g. Yesterday I went hiking with my father and my brother.

h. Two days ago I played guitar with my friend in the living room.

i. Last weekend I went for a walk on the beach with my girlfriend.

j. Last week I visited an art gallery with my sisters.

k. Three days ago I went to the sports centre with my cousins.

8. Write two paragraphs in the first person singular (I) about Nerea and Mark. NOTE: you cannot repeat the same information twice

Nerea (14 years old from Spain)	**Mark** (13 years old from England)
• Say your name, age and nationality	• Say your name, age and nationality
• Describe your physique and personality (4 details)	• Describe your physique and personality (6 details)
• Say you live in the east of Spain, near Valencia, on the coast	• Say you live in the north-west of England, near Manchester, in the countryside
• Describe your neighbourhood: say what there is to see and do (4 details minimum)	• Describe your town: size, what is there to see and do (4 details minimum)
• Say one thing you like and one that you dislike about your neighbourhood	• Say one thing you like and one that you dislike about your town
• Say 4 things that you did last weekend in your neighbourhood	• Say 4 things that you did last weekend in your neighbourhood

1. Hola, soy Alejandro. Tengo dieciocho años y mi cumpleaños es el catorce de septiembre. Vivo cerca de Alicante, una ciudad en el sureste de España. Vivo en el campo con mis padres y mi hermana María. Me llevo bien con mi hermana porque es muy amable y siempre me ayuda.

2. Me gusta Alicante porque hay muchas cosas que hacer. Por ejemplo, en el centro se puede hacer de todo; hay muchos restaurantes, muchas tiendas y varios parques bonitos. También se puede hacer deporte, ir de compras o hacer turismo.

3. En mi calle no hay mucho que hacer. Como vivo en el campo, hay pocas tiendas y restaurantes. Al lado de mi casa hay un parque pequeño donde se puede jugar al fútbol. Solo hay cinco casas en mi calle; mi casa está en la esquina. Mi casa es muy grande. Hay cuatro dormitorios, un salón, una cocina, un comedor, una sala de juegos y un garaje. En mi dormitorio tengo un ordenador y una televisión. Veo la tele todas las noches.

4. Este fin de semana voy a ir al centro comercial con mi hermana a ver una película de acción en el cine. Creo que será muy divertido y emocionante. Después vamos a ir a un restaurante a comer. Para la cena voy a pedir *(order)* una hamburguesa y patatas fritas y un zumo de naranja. Creo que mi hermana va a pedir lo mismo *(the same)*.

5. El fin de semana pasado visité el castillo de Santa Bárbara, un icono alicantino. El castillo está ubicado *(located)* en la costa y tiene un museo muy interesante. Visité el castillo con mis padres porque les encanta la historia y la cultura española. En mi opinión fue bastante divertido pero también fue agotador.

6. Anteayer fui a ver un partido de fútbol del Hércules CF en el estadio José Rico Pérez. El estadio está bastante cerca del centro de Alicante, pero un poco lejos de mi casa. Fui al partido con mi mejor amigo, Juanma. Juanma también vive en el campo con sus padres y su hermana mayor. Después del partido jugué a la Play en mi dormitorio hasta las once y media.

Alejandro, 18 años. Alicante, España

1. Answer the following questions in English

a. When is Alejandro's birthday?

b. Why does he get along with his sister?

c. How does he feel about his city?

d. List two things you can do in his city.

e. What is on Alejandro's street?

f. What does he do every night?

g. What will he do this weekend?

h. What will he order to eat?

i. Who did he visit the castle with?

j. Who did he watch the football match with?

2. Find the Spanish equivalent in Alejandro's text

a. In the countryside (1)

b. I get on well with (1)

c. One can do (2)

d. Few shops (3)

e. There are only (3)

f. A games room (3)

g. An action film (4)

h. (She) is going to order (4)

i. Is located (5)

j. They love (5)

k. The day before yesterday (6)

l. Near my house (6)

m. Until 11:30 (6)

3. Complete the translation of paragraph 5

___________ ________________, I visited the ________________ of Santa Bárbara, an ____________ of Alicante. The castle ________ located on the ____________ and it ___________ a very interesting ______________. I ________________ the castle with my ________________ because ___________ love history ________ Spanish culture. In ________ opinion, it was ____________ fun but ____________ a bit ________________.

Juan y Sara son amigos. Están hablando de lo que hicieron el fin de semana pasado.	
Juan	¿Qué tal, Sara? ¿Todo bien?
Sara	Buenos días, Juan. Sí, todo bien. Bueno, estoy supercansada.
Juan	¿Por qué?
Sara	El fin de semana pasado estuve muy ocupada *(busy)*, hice muchísimas cosas.
Juan	¿Qué hiciste?
Sara	El viernes por la noche fui de compras con mis padres al centro comercial. También vimos una película de terror en el cine.
Juan	¡Qué guay! A mí no me gustan las películas de terror, me dan mucho miedo *(fear)*. ¿Y qué hiciste el sábado?
Sara	El sábado visité las ruinas romanas en el casco antiguo. También fui a la plaza mayor a tomar un café con mis amigas. Por la tarde hice footing en el bosque. ¿Y tú?
Juan	No me soprende que estés cansada. El sábado vi un espectáculo de flamenco en el centro de la ciudad. Fui con mi abuela.
Sara	Ay, ¡qué chulo! ¿Te llevas bien con tu abuela?
Juan	Sí, es muy simpática y graciosa. Además, vivo con ella así que tengo que llevarme bien con ella. ¿Con quién vives tú?
Sara	Vivo con mis padres y mi hermana mayor. ¿Qué hiciste el domingo?
Juan	Pues no hice nada. Cuando llueve siempre me quedo en casa y veo una película en el salón. ¿Y tú?
Sara	Todos los domingos jugamos al tenis en el polideportivo. Luego cenamos en casa, siempre comemos pollo asado y arroz.
Juan	¿Jugáis cuando hace mal tiempo?
Sara	¡Claro! También hay pistas cubiertas.

4. True (T), False (F) or Not Mentioned (NM)?

Juan and Sara are cousins.	
Juan is feeling really tired.	
Sara was very busy at the weekend.	
Sara watched a horror film.	
Juan loves horror films.	
Juan played rugby in the park.	
Sara had coffee with her friends in the old town.	
Sara went jogging in the woods.	
Juan watched a flamenco show on Saturday.	
Juan lives close to his grandmother.	
Sara has a pet cat.	
Juan did not do anything on Sunday.	
Every Sunday, Sara eats roast chicken and rice.	

5. Complete the statements

a. _____________ did many things last _____________.

b. _____________ is _____________ of horror films.

c. _____________ visited the roman ruins in the _________ _____________.

d. Juan's grandmother is very _____________ and _____________.

e. _____________ stays at home when it _____________.

Unit 11
Saying what I did & am going to do at the weekend

In this unit you will learn:

- To describe what you did last weekend
- To give your opinion on the activities you did last weekend
- To describe what you are going to do next weekend
- To predict what your plans next weekend will be like

You will revisit:

- Time markers
- Free-time activities
- Activities in the preterite
- Expression opinions

UNIT 11. Saying what I did & am going to do at the weekend

¿Qué hiciste el fin de semana pasado?	*What did you do last weekend?*
¿Cómo fue?	*How was it?*
¿Qué vas a hacer el próximo fin de semana?	*What are you going to do next weekend?*
¿Qué va a hacer tu hermano/a?	*What is your brother/sister going to do?*

El fin de semana pasado *Last weekend*	**yo**	**fui**	*I went*	**a casa de mi amigo/a**	*to my friend's house*	
		fuimos	*we went*	**al estadio**	*to the stadium*	
	mi amigo/a y yo *my friend and I*	**hice**	*I did*	**deporte**	*sport*	
		hicimos	*we did*	**mis deberes**	*homework*	
El viernes pasado *Last Friday*	**nosotros** *we – (m / mixed)*	**jugué**	*I played*	**a videojuegos**	*videogames*	
		jugamos	*we played*	**en mi ordenador**	*on my computer*	
		toqué	*I played*	**el piano**	*piano*	
El domingo pasado *Last Sunday*	**nosotras** *we (f)*	**tocamos**	*we played*	**la guitarra**	*guitar*	
		vi	*I saw*	**un partido de fútbol**	*a football match*	
		vimos	*we saw*	**una película**	*a film*	

Fue *It was*	**bastante** **un poco** **muy**	**aburrido** *boring* **divertido** *fun* **interesante**
No fue nada *It was not … at all*		

El próximo fin de semana *Next weekend*	**voy a** *I am going*	**hacer** *to do*	**deporte** **los deberes**	*sport*	
		ir *to go*	**a una fiesta** **al centro comercial** **de compras**	*to a party* *to the shopping mall* *shopping*	
	mi hermana va a *my sister is going*	**jugar** *to play*	**al baloncesto** **en mi ordenador**	*basketball* *on my computer*	
El próximo sábado *Next Saturday*	**mi hermano y yo vamos a** *my brother and I are going*	**tocar** *to play*	**la batería**	*drums*	
El próximo domingo *Next Sunday*	**mis padres van a** *my parents are going*	**ver** *to see*	**un concierto** **un partido de fútbol** **una película**	*a concert* *a football match* *a film*	

Será *It will be*	**bastante** *quite* **un poco** *a bit* **muy** *very*	**agotador** *exhausting* **apasionante** *exciting* **guay** *cool*
No será nada *It won't be … at all*		

Author's notes:

1) **Nosotros** is the personal pronoun for "we". You use it when talking about a male or mixed gender group (regardless of the ratio of girls and boys). **Nosotras** is "we" for an all girl group.

2) Don't forget there are two verbs to say "I play": **tocar** (for instruments) and **jugar** (for sports)

1. Multiple choice: cross out the word that was <u>not</u> said

e.g.	**Próximo**	**Ir**	~~Fiesta~~
a.	Sábado	Jugar	Fútbol
b.	Próximo	Hacer	Caballo
c.	La	Hermana	Va
d.	De	Fui	Al
e.	Viernes	Jugamos	Partido
f.	Domingo	Vosotros	Ordenador
g.	Sábado	Hice	Deberes

2. Dictation

a. _ _ _ _ _ _ _

b. _ _ _ _ _ _ _

c. _ _ _ _ _ _ _ _ _

d. _ _ _ _ _ _ _

e. _ _ _ _ _

f. _ _ _ _ _ _ _

g. _ _ _ _ _ _ _ _ _ _ _

h. _ _ _ _ _

3. Fill in the blanks

a. El fin de semana pasado ______________ al estadio.

b. Este viernes ______________ a ver una película.

c. Voy a tocar ___ ______________ con mi ______________.

d. El viernes pasado ______________ en mi ordenador.

e. El domingo pasado ______________ deporte.

f. El próximo finde ______________ a ir de compras.

g. Pienso que ______________ muy aburrido.

h. En mi opinión ______________ bastante guay.

4. Spot the intruders

Hola, soy estoy Vicente y este fin de la semana voy a hacer deporte en el polideportivo. Vamos Voy a jugar al fútbol baloncesto. Mis hermanos padres van a ir de fiesta compras pero yo él no voy a ir porque será bastante muy aburrido. El próximo fin de semana pasado mi amigo y yo fuimos vimos una película en el cine y fue un poco muy guay.

5. Faulty translation: one column contains a mistake - listen and correct the errors

e.g.	~~Last weekend~~ *Last Friday*	**we went**	**to the stadium.**
a.	Next weekend	we are going	to ride a bike.
b.	Next Friday	my parents are going	to watch a concert.
c.	In my opinion,	it will be	very fun.
d.	Next Sunday	my sister is going	to play basketball.
e.	Last weekend	I did	sport.
f.	I think that	it will be	a bit exciting.
g.	Last Friday	we watched	a football match.
h.	Next Sunday	I am going	to go to the beach.

6. Listening slalom: follow the speaker from top to bottom and number the boxes

a	b	c	d	e
Next weekend	Last weekend	Next Sunday	Last Saturday	Last Friday
my parents are going	I	my sister is going	we	my friend and I
went	to ride	watched	to watch	played
a horse	a film	a football match	to the stadium	guitar
in the stadium.	in the city centre.	in the park.	at my friend's house.	at the shopping mall.

7. Narrow listening: gapped translation

a. I ____________ lots of plans this __________________. First, I am going to go to the ______________ ______________ with my ______________. We are going to __________________ and after ________ are going to go to a ________________. I think that it will be ______________ fun and it won't be ________________ at all.

b. My __________________ are going __________________ a football match in the __________________________. Last __________________, my friends and I went to the __________________ but we didn't ______________ a __________________. Last ________________, I ______________ a ________________ at home and it ______________ very ________________.

8. Listen to Eugenio and answer the questions in English

Part 1 – a.

1. How old is Eugenio?
2. What will Eugenio do first next weekend?
3. Where will this activity take place?
4. What will Eugenio do after?
5. How does Eugenio think this activity will go?

Part 2 – b.

1. When will Eugenio ride a horse?
2. How does he think riding a horse will be?
3. Who did he go to the sports centre with?
4. What happened in the city centre?
5. How was this event? (2 details)

UNIT 11. What I did & am going to do at the weekend: VOCAB BUILDING

1. Match: near future recap

Vamos a ir de compras	We are going to play the flute
Vamos a jugar al baloncesto	We are going to do homework
Vamos a ver una película	We are going to go to the stadium
Vamos a leer un libro	We are going to go to a concert
Vamos a hacer deporte	We are going to do swimming
Vamos a hacer natación	We are going to do sport
Vamos a ir al estadio	We are going to play videogames
Vamos a hacer los deberes	We are going to read a book
Vamos a jugar a videojuegos	We are going to watch a film
Vamos a ir a un concierto	We are going to go shopping
Vamos a tocar la flauta	We are going to play basketball

2. Complete with *ir, hacer, jugar, tocar* or *ver*

a. Voy a ____________ de compras.

b. Voy a ____________ a un concierto.

c. Vamos a ____________ al tenis.

d. Vamos a ____________ al centro comercial.

e. Voy a ____________ al campo.

f. Voy a ____________ deporte.

g. Voy a ____________ una película en el cine.

h. Voy a ____________ al estadio.

i. Voy a ____________ el violín en el colegio.

3. Complete with the missing letters

a. Vo _ a v _ r un _ pel _ cul _ .

b. V _ y a i _ a _ estadi _ .

c. Va _ os a hac _ r deport _ .

d. V _ _ os a j _ _ ar al balonce _ t _ .

e. _ oy a i _ al parq _ _ .

f. Ser _ diverti _ _ .

g. Vamo _ a to _ _ r el pi _ _ o.

h. _ _ mos a i _ al centr _ co _ ercia _ .

i. V _ _ os a ha _ _ r nataci _ n.

j. V _ y a mont _ _ en b _ c _ .

4. Faulty translation: correct the mistakes in the English translations below (not all are wrong)

a. El próximo sábado voy a ver una película.   *Next Friday I am going to watch a film.*

b. El próximo fin de semana vamos a montar en bici.   *Next weekend I am going to ride a horse.*

c. Mi amigo y yo vamos a hacer senderismo.   *My friend and I are going to go hiking.*

d. El domingo por la tarde voy a ir de compras.   *Sunday morning I am going to go shopping.*

e. El próximo sábado mi tía va a ir a la piscina.   *Next Saturday my aunt is going to go to the beach.*

f. El próximo viernes voy a hacer mis deberes.   *On Friday my brother is going to do his homework.*

g. Voy a salir con mi amiga por la mañana.   *I'm going to go out with my friend in the afternoon.*

UNIT 11. What I did & am going to do at the weekend: VOCAB BUILDING

5. Sentence puzzle: rewrite the sentences in the correct order

a. próximo El vamos sábado al estadio a ir

b. El fin de a voy ir semana al próximo comercial centro

c. El vamos a ir de fin semana de próximo compras

d. El tocar por domingo voy a la mañana el piano

e. padres Mis a van una el película cine ver en

f. hermana Mi a va a ir piscina la amigas con sus

g. El hermano viernes mi va a próximo ir de marcha

6. Multiple choice: choose the correct translation

		1	2	3
a.	**Hacer deporte**	To ride a bike	To do sport	To do hiking
b.	**Ir de compras**	To go compare	To go shopping	To do nothing
c.	**Ver una película**	To watch a game	To go running	To watch a film
d.	**Tocar la batería**	To play drums	To touch a battery	To play piano
e.	**Ir a un concierto**	To play guitar	To go to a concert	To watch a film
f.	**Montar en bici**	To ride a bike	To ride a horse	To play games
g.	**Leer un libro**	To read an article	To read a magazine	To read a book
h.	**Ir de paseo**	To go for a walk	To go running	To stay at home

7. Find in the wordsearch the Spanish translations of the phrases below and write them as shown in the example

```
O E S A P N U R A D W E W V M G B O A D
D D T Z S C X R Z Q T Q E O I Q C D I B
I L Z E M W O T D R S R N S U L H I K R
T B R L K E C E O D U T E E B R R R X H
R Á P W O Q T P Y N A B D H C S H R Q V
E S F B J B E N A R J K H U T S T U J J
V Z T U F D S P A L E E R U N L I B R O
I Q G H R D E C I N S K B J O H O A R D
D A A E C L A J Y O O B R H M J F B O R
R J C G Í B Y B Q X T I K V R F I K D F
T A F C A L Y E V V G H S E G I U S X Z
H W U L E A I C I B N E R A T N O M J L
P L L A D A N R E C A H O N P C R O H Y
A O Y W F Z X U J O O A G S L A X A A O
G E Z Z R I E W O L M S T M I Y U M S W
```

e.g. Leer un libro
To read a book

a. Boring

b. Exciting

c. It will be

d. To do nothing

e. To do sport

f. To go for a walk

g. To play

h. To ride a bike

i. To ride a horse

j. To watch a film

k. Fun

UNIT 11. What I did & am going to do at the weekend: VOCAB BUILDING

8. Translate into English

a. El próximo sábado mi novia y yo vamos a ver una película.

b. El próximo fin de semana mi hermano y yo vamos a jugar al bádminton.

c. El próximo viernes mis padres van a ver un espectáculo de flamenco.

d. El próximo domingo por la tarde voy a ir de compras con mi madre.

e. El próximo fin de semana mi hermana va a ir a la piscina con su novio.

f. El próximo fin de semana voy a hacer mis deberes de matemáticas.

g. El próximo sábado por la mañana voy a ir al parque con mi hermano menor.

h. Después, mi hermano y yo vamos a ir a comer al restaurante italiano cerca de mi casa.

i. El próximo domingo por la mañana voy a ir a la iglesia con mi familia.

9. Match

Fui de compras	I went to the library
Leí un libro	I played the ukulele
Vi una película	I rode a horse
Monté a caballo	We did sport
No hice nada	I watched a film
Fui a la biblioteca	We did jogging
Hicimos deporte	I played basketball
Jugué al baloncesto	I read a book
Toqué el ukelele	We didn't do anything
Hicimos footing	I didn't do anything
No hicimos nada	I went shopping

10. Complete the past tense verbs with the missing letters

a. Fu _ de compras.

b. Fuimo _ al campo.

c. Hic _ mos deporte.

d. V _ una película.

e. F _ i al estadio.

f. Le _ un libro.

g. J _ gamos al baloncesto.

h. V _ mos monumentos.

i. No hi _ e nada.

11. Choose the correct verb and cross out the wrong ones

a. Hice / Vi / Jugué al baloncesto.   *I played basketball.*

b. No hice / vi / jugué nada.   *I didn't do anything.*

c. Toqué / Vi / Jugué la batería.   *I played drums.*

d. Fui / Vi / Escuché música.   *I listened to music.*

e. Vi / Jugué/ Fui de compras.   *I went shopping.*

f. No vi / jugué / hice nada.   *I didn't see anything.*

g. Hicimos / Vimos / Fuimos pesas.   *We did weights.*

h. Vi / Hice / Leí un libro.   *I read a book.*

12. Anagrams: rewrite the jumbled-up words correctly

a. uiF ed ompcras

b. iV nau lículape

c. oN cehi adan

d. éugJu la cebastolon

e. uFiosm la staeiod

f. iciHosm portdee

g. oN cehi ism beresde

h. ugJamos la niste

UNIT 11. Saying what I did & am going to do at the weekend: TRANSLATION

1. Slalom writing

e.g. Yesterday I rode my bike in the park.

a. Last Saturday I went shopping with my girlfriend.

b. Last Friday I did my homework after school.

c. Last Sunday I didn't do anything. I only watched a film.

d. Three days ago I went to the gym with my older brother.

e. The day before yesterday I played basketball with my friends.

f. Next Saturday I am going to the stadium with my cousin.

g. Next Friday I am going to do sightseeing in the old town.

Ayer	voy a hacer	turismo	con mi	con mi primo.
El viernes pasado	**monté en**	nada.	Solo vi	**parque.**
Hace tres días	fui de	**bici**	**en el**	mayor.
Anteayer	hice	baloncesto	después	amigos.
El sábado pasado	fui al	ir al	con mis	una película.
El próximo sábado	no hice	mis deberes	con mi hermano	novia.
El próximo viernes	jugué al	compras	estadio	antiguo.
El domingo pasado	voy a	gimnasio	en el casco	del colegio.

2. Translate into English (preterite)

a. Fui a la piscina.

b. Fui de compras con mi amigo.

c. Fuimos a la bolera *(bowling alley)*.

d. Mi amigo y yo hicimos deporte.

e. Toqué la guitarra.

f. Hice natación.

g. Fui al estadio.

3. Translate into English (near future)

a. Vamos a jugar al baloncesto.

b. Voy a hacer turismo.

c. Vamos a comer tapas.

d. Voy a leer una novela.

e. Vamos a ver dibujos animados.

f. Vamos a ir al estadio.

g. Voy a tocar el violín.

4. Complete the hidden sentences
HINT: they are all in the past tense

a. T _ _ _ _ e _ p _ _ _ _ .

b. F _ _ d _ c _ _ _ _ _ _ _ .

c. J _ _ _ _ a _ b _ _ _ _ _ _ _ _ _ _ _ .

d. F _ _ _ _ _ a l _ b _ _ _ _ _ _ .

e. F _ _ al e _ _ _ _ _ _ _ .

f. N _ h _ _ _ n _ _ _ .

g. H _ _ _ m _ _ d _ _ _ _ _ _ _ .

h. J _ _ _ _ _ _ a _ t _ _ _ _ .

i. F _ _ a l _ p _ _ _ _ _ _ .

j. M _ _ _ _ a c _ _ _ _ _ _ _ .

k. L _ _ u _ _ n _ _ _ _ _ .

UNIT 11. Saying what I did & am going to do at the weekend: WRITING

1. Complete the table using the words listed below. NOTE: three of the words are distractors
HINT: all the sentences are in the past tense

coche	colegio	amigo	bici
piscina	vi	el	pingüino
centro	hice	compras	ayer
cine	viernes	hace	parque
pasada	jugué	película	pasado
tele	fui	semana	estadio

¿Cuándo?	¿Qué hiciste?	¿Dónde? / ¿Con quién?
a. El sábado __________	monté en __________	en el __________.
b. El __________ pasado	_______ un partido de fútbol	en la __________.
c. ______ domingo pasado	fui de __________	en el ________ comercial
d. __________	__________ natación	en la _________ municipal.
e. __________ tres días	vi una __________	en el ______ cerca de mi casa.
f. La semana __________	__________ al baloncesto	en mi ____________.
g. El fin de _______ pasado	__________ a una fiesta	en la casa de mi _______.

2. Complete the table below with the missing verb forms, as shown in the example

PAST (Preterite)	PRESENT (Present indicative)	FUTURE (Immediate future)
Fui al cine	*Voy* al cine	*Voy a ir* al cine
	Vamos de compras	Vamos a ir de compras
		Voy a hacer mis deberes
Monté en monopatín *I skateboarded*	Monto en monopatín *I skateboard*	
	Voy al estadio	
	Toco el bajo *(bass)*	
Fui a una fiesta	Voy a una fiesta	
	Monto en bici	Voy a montar en bici
	Veo una película	
Vi dibujos animados		

UNIT 11. Saying what I did & am going to do at the weekend: READING 1

El fin de semana pasado no hice nada especial. El viernes después del colegio volví (*I came back)* a mi casa a eso de las cuatro. Comí un bocadillo de queso y me relajé (*I relaxed)* un rato escuchando música. Después, como siempre, hice mis deberes y fui al gimnasio con mi hermano mayor. Fue agotador pero divertido. Por la tarde vi una película de acción en la tele. ¡No fue nada apasionante! El actor principal se llama Esteban Gaviota. ¡Es muy malo!

El sábado por la mañana fui de compras con mi madre. Compré (*I bought)* una camiseta y unos vaqueros. Por la tarde toqué la guitarra en el parque cerca de mi casa con mi mejor amigo y luego, a eso de las siete, fui al cine con mi novia, Arancha. Lo pasé muy bien con ella. ¡Es muy inteligente y graciosa!

El domingo no hice nada. Me levanté (*I got up)* muy tarde, luego fui a la iglesia con mis padres y después me relajé jugando en mi ordenador y escuchando música. No fue nada especial.

Fue un fin de semana muy relajante.

Sergio, 15 años. Oviedo, España

1. Find the Spanish equivalent in the text

a. I didn't do anything special

b. I came back home

c. I ate a cheese sandwich

d. I did my homework

e. I went to the gym

f. It was tiring

g. I watched a film

h. It wasn't exciting at all

i. I went shopping

j. In the afternoon

k. I played guitar

l. With my girlfriend

m. I had a good time with her

n. She is very clever and funny

o. I went to church

p. Afterwards I relaxed

q. Nothing special

2. Answer the questions in the first person, as if you were Sergio

a. ¿A qué hora volviste a casa el viernes pasado?

b. ¿Qué comiste?

c. ¿Qué hiciste para relajarte?

d. ¿Con quién fuiste al gimnasio?

e. ¿Cómo fue el entrenamiento?

f. ¿Qué tipo de película viste en la tele?

g. ¿Adónde fuiste el sábado por la mañana?

h. ¿Con quién?

i. ¿Qué compraste?

j. ¿A qué hora fuiste al cine con tu novia?

k. ¿Cómo es Arancha?

l. ¿Adónde fuiste el domingo por la mañana?

3. Spot and correct the mistakes in these sentences from Sergio's text

a. No hice nada special (1 mistake)

b. El viernes, despues colegio, volvi a casa a eso de las cuatro (3)

c. Comi un bocadillo queso (2)

d. Hace mis deberes y fue al gimnasio (2)

e. Ví una pelicula (2)

f. El zapato por la manana (2)

g. Fuí de compras (1)

h. Compre una camiseta (1)

i. El domingo hice nada (1)

j. Me levante tarde (1)

k. Me relajé escuchar música (1)

l. Fui un fin de semana muy relajante (1)

UNIT 11. Saying what I did & am going to do at the weekend: READING 2

El sábado pasado por la mañana fui de paseo por el centro con mi hermana mayor. Fui a mi tienda de ropa favorita y compré un vestido rosa muy guay. Por la tarde salí *(I went out)* con mi novio. Fuimos al parque cerca de mi casa y luego, a eso de las siete, fui al restaurante italiano con mi familia. El restaurante está a cien metros de mi casa, así que fuimos allí a pie. ¡Comimos muy bien!

El domingo no hice nada especial. Me levanté *(I got up)* bastante tarde, luego fui a la piscina con mi hermana mayor y después me relajé leyendo un libro y tocando la guitarra. Fue un fin de semana muy relajante.

Amparo, 13 años. Sevilla, España

El sábado pasado por la mañana fui de paseo por el centro con mi hermana menor. Fui a mi tienda de ropa favorita y compré una falda rosa muy guay. Por la tarde salí con mi mejor amigo, Daniel. Fuimos al centro comercial cerca de mi casa. Miramos escaparates y tomamos un helado. Luego fui al restaurante japonés con mi familia. El restaurante está al lado de mi casa. Es muy bueno. Comimos muy bien.

El domingo no hice nada especial. Me levanté temprano para hacer footing con mi madre. ¡Estoy intentando ponerme en forma! Luego me relajé escuchando música y jugando a videojuegos en línea hasta las cinco de la tarde. Luego vi una película en la tele e hice mis deberes.

Lorène Carver, 15 años. Montpellier, Francia

1. Tick the phrases below that are contained in Amparo's text

a. Fui de paseo	g. Por la tarde
b. Fuimos allí	h. A cien metros
c. Fui de compras	i. En coche
d. Monté en bici	j. Con mi novio
e. No hice nada	k. Compramos
f. Fui a la piscina	l. Compré

2. *Amparo*, *Lorène* or *Neither* of them?

a. Went to the park with her boyfriend.

b. Relaxed reading a book.

c. Had an ice cream with her best friend.

d. Went to the restaurant by car.

e. Went for a walk with her younger sister.

f. Went window shopping.

g. Relaxed playing guitar.

h. Lives right next to a restaurant.

i. Went to the pool on Sunday morning.

j. Woke up early to go jogging.

3. Find the Spanish equivalent in Lorène's text. HINT: they are not listed in the same order as in the text

a. In the morning

b. I did my homework

c. Next to my house

d. I didn't do anything special

e. Early

f. I am trying to get fit

g. With my best friend

h. We went window shopping

i. We ate very well

j. I went to my favourite shop

k. I relaxed

4. Translate the words underlined below. HINT: the sentences are from Lorène's text

a. <u>Salí</u> con mi mejor amigo

b. Una falda rosa muy <u>guay</u>

c. <u>Comimos</u> muy bien

d. Me levanté <u>temprano</u>

e. <u>Miramos</u> escaparates

f. <u>Estoy intentando</u> estar en forma

g. Me relajé <u>escuchando música</u>

UNIT 11. Saying what I did & am going to do at the weekend: READING 3

Silvia: El domingo pasado no hice nada especial. Por la mañana fui a la biblioteca y luego, por la tarde, fui al centro comercial cerca de mi casa. Luego hice mis deberes de matemáticas. Cuando terminé mis deberes vi una película romántica en la tele. Fue bastante aburrida.

Marcela: El domingo pasado no fue nada divertido. Solo hice mis deberes, jugué con mi perro en el jardín y ayudé a mis padres con las tareas domésticas. A eso de las siete de la tarde fui a la casa de mis abuelos con mi madre y cenamos allí.

Paco: El domingo pasado fue muy apasionante porque hice mucho deporte con mis mejores amigos. Por la mañana hice ciclismo de montaña con mi amiga Ana. Fue muy agotador, ¡pero también muy divertido! Por la tarde hice escalada con mi mejor amigo, Pablo, en el parque de mi barrio. Hay un muro de escalada muy alto allí. ¡Fue apasionante! Luego hice pesas con mi amigo Juan. ¡Fue fenomenal! ¡Todavía me duelen los brazos!

Susana: El domingo pasado no hice nada de nada. Solo dormí, comí y vi la tele.

Julián: El domingo pasado lo pasé muy bien. Pasé todo el día con mi novia. Por la mañana fuimos de compras al centro. Luego tomamos algo en una cafetería y dimos una vuelta por el casco antiguo. Hicimos turismo y sacamos muchísimas fotos en el castillo. Luego fuimos al parque de atracciones cerca del puerto. ¡Fue muy divertido! ¡Lo pasamos bomba!

1. Find someone who...

a. ...went to an amusement park last Sunday.

b. ...didn't do anything special.

c. ...went rock climbing in the afternoon.

d. ...had a nice day with his girlfriend.

e. ...went mountain biking.

f. ...who still had sore arms from their workout.

g. ...spent the evening with their grandparents.

h. ...watched a romantic film on TV.

i. ...spent the whole Sunday eating, sleeping and watching television.

j. ...took a lot of pictures in a castle.

k. ...helped their mother with the chores.

2. Find the Spanish equivalent

a. Last Sunday

b. I went to the library

c. When I finished my homework

d. It was quite boring (f)

e. I helped my parents with the house chores

f. We had dinner there

g. I did a lot of sport

h. With my best friends

i. My neighbourhood park

j. I did weights

k. My arms still hurt

3. Tick or cross? Tick the phrases below that are contained in the text above and then cross the ones that are not.

a. Lo pasé muy bien	f. Lo pasamos bomba	k. Hice pesas
b. Hice vela	g. Fue interesante	l. Por la mañana
c. Saqué muchas fotos	h. Tomamos algo	m. Hicimos turismo
d. Toqué la trompeta	i. El casco antiguo	n. No hice nada de nada
e. Cenamos allí	j. Fui a la piscina	o. Me metí en internet

UNIT 11. Saying what I did & am going to do at the weekend: WRITING

---

1. Sentence puzzle: rewrite the sentences in the correct order

a. levanté Me temprano — *I got up early*

b. Saqué fotos muchas — *I took many pictures*

c. hice No especial nada — *I didn't do anything special*

d. al Fui solo cine — *I went to the cinema alone*

e. Me escuchando relajé música — *I relaxed listening to music*

f. turismo Hicimos en el centro — *We did some sightseeing in the centre*

g. Hicimos campo en el ciclismo — *We did some biking in the countryside*

h. en colinas senderismo Hicimos las — *We did some hiking on the hills*

i. sábado fuimos El de pasado compras — *Last Saturday we went shopping*

j. la Por con tarde novia mi salí — *In the afternoon I went out with my girlfriend*

---

2. Complete the translation

a. *I had a great time.*   L _ p _ _ _ b _ _ _ _ .

b. *I went to the old part of town.*   F _ _ a _ c _ _ _ _ a _ _ _ _ _ _ .

c. *Last Saturday.*   E _ s _ _ _ _ _ p _ _ _ _ _ .

d. *I played drums.*   T _ _ _ _ l _ b _ _ _ _ _ _ .

e. *We did some sightseeing.*   H _ _ _ _ _ _ t _ _ _ _ _ _ .

f. *I went to the stadium with my dad.*   F _ _ a _ e _ _ _ _ _ _ c _ _ m _ p _ _ _ _ .

g. *I relaxed listening to music.*   M _ r _ _ _ _ _ e _ _ _ _ _ _ _ _ _ _ m _ _ _ _ _ .

h. *I did not do anything special.*   N _ h _ _ _ n _ _ _ e _ _ _ _ _ _ _ .

i. *I got up late.*   M _ l _ _ _ _ _ _ t _ _ _ _ .

j. *In the morning I went to the park.*   P _ _ l _ m _ _ _ _ _ f _ _ a _ p _ _ _ _ _ .

---

3. Rewrite the present tense sentences in the preterite and near future tenses

Preterite tense	Present (indicative) tense	Near future tense
Monté en bici	Monto en bici	Voy a montar en bici
	Voy al estadio	
	Hago mis deberes	
	Toco el piano	
	Juego al baloncesto	
	Lo paso bomba	
	Como un bocadillo	
	Escucho música	

4. Split sentences

Comí	un partido de fútbol en la tele.
Me relajé	en la piscina municipal.
No hice	temprano.
Compré	carne y ensalada.
Vi	la batería.
Fui	un vestido rosa.
Hice natación	leyendo.
Me levanté	al baloncesto.
Toqué	al centro comercial.
Jugué	nada.

5. Translate into Spanish

a. I had a great time.

b. I went to the cinema.

c. We did sightseeing.

d. I am going to play basketball.

e. I didn't do anything.

f. We went shopping.

g. We are going to go to a party.

h. I played guitar.

6. Complete with the missing verbs. Please note: use the first person singular of the preterite (e.g. fui, hice, etc.)

a. _____________ al parque con mi perro.

b. _____________ una camiseta.

c. Ayer ______ una serie en la tele.

d. ___________ el piano en casa.

e. ____________ a las cartas con mi abuelo.

f. Me ____________ escuchando música.

g. El sábado me _____________ temprano.

h. _________ a la fiesta de mi primo.

i. No _________ nada el domingo pasado.

j. _____________ al tenis.

k. _____________ muchas fotos.

l. __________ al estadio con mi padre.

m. __________ una revista en el salón.

7. Write a paragraph in which you include as much of the information below as possible

Things to see in your neighbourhood	shops a medieval castle a big museum
Things one can do in your neighbourhood	eat well go shopping go to concerts go to the cinema
Sports facilities	a big sports centre gyms a swimming pool a climbing wall *(rocódromo)*
Things you did last weekend	went shopping watched a football match played piano
Things you are going to do next weekend	go to a concert play basketball with friends go sightseeing in the old town

8. Write a 200 word description of your neighbourhood including the following information

- Where it is located.
- What one can see and do in your neighbourhood (*se puede + verb*).
- A brief description of your street.
- What sports facilities can be found.
- What you usually do at the weekend (**present tense**).
- What you are planning to do next weekend (**near future tense**).
- What you did last weekend (**preterite tense**).

TERM 3 - BRINGING IT ALL TOGETHER – 11

1. Hola. Soy Pedro y tengo trece años. Vivo en Ciudad de Panamá. Es la capital de Panamá, un país en América Central. Vivo en un piso moderno en un barrio que se llama Casco Viejo. Me gusta mi barrio porque es muy seguro y está bien cuidado. Además, cerca de mi casa hay muchas cosas que hacer y ver. Vivo con mis padres, mi hermano menor y mi hermana mayor.

2. En mi barrio hay varios bares y restaurantes muy buenos, así que siempre se puede comer bien. También hay un centro comercial, un polideportivo y una calle peatonal en el centro de la ciudad. El polideportivo tiene muchas instalaciones; se puede jugar al fútbol, al tenis y al baloncesto, y también se puede hacer natación y footing.

3. Vivo en una calle donde hay varias cosas. Mi casa está entre una biblioteca y una carnicería. Enfrente de mi casa hay una panadería muy antigua. Detrás de mi casa hay un parque y un campo de fútbol. Mi casa está a diez minutos a pie de la estación de tren. Antes de ir al colegio tengo que pasear al perro a las ocho menos cuarto. Entre semana suelo ir a la panadería después del colegio pare comprar pan.

4. El fin de semana pasado hice deporte en el polideportivo con mi hermano menor y mis amigos. Fue muy divertido aunque hizo mal tiempo. Cuando hace mal tiempo tengo que llevar una chaqueta deportiva y un gorro. Fuimos al polideportivo a las once y media y volví a casa a las cinco de la tarde.

5. El domingo pasado mi familia y yo fuimos en tren al centro de la ciudad y fuimos de compras en el centro comercial. Después vimos una película en el cine y comimos en un restaurante chino a las diez. Por la noche jugué a videojuegos en mi dormitorio.

6. El próximo fin de semana voy a jugar en mi ordenador con mi hermano menor porque va a hacer mal tiempo. Sin embargo, mi hermana va a ir a una fiesta con sus amigas en el casco antiguo. Mis padres van a ir a un concierto en la plaza mayor y a comer una pizza juntos.

Pedro, 13 años. Ciudad de Panamá, Panamá

1. Answer the following questions in English

a. Where is Panama?

b. Why does Pedro like his neighbourhood?

c. Who does Pedro live with?

d. What is there in Pedro's neighbourhood?

e. What is opposite Pedro's house?

f. What is behind Pedro's house?

g. What must Pedro wear when the weather is bad?

h. How did Pedro and his family get to the mall?

i. Where did Pedro eat last Sunday?

j. What will his parents do next weekend?

2. Find the Spanish equivalent in Pedro's text

a. That is called (1)

b. Many things to do (1)

c. One can always (2)

d. Lots of facilities (2)

e. Between a library (3)

f. Before school (3)

g. I tend to go (3)

h. It was very fun (4)

i. I returned home (4)

j. We went shopping (5)

k. In my bedroom (5)

l. The weather will be bad (6)

m. The old town (6)

3. Complete the translation of paragraph 5

Last ______________, my family and I ____________

on the ________________ to the ________________

centre and we went ________________ at the

________________ ____________. ______________, we

________________ a ________________ in the cinema

and ______ ate at a Chinese restaurant at __________.

At ______________, I played ________________

in my ________________.

Mónica está hablando con su madre, Manoli. Están hablando se sus planes para este fin de semana.	
Mónica	Mamá, ¿qué haces este fin de semana?
Manoli	Ay hija, no sé *(I don't know)*. A ver, el sábado voy a hacer footing en el parque con tu tía. ¿Por qué?
Mónica	Porque quiero ir de compras con mis amigas. ¿Puedo salir con ellas el sábado a las tres de la tarde?
Manoli	Claro que sí. ¿Vas a comer en casa o con las amigas?
Mónica	Quiero comer con las amigas en un restaurante muy bueno en el centro comercial. ¿Puedo?
Manoli	Si quieres, sí. ¿Vas a ver una película en el cine también?
Mónica	No, voy a volver a casa y ver la tele en el salón. Y tú, ¿qué vas a hacer el domingo?
Manoli	El domingo no voy a hacer nada. El domingo pasado monté en bici en las montañas y este domingo quiero relajarme y preparar una cena buena para todos.
Mónica	¿Con quién montaste en bici?
Manoli	Con tu tía. También fuimos a un concierto en la plaza mayor. Fue muy divertido pero también muy agotador.
Mónica	Pues claro. ¿Comísteis?
Manoli	Sí, comimos en mi restaurante favorito. ¿Quieres comer allí el domingo?
Mónica	¡Sí! Será muy guay. ¡Vamos a descansar las dos!
Manoli	Sí. Entonces no voy a cocinar este domingo. ¡Qué suerte!

4. True (T), False (F) or Not Mentioned (NM)?

Manoli is going jogging this weekend.	
Mónica wants to go shopping this weekend.	
Manoli tells Mónica that she is not allowed to go.	
Mónica wants to eat at home.	
Mónica is going to the cinema.	
Manoli is going to play chess.	
Manoli is not going to do anything this Sunday.	
Mónica will ride her bike this weekend.	
Manoli rode her bike with her sister.	
Manoli watched a film last weekend.	
Manoli ate at her favourite restaurant last weekend.	
Manoli decides not to cook this weekend.	
Manoli is unhappy about changing her plans.	

5. Complete the statements

a. _____________ asks for permission to go out this _____________ .

b. _____________ allows _____________ to go shopping this weekend.

c. _____________ is going to watch TV in the _____________ _____________ .

d. _____________ wants to have a relaxing Sunday.

e. _____________ decides not to _____________ this weekend.

TERM 3 – MIDPOINT – RETRIEVAL PRACTICE

1. Answer the following questions in Spanish

¿Adónde fuiste el fin de semana pasado?	
¿Con quién fuiste?	
¿Qué hiciste el sábado?	
¿Cómo fue?	
¿A qué jugaste ayer? ¿Dónde?	
¿Viste alguna película o serie la semana pasada?	
¿Qué sitios de interés visitaste?	
¿Qué vas a hacer el próximo fin de semana?	
¿Con quién vas a hacerlo?	
¿Cómo será?	
¿Qué va a hacer tu amigo?	

2. Write a paragraph in the first person singular (I) providing the following details

a. Your name is Arturo and you live in Barcelona.

b. You live in a small neighbourhood with a park, a sports centre and a town square.

c. Last weekend, you went to the park with your friends and your brother.

d. Last Saturday, you went hiking in the woods with your father. It was tiring but fun.

e. Yesterday, you played tennis with your mum at the sports centre.

f. Last week, you watched a film at the cinema near your house with your cousins.

g. Three days ago, you visited the modern art gallery in the city centre.

h. Tomorrow, you are going to play piano at home with your brother.

i. Next weekend, you are going to go shopping at the shopping mall with your best friend.

j. You think it will be quite exciting and cool but also a bit tiring.

k. Your best friend is going to go to a concert with her cousins.

Unit 12
Making after-school plans with a friend

In this unit you will learn:
- To make plans with other people
- To say what you would like to do today
- To accept or reject plans with reasons why
- To arrange when and where you will meet a friend

You will revisit:
- Free-time activities
- Locations
- Places in town
- Expressing opinions
- Times of day

UNIT 12. Making after-school plans with a friend

¿Qué quieres *What do you want* ¿Qué te gustaría *What would you like*	hacer *to do*	esta mañana? esta tarde? este fin de semana?	*this morning?* *this afternoon?* *this weekend?*	hoy? mañana?	*today?* *tomorrow?*

Hoy	*me apetece *I fancy 'to'* me gustaría *I would like to* quiero *I want to*	dar una vuelta en bici ir al cine ir de tiendas jugar al baloncesto	*go for a bike ride* *go to the cinema* *go shopping* *play basketball*

¿Te gustaría *Would you like to*	dar una vuelta ir a casa de Pablo ir al parque jugar a la Play	*go for a walk* *go to Pablo's house* *go to the park* *play on the PlayStation*	conmigo? *with me?* juntos? *together?*

Lo siento, *Sorry,*		no me apetece no tengo ganas	*I don't fancy it* *I don't feel like it*	no quiero *I don't want to*
Bueno, *Well,*	me apetece, pero *I fancy it, but* me gustaría, pero *I would like to, but*	no puedo	*I can't*	
		tengo que *I have to*	ayudar a mi madre/padre estudiar hacer las tareas domésticas ir a casa de mis abuelos trabajar	*help my mum/dad* *study* *do the chores* *go to my grandparents' house* *work*
Sí, me apetece *Yes, I fancy it*		¡Qué guay!	*(How) Great!*	

Está bien *It's fine* No pasa nada *No problem* Vale *OK*	podemos *we can*	ir a casa de Pablo ir al estadio jugar a la consola quedarnos en casa	*go to Pablo's house* *go to the stadium* *play on the games console* *stay at home*

¡Fantástico! ¡Genial! *Great!*	¿A qué hora *At what time* ¿Dónde *Where*	quedamos? *shall we meet?*

Quedamos *Let's meet* Vamos a quedar *We are going to meet*	enfrente *opposite*	de la casa de Paco *Paco's house* del centro comercial *the shopping mall* del cine *the cinema*	a las *at*	cinco seis siete	y cuarto y media menos diez
Genial, nos vemos luego *Great, we'll see each other later*			Hasta luego *See you later*		

Author's note: In Spanish, we use "me apetece" to say that we fancy doing something. It can be used in the same way as "me gusta" or "me gustaría", followed by an infinitive.

1. Multiple choice: cross out the word that was <u>not</u> said

e.g.	Quieres	Hacer	~~Mañana~~
a.	Queréis	Jugar	Chicos
b.	Me	Dar	Bosque
c.	Le	Conmigo	Tarde
d.	Apetece	Que	Deberes
e.	Nada	Ver	Estadio
f.	Genial	Hora	Quedamos
g.	Enfrente	Los	Hasta

2. Dictation

a. Q _ _ _ _ _ _

b. A _ _ _ _ _ _

c. G _ _ _ _ _ _ _

d. D _ _ _ _ _ _ _ _

e. T _ _ _ _ _ _ _

f. Q _ _ _ _ _ _ _ _

g. G _ _ _ _ _

h. Q _ _ _ _ _ _ _ _

3. Fill in the blanks

a. ¿Qué _______________ hacer este fin de semana?

b. Hoy no _______________ ir al cine.

c. ¿Te gustaría ir a casa de Pablo _______________?

d. Lo _______________, hijo (*son*), no me apetece.

e. Bueno, me _______________ pero tengo que estudiar.

f. Está bien. Podemos _______________ en casa.

g. ¡Fantástico! A qué hora _______________?

h. Vamos a _______________ enfrente del cine a las ocho.

4. Spot the intruders

a.	¿Qué quieres queréis hacer hoy mañana, María?
b.	Hoy no me gustaría ir de tiendas e ir al la cine. ¿Te gustaría ir al centro comercial juntos conmigo?
c.	Bueno, me gustaría apetece pero tengo que hacer las los tareas domésticas deberes.
d.	No pasa nada. Podemos hacer las tareas domésticas y e jugar ir al centro comercial luego después.
e.	¡Fantástico! ¡Genial! ¿A qué la hora quedamos?
f.	Vamos a quedar en tu mi casa a las seis siete y cuarto media.
g.	Genial, no nos vemos luego.
h.	Hasta luego, Daniel.

5. Faulty translation: listen and identify the errors

e.g. What do you ~~guys~~ want to do this weekend?

a. What do you want to do this morning?

b. Today, I would like to play basketball.

c. Would you like to go for a walk in the centre with me?

d. Well, I fancy it but I have to help my mum.

e. Ok, we can play basketball.

f. Great! At what time shall we meet?

g. Let's meet opposite the cinema at 5.

h. What do you guys want to do today?

i. Today I want to go for a bike ride.

6. Listening slalom: follow the speaker from top to bottom and number the boxes

a	b	c	d	e
Today	This afternoon	Tomorrow	It's fine	This weekend
I would like to	would you like to	wouldn't you like to	I don't want to	we can
go to the cinema	go shopping	help my mum	play basketball	go for a walk
in the centre	at home	in the neigbourhood	at the shopping mall	at the sports centre
at 4:15.	with me?	with you.	wth my brother?	at 5:30.

7. Narrow listening: gapped translation

a. What do ___________ want to do ___________________? Would you like to go to the _____________?

b. This weekend I want to _______________________ at the park with my ___________________.

c. _______________ I fancy going shopping at the _______________. Would you like ____________ with me?

d. Well, I fancy it, ___________ I have to _______________________ at ___________________.

e. _______________________, _______________ can go to the ___________________ tomorrow.

f. _______________, I would _________________ to, but I can't. I have to ___________________.

g. _________________! Let's meet _________________ Paco's house at _________________.

h. It's _________________, we'll see each other _______________ in the ___________________.

8. Listen to the two conversations and answer the questions in English

Conversation 1

a. What does Alba fancy doing? (2 details)

b. Why can't Julio go with her?

c. When can he go with her?

d. When will they meet?

e. Where will they meet?

Conversation 2

a. Where does Carmen want to go?

b. What does she want to do there?

c. Does Rodrigo want to go with Carmen?

d. Why can't Rodrigo go with Carmen?

e. What is Carmen's solution to the problem?

UNIT 12. Making after-school plans with a friend: VOCAB BUILDING

1. Match

Dar una vuelta en bici	To not do anything
Jugar al baloncesto	To go out with my best friend
Ver una película	To go for a bike ride
Ir al estadio	To go out with my girlfriend
No hacer nada	To study
Hacer pesas	To play basketball
Hacer natación	To do weights
Salir con mi novia	To stay at home
Quedarme en casa	To watch a film
Salir con mi mejor amigo	To go to a friend's house
Estudiar	To go on the internet
Ir a casa de un amigo	To do swimming
Meterme en internet	To go to the stadium

3. Sort the sentences in the categories below

1. Jugar al ajedrez	9. Escribir un ensayo
2. Estudiar	10. Memorizar palabras
3. Limpiar el suelo	11. Poner la mesa
4. Hacer los deberes	12. Repasar para un examen
5. Ver una película	13. Jugar a videojuegos
6. Mirar escaparates	14. Hacer la cama
7. Hacer natación	15. Ver un partido de tenis
8. Hacer pesas	16. Lavar el coche

Tareas domésticas *(House chores)*	Pasatiempos *(Hobbies)*	Trabajo escolar *(School work)*

5. Translate into English

a. Quiero dar una vuelta en bici esta tarde.

b. Quiero ir al estadio con mi padre mañana.

c. Hoy tengo que estudiar antes de *(before)* salir con mi novio.

d. No me apetece hacer deporte hoy.

e. Quiero jugar al ajedrez con mi hermano.

f. Tengo que repasar para mi examen de matemáticas.

g. Tenemos que ayudar a nuestra madre hoy.

2. Complete with the appropriate option

a. Quiero _________ una vuelta en bici.

b. No quiero ___________ nada.

c. Me gustaría ___________ con mis amigos.

d. Tengo que ___________ el suelo ahora.

e. Tenemos que ___________ el coche de papá.

f. Queremos ___________ a la casa de Felipe.

g. Nos gustaría ___________ una película en el cine.

h. Quiero ___________ a mi madre con las tareas domésticas.

ayudar	hacer
dar	ver
fregar	lavar
salir	ir

4. Sentence puzzle: rewrite the sentences in the correct order

a. ¿hora A qué quedamos?

b. quiero ir al tarde cine Esta

c. enfrente Quedamos del cine

d. a casa hoy No me ir de apetece Paco la

e. ¿Qué hoy hacer quieres?

f. contigo puedo salir No hoy

g. que Tengo a mi madre ayudar

h. apetece Me al contigo ir cine

UNIT 12. Making after-school plans with a friend: VOCAB BUILDING

6. Multiple choice: choose the correct translation

		1	2	3
a.	**¿Qué tal?**	What?	What is it?	How are you?
b.	**¿Adónde quieres ir?**	Where are you?	Where shall we meet?	Where do you want to go to?
c.	**¿Qué quieres hacer?**	What do you want to do?	Where is it?	What do you want to see?
d.	**¿Dónde quedamos?**	Where are you?	Where shall we go?	Where shall we meet?
e.	**¿Te apetece?**	Do you like?	Do you fancy it?	Are you free?
f.	**¡Qué guay!**	How cool!	How crazy!	How boring!
g.	**¿A qué hora quedamos?**	Where are we going?	What time shall we meet?	What time are you free?
h.	**Hasta luego**	Hello	See you later	See you tomorrow
i.	**No pasa nada**	Not a problem	I have nothing	No raisin nothing
j.	**No tengo ganas**	I have no gains	I don't have it	I don't feel like it

7. Match

¿Qué tal?	What are we going to do?
¿Qué quieres hacer esta tarde?	Who are we going with?
¿Te apetece?	Where shall we meet?
¿Dónde quedamos?	Do you fancy it?
¿A qué hora quedamos?	How are you?
¿Con quién vamos?	Why can't you come?
¿Por qué no puedes venir?	At what time shall we meet?
¿Qué vamos a hacer?	What do you want to do this evening?

8. Match questions and answers

¿Qué tal?	No, no tengo ganas, prefiero ir al cine.
¿Qué quieres hacer esta tarde?	Enfrente de la parada del autobús.
¿Te apetece?	A las siete y media.
¿Dónde quedamos?	Estoy muy bien, gracias.
¿A qué hora quedamos?	Porque tengo que estudiar para un examen.
¿Con quién vamos?	Quiero ir al parque.
¿Por qué no puedes venir?	Vamos a jugar a la Play y escuchar música.
¿Qué vamos a hacer?	Con Pablo y Miguel.

UNIT 12. Making after-school plans with a friend: VOCAB BUILDING

9. Complete with the missing letters

a. H _ _ _	*Hi*
b. ¿D _ _ _ _ ?	*Where?*
c. Me a _ _ _ _ _ _	*I fancy it*
d. T _ _ _ _ que	*I have to*
e. Nos v _ _ _ _	*See you*
f. L _ _ _ _	*Later*
g. L_ s _ _ _ _ _	*Sorry*
h. No p _ _ _ _	*I can't*
i. Me g _ _ _ _ _ _ _	*I would like*
j. No q _ _ _ _ _	*I don't want*
k. V _ _ _	*OK*
l. No pasa n _ _ _	*No problem*
m. Vamos a que _ _ _	*Let's meet up*
n. ¿A q _ _ ho _ _ ?	*At what time?*

10. Complete with the most suitable option

Marcelo: _______ Pablo, ¿qué tal?

Pablo: Hola Marcelo. Bien, ________.

Marcelo: ¿______ quieres hacer hoy?

Pablo: Hoy me gustaría ______ un paseo en bici. ¿Y tú?

Marcelo: No sé, no me ______. Yo quiero ir al cine.

Pablo: ______, pues no pasa nada. Podemos ir al cine.

Marcelo: Fantástico. ¿A qué _______ quedamos?

Pablo: Vamos a ________ a las siete

Marcelo: Muy _______, ¿dónde quedamos?

Pablo: Vamos a quedar enfrente ______ cine

Marcelo: Genial, nos vemos ________.

Pablo: Vale, guay, ________ luego.

hasta	hola	quedar	del
apetece	hora	gracias	vale
qué	dar	bien	luego

11. Complete with the most suitable option

Manuel: _______ Sergio, ¿qué tal?

Sergio: Hola Manuel. ______ bien, gracias.

Manuel: ¿Qué ________ a hacer hoy?

Sergio: Hoy me gustaría ______ al cine. ¿Y tú?

Manuel: No sé, no ______ apetece. Yo ________ ir a casa de Miguel. Hay una fiesta.

Sergio: Vale, pues no pasa ______. Podemos ir a la ________ de Miguel

Manuel: Fantástico. ¿______ qué hora quedamos?

Sergio: Vamos a quedar a las ocho.

Manuel: Muy bien, ¿dónde ________?

Sergio: Vamos a quedar enfrente de la parada de ________ cerca de mi casa.

Manuel: Genial, nos ______ luego

Sergio: Vale, guay, hasta luego.

fiesta	ir	me	a
nada	hola	muy	quiero
vamos	quedamos	vemos	autobús

12. Faulty translation: correct the English

a. **¿Qué tal?**	*Who are you?*
b. **Hasta luego.**	*See you tomorrow.*
c. **¿A qué hora quedamos?**	*Why do we meet?*
d. **Nos vemos luego.**	*Nice to see you.*
e. **Vale.**	*It's not OK.*
f. **No pasa nada.**	*There is a problem.*
g. **Podemos ir.**	*We must go.*
h. **Muy bien.**	*Very badly.*
i. **No me apetece.**	*I really want to.*

j. **¿Qué quieres hacer hoy?**

What do you want to do this evening?

k. **Quiero dar una vuelta en el centro.**

I want to go to the shopping mall.

l. **Tengo que hacer las tareas.**

I have to wash the dishes.

UNIT 12. Making after-school plans with a friend: READING 1

Susana: Hola Marta, ¿qué tal?

Marta: Hola Susana. Bien, gracias. Estoy un poco cansada hoy.

Susana: ¿Qué quieres hacer esta tarde?

Marta: Hoy me gustaría mirar escaparates en el centro comercial. ¿Y tú?

Susana: No sé. No me apetece hoy, lo siento. Mañana, tal vez. Hoy prefiero ir a casa de Amparo. ¿Te apetece?

Marta: Vale. No pasa nada. Podemos ir a casa de Amparo, claro que sí.

Susana: Genial. ¿A qué hora quedamos?

Marta: ¿A las seis?

Susana: No, a las seis no puedo porque tengo que ayudar a mi madre con las tareas hasta las siete.

Marta: ¿Y a las siete y media?

Susana: Muy bien. ¿Dónde quedamos?

Marta: Vamos a quedar en la cafetería al lado del colegio.

Susana: Genial, nos vemos luego.

Marta: Vale, guay, hasta luego.

---

1. Find the Spanish equivalent in the text

a. How are you?

b. What do you want to do this evening/afternoon?

c. At what time shall we meet?

d. We'll see each other later

e. Where shall we meet?

f. OK, cool

g. I would like to go window shopping

h. Next to school

i. Of course

j. I am sorry

k. To Amparo's house

l. I must help my mother with the chores

2. Answer in English

a. How is Marta feeling today?

b. What does Marta want to do this evening?

c. What does Susana want to do instead?

d. At what time does Marta want to meet?

e. Why can't Susana meet at six?

f. Where are they going to meet?

3. Spot and correct the grammar and spelling mistakes

a. ¿Qué hora quedamos?

b. Tengo ayudar mi madre.

c. Vale. No pasa nadie.

d. No apetece.

e. Hasta luegos.

f. ¿Donde quedamos?

g. ¿Qué quieres hacer esto tarde?

h. ¿A las siete media?

Juan: Hola Conchi, ¿qué tal?

Conchi: Hola Juan. Bien, gracias. Estoy un poco aburrida.

Juan: ¿Qué hiciste el sábado pasado?

Conchi: Nada especial. Hice mis deberes, arreglé mi dormitorio y paseé al perro. ¿Y tú?

Juan: Hice footing, corté el césped y di una vuelta en bici en el parque con Paco. ¿Qué quieres hacer esta tarde?

Conchi: Hoy me gustaría ir de tiendas. ¿Y tú?

Juan: No sé, cariño. No me apetece ir de tiendas hoy, lo siento. Mañana, tal vez. Hoy prefiero ir al cine. ¿Te apetece?

Conchi: Vale. No pasa nada. ¿Al cine? ¿Qué película quieres ver?

Juan: ¿La última película de La Guerra de las Galaxias?

Conchi: Genial. ¿A qué hora quedamos?

Juan: ¿A las cuatro?

Conchi: No, a las cuatro no puedo porque tengo que ayudar a mi hermano con sus deberes.

Juan: ¿Y a las cinco?

Conchi: No, a las cinco no puedo porque tengo que lavar y planchar la ropa ¿A las seis y media?

Juan: Muy bien, ¿dónde quedamos?

Conchi: Vamos a quedar delante de tu casa.

Juan: Genial, nos vemos luego.

Conchi: Vale, guay, hasta luego.

---

1. Find the Spanish equivalent in the conversation above	**2. Answer in English**
a. I am a bit bored	a. How is Conchi feeling?
b. Nothing special	b. What three things did she do this morning?
c. I tidied my bedroom	c. What three things did Juan do?
d. I mowed the lawn	d. What does Conchi want to do this evening?
e. I would like to go shopping	e. How about Juan?
f. I don't know, darling	f. Why can't Conchi meet at 4?
g. Not a problem	g. Why can't she meet at 5?
h. The latest film	h. At what time can she meet him?
i. I have to do the laundry and iron.	i. Where are they going to meet?
j. In front of your house	
k. Great	

UNIT 12. Making after-school plans: WRITING & TRANSLATION

1. Complete the table

Español	English
Lo siento	
	I am fine
	Great
No puedo	
No me apetece	
Esta tarde	
	In front of your house
	At what time?
¿Dónde quedamos?	
¿A qué hora quedamos?	
No pasa nada	

2. Complete with a suitable word

a. ¿Qué quieres ___________?

b. ¿Dónde _______________?

c. A las cinco y ___________.

d. Vamos a _________ enfrente de tu casa.

e. Hola. ¿Qué ___________?

f. Estoy un poco ___________.

g. No, no me ____________.

h. Quiero ir al _________ contigo.

i. Tengo que ayudar a mi ___________ en la cocina.

j. Tengo que ___________ al perro.

3. Complete

a. *Where shall we meet this evening?* ¿D_________ q_______________ e_________ t___________?

b. *What do you want to do?* ¿Q________ q_______________ h_________?

c. *OK. Not a problem.* V______. N____ p__________ n____________.

d. *I have to help my parents.* T_________ q____ a_____________ a m______ p__________.

e. *Sorry. I don't fancy it.* L___ s_________. N__ m___ a________________.

f. *Let's meet opposite the cinema.* Q____________ e____________ d_____ c________.

g. *I must tidy my bedroom.* T_________ q______ a_____________ m_ d____________.

h. *We can go to the park with them.* P______________ i__ a__ p__________ c_____ e________.

i. *At what time shall we meet?* ¿A q_____ h_________ q________________?

j. *See you later .* N______ v_________ l_____________.

4. Translate into Spanish

a. Not a problem.

b. Do you want to go shopping?

c. I don't like it.

d. I can't because I have to study.

e. What do you want to do?

f. I have to help my father.

g. I have to iron the clothes.

h. Where shall we meet?

i. Let's meet at the bus stop near my house.

j. At what time shall we meet?

k. I would like to do swimming.

l. I am sorry, I have to do my homework.

UNIT 12. Making after-school plans: WRITING & TRANSLATION

<table>
<tr><td valign="top">

5. Answer each of the questions with a full sentence, as in the example

e.g. ¿Cómo te llamas? – Me llamo Mark.

a. Hola, ¿qué tal?

b. ¿Qué hiciste ayer?

c. ¿Qué quieres hacer hoy por la tarde?

d. ¿Quieres venir conmigo al centro comercial?

e. ¿A qué hora quedamos?

f. ¿Dónde quedamos?

g. ¿Qué vas a hacer mañana?

h. ¿Quieres salir conmigo otra vez?

i. ¿Te gustaría ir al cine?

j. ¿Qué te gustaría hacer después del cine?

</td><td valign="top">

6. Write the questions for the answers below

e.g. Voy a ir al estadio con mi padre esta tarde.
¿Qué vas a hacer esta tarde?

a. Quiero jugar a la Play.

b. Porque es aburrido.

c. Ayer no hice nada. Solo descansé.

d. Quedamos enfrente de la piscina municipal.

e. No, no me apetece.

f. Sí, quiero ir al cine.

g. Lo siento, el viernes no puedo. Estoy ocupada.

</td></tr>
</table>

7. Translate *a* and *b* into English, and *c* into Spanish

a. Marina y Julio	b. Marcelo y Enrique	c. Ana y Consuelo
M. Hola Julio. ¿Qué tal? *J. Todo bien, Marina. ¿Y tú?* M. Bien, pero estoy muy cansada. *J. ¿Por qué?* M. Ayer por la tarde hice footing y luego natación. También, me levanté muy temprano hoy. *J. Ay. ¿Entonces no puedes salir esta tarde?* M. ¡Sí, claro que puedo! ¿Adónde quieres ir? *J. ¿A la fiesta de Fernando?* M. Sí, vale, guay. Me apetece. ¿Dónde quedamos? *J. ¿Quedamos en mi casa a las siete?* M. Genial. Nos vemos luego.	M. Hola Enrique. ¿Cómo estás? *E. Muy bien, Marcelo. ¿Y tú?* M. ¿Qué hiciste el sábado pasado? *E. Hice la compra con mi madre. ¿Y tú?* M. Ayudé a mi padre en el jardín. ¡Fue aburrido! *E. ¿Quieres venir conmigo al estadio hoy?* M. Sí. ¡Qué guay! ¿Dónde quedamos, y a qué hora? *E. Vamos a quedar en la parada de autobús enfrente de mi casa, a las tres.* M. Vale, perfecto. Nos vemos allí a las tres.	A. Hi Ana. Do you want to go out this afternoon? *C. Yes, but first I have to help my mother until 4:00.* A. Ok. Do you want to go to the cinema this evening? *C. No. I am sorry, but I don't feel like it. I would like to go to the town centre and do some window shopping (mirar escaparates).* A. OK, not a problem. At what time shall we meet? At 4:30? *C. I cannot at 4:30. I have to help my brother with his homework. Let's meet at 5:00.* A. OK. At five. Where shall we meet? *C. Let's meet at your house.*

1. Buenos días, soy Agustín y vivo en Ciudad de México, la capital de México. Cerca de mi casa hay muchas cosas. En mi calle hay una iglesia pequeña, una zapatería y un teatro. Mi casa también está al lado de la casa de mi mejor amigo Tomás.

2. Vivo en la Zona Rosa, un barrio en la capital con muchas cosas que hacer. Me encanta mi barrio porque se puede hacer de todo; hay museos, tiendas, restaurantes, bares y muchos edificios antiguos y modernos. Además, mi barrio es muy seguro aunque sí hay bastante tráfico.

3. El fin de semana pasado estuve muy ocupado. El sábado fui a casa de mi primo y montamos a caballo todo el día. Fue superagotador, pero muy interesante. El domingo mi hermano y yo vimos un partido de fútbol en el estadio y en mi opinión no fue nada divertido porque perdió mi equipo favorito.

4. Ayer no hice mucho. Hacía mal tiempo, así que me quedé en casa y vi una serie en Netflix en mi dormitorio. En mi dormitorio tengo una televisión nueva y una cama muy cómoda *(comfortable)*. Luego hice mis deberes y me acosté a eso de las diez.

5. Hoy hace buen tiempo así que me apetece dar una vuelta en bici por el parque con mi mejor amigo Tomás. Normalmente quedamos enfrente de la iglesia a las doce y media. Siempre nos llevamos una pelota *(ball)* para jugar al fútbol. También me gustaría tomar un helado en la cafetería que está en el parque.

6. El próximo fin de semana quiero ir al cine a ver una película con mi hermano. Vamos a ir al cine a las siete y media y vamos a ver una comedia. Creo que será muy divertido. Luego me gustaría comer en un restaurante italiano que está al lado del cine. El sábado mis padres van a ir a un restaurante, pero yo voy a quedarme en casa y voy a pedir una pizza a domicilio, ¡qué *padre! *(how cool)*

Agustín, 15 años. Ciudad de México, México

In Mexico you will often hear 'padre' or 'chévere' for 'cool' instead of 'chulo' or 'guay', which are more common in Spain.

1. Answer the following questions in English

a. What is on Agustín's street?

b. Who does Agustín live next door to?

c. What does Agustín think of his neighbourhood?

d. What is a negative of Agustín's neighbourhood?

e. What did Agustín do last Saturday?

f. What did Agustín think of the football match?

g. What did Agustín do yesterday?

h. What does Agustín have in his bedroom?

i. What time will Agustín go to the cinema?

j. What food is Agustín going to order on Saturday?

2. Find the Spanish equivalent in Agustín's text

a. There are lots (1)

b. Next to (1)

c. There are museums (2)

d. Even though (2)

e. Very busy (3)

f. We watched (3)

g. I stayed at home (4)

h. I did my homework (4)

i. We meet (5)

j. I would like (5)

k. I want to go (6)

l. We are going to go (6)

m. They are going to (6)

3. Complete the translation of paragraph 5

_______________ the weather is _____________

therefore I _____________ going for a bike ride in

the _______________ with my ___________ friend,

Tomás. _______________ we meet _______________

the church at _____________. We

_______________ take a ball to _____________

football. I _______________ also _____________ to

have an ___________ _____________ at the café

that is ______ the _______________.

TERM 3 - BRINGING IT ALL TOGETHER – 12

Hoy es viernes. Damián y Nerea están casados *(married)*. Están hablando de lo que van a hacer este fin de semana.	
Nerea	Cariño *(Dear)*, ¿qué quieres hacer hoy?
Damián	No sé. Me apetece ir al gimnasio. ¿Te gustaría venir *(to come)* conmigo?
Nerea	No. Yo no quiero hacer ejercicio. Me apetece ver una película y pedir una pizza.
Damián	Nerea… ¿Otra vez pizza?
Nerea	Sí, ¿no te apetece pedir una pizza y nos quedamos tranquilos en casa?
Damián	Claro que me apetece, pero tengo que ir al gimnasio.
Nerea	Vale, vale, está bien. ¿Y si quedamos enfrente del gimnasio a las ocho y media?
Damián	¿Por qué?
Nerea	Así puedes ir al gimnasio y después podemos ir a comer en un restaurante.
Damián	Vale perfecto. ¿Y qué quieres hacer mañana? ¿Te gustaría ir al parque a dar una vuelta?
Nerea	Sí, me apetece. ¡Qué guay! ¿A qué hora quieres ir al parque?
Damián	Primero tengo que ir a casa de mis abuelos a ayudar con las tareas domésticas. ¿Quedamos enfrente del parque a la una?
Nerea	¡Genial! ¿Y después qué te apetece hacer?
Damián	Me gustaría jugar a la Play con mis amigos.
Nerea	¿Te gustaría jugar a la Play conmigo?
Damián	Nerea, por favor…

4. True (T), False (F) or Not Mentioned (NM)?

Damián and Nerea are married.	
Damián wants to go to the gym.	
Damián doesn't ask Nerea to go to the gym with him.	
Nerea wants to go to the gym.	
Damián wants to order a pizza.	
Damián has to go to the gym.	
Nerea will meet Damián opposite the gym at 9:30.	
Damián asks Nerea to go for a walk in the park tomorrow.	
Damián has to help his parents.	
Damián wants to walk his dog.	
Damián and Nerea will meet opposite the park at 13:00.	
Damián wants to play basketball afterwards.	
Damián doesn't want to play videogames with Nerea.	

5. Complete the statements

a. ________________ tries to convince ________________ to order a pizza.

b. Damián wants to go to the ________________.

c. The couple agree to ________ ________ ________ ________________ after the gym.

d. Nerea fancies going to the ________________ tomorrow.

e. Damián wants to play ________________ with his ________________.

Unit 13
A future trip to Cádiz

In this unit you will learn:
- To talk about an upcoming trip to Cádiz
- To describe events you will do and would like to do on holiday
- To give future tense opinions

You will revisit:
- Holidays
- Locations
- Adjectival agreement
- Time markers
- Free-time activities
- Expressing opinions

Unit 13. (OPTIONAL) A future trip to Cádiz

¿Adónde vas a ir este verano?			*Where are you going to go this summer?*	
¿Cómo vas a viajar?			*How are you going to travel?*	
¿Dónde vas a quedarte?			*Where are you going to stay?*	
¿Qué vas a hacer?			*What are you going to do?*	
¿Qué lugares vas a ver/visitar?			*What places are you going to see/visit?*	

Este verano *This summer*	**voy a ir** *I'm going to go*	**a Cádiz** *to Cadiz*	**Voy a viajar** *I am going to travel* **Vamos a viajar** *We are going to travel*	**en avión** *by plane* **en coche** *by car*

El viaje *The trip*	**El vuelo** *The flight*	**a España** *to Spain*	**dura X horas** *takes X hours*

(No) Me gusta *I (don't) like*	**viajar** *to travel*	**en avión** *by plane* **en barco** *by boat* **en coche** *by car* **en tren** *by train*	**porque es** *because it is*	**apasionante** *exciting* **cómodo** *comfortable* **divertido** *fun* **incómodo** *uncomfortable* **lento** *slow* **rápido** *fast*

En Cádiz *In Cádiz*	**voy a alojarme** *I am going to stay* **vamos a alojarnos** *we are going to stay*	**en** *in*	**un albergue** *a hostel* **un hotel** *a hotel*	**barato** *cheap* **básico** *basic* **caro** *expensive* **de lujo** *luxury*

El hotel *The hotel*	**está** *is*	**cerca** *near* **lejos** *far*	**del casco antiguo** *from the old town* **del centro** *from the town centre* ***del Puerto de Santa María** *from the Port of Santa María* **de la catedral** *from the cathedral* **de la playa de la Caleta** *from the Caleta beach*

Durante el viaje	*During the trip*

me gustaría *I would like*	**comer** *to eat* **probar** *to try*	**marisco** *seafood* **platos típicos** *typical dishes* **tapas** *tapas*
voy a *I'm going*	**dar un paseo por** *to go for a walk around* **ver** *to see* **visitar** *to visit*	**el barrio de la Viña** *the Viña neighbourhood* **el casco antiguo** *the old town* **el Parque Genovés** *the Genovés Park* **el jardín botánico** *the botanical gardens* **la Plaza de las Flores** *the flower market*

El primer día *On the first day* **El segundo día** *On the second day* **Por la mañana** *In the morning* **Por la tarde** *In the afternoon*	**voy a ir** *I am going to go* **vamos a ir** *we are going to go*	**al museo** *the museum* **al parque** *the park* **a la playa** *to the beach* **a un espectáculo** *to a show*

Finalmente *Finally*	**voy a** **vamos a**	**volver a casa** *go back home*	**en autocar** *by coach* **en avión** *by plane*	**en coche** *by car* **en tren** *by train*

Creo que el viaje a Cádiz será *I believe the trip to Cádiz will be*	**genial** *great* **inolvidable** *unforgettable*	**la leche** *awesome*

El viaje me hace mucha ilusión	*I'm really looking forward to the trip*

***Author's note:** El Puerto de Santa María is a small town located on the bay of Cádiz, about 10km northeast of Cádiz city, the region's capital. It is famous for its sherry, seafood and stunning beaches.*

---

1. Partial dictation

a. ¿A _ _ _ _ _ v _ _ a i _ ?

b. V _ _ a q _ _ _ _ _ _ _

c. V _ _ _ _ _ e _ a _ _ _ _

d. E _ c _ _ _ _ _

e. V _ _ a a _ _ _ _ _ _ _

f. U _ a _ _ _ _ _ _ _

g. E _ _ _ l _ _ _ _ _

h. M _ g _ _ _ _ _ _ _

i. U _ e _ _ _ _ _ _ _ _ _ _

j. S _ _ _ g _ _ _ _ _

---

2. Listen and fill in the gaps

a. Este verano, _________ a ir de vacaciones a __________.

b. El _______________ a España dura ____________ horas.

c. Me gusta viajar en ____________ porque es ____________.

d. En Cádiz voy a ____________ en un hotel ____________.

e. El hotel está _______________ de la _________________.

f. Durante el viaje, me ______________ comer ____________.

g. También ________ a dar un paseo por el _____________.

h. El _______________ día vamos a ir a la _____________.

i. Finalmente voy a ____________ a casa en ____________.

j. Creo que el ____________ a Cádiz será _______________.

---

3. Spot the intruders

Este pasado verano, voy a fui ir de vacaciones a al Cádiz con mi amigo familia. Me gusta encanta viajar viajé en avión porque es rápido cómodo. Vamos Voy a quedarnos en un hotel de lujo barato en el centro. El albergue hotel está cerca del centro casco antiguo. Durante el viaje, me gustaría jugar visitar el jardín de botánico y a la playa del de la Caleta.

---

4. Multiple choice: cross out the word that was <u>not</u> said

e.g.	This	~~We~~	Chile
a.	Summer	To Go	México
b.	Travel	Car	Fun
c.	Journey	Takes	Days
d.	I	Fly	Basic
e.	Hotel	Far	Beach
f.	Second	Go	Show
g.	Finally	Home	Plane

---

5. Faulty translation: listen, identify and correct the errors

*e.g. Where are you going to go ~~next~~ **this** summer?*

a. This winter I am going to spend three weeks in Cádiz.

b. This summer I am not going on holiday to Chile; I am going to Spain.

c. I like to travel by plane because it is comfortable.

d. In Cádiz I am going to stay in a basic hostel.

e. The hotel is far from Puerto de Santa María.

f. During the trip I am going to try tapas.

g. In the afternoon I am going to go to the park.

---

6. Listening slalom: follow the speaker from top to bottom and number the boxes

a.	b.	c.	d.	e.
During the trip	On the first day	On the second day	In the morning	Finally
I am going	I would like	I'm not going	I don't want	we are going
to try	to watch	to visit	to eat	to go
typical dishes	tapas	for a walk	a show	the castle
in the park.	on the beach.	in the old town.	in a restaurant.	in the centre.

7. Narrow listening: gapped translation

a. _______________ are you going on holiday _______________ summer?

b. This _______________, I am going on holiday to _______________ with my _______________.

c. The _______________ to Madrid takes _______________ hours but it is very _______________.

d. In Cádiz, _______________ going to stay in a _______________ hotel in the _______________.

e. The _______________ is very _______________ from the _______________ _______________.

f. During the trip, I would like _______________ seafood and other _______________ _______________.

g. On the _______________ day, I am not going to go to the _______________ with my _______________.

h. In my opinion, _______________ that the _______________ to Cádiz will be _______________.

8. Listen to the two conversations and answer the questions in English

Conversation 1: Hugo & Damián

a. How is Hugo feeling?

b. Where is he going on holiday to?

c. Who is he going on holiday with?

d. Where is Damián going on holiday?

e. Where is Damián staying? (3 details)

f. What will Damián do in Rome? (any 2 details)

Conversation 2: Isabela & Elena

a. How is Isabela feeling?

b. Where is Isabela going on holiday?

c. Where will Isabela's family stay?

d. Why aren't they going to the beach?

e. How long will the flight last?

UNIT 13. A future trip to Cádiz: VOCAB BUILDING

1. Match

Este verano	Because it is slow
El vuelo a España	The first day
El viaje	It is near
Un albergue barato	Go for a walk around
Porque es lento	The trip
Está cerca	Try typical dishes
Será le leche	It will be unforgettable
Voy a alojarme	This summer
Comer marisco	A cheap hostel
Dar un paseo por	I am going to stay
Probar platos típicos	The flight to Spain
El primer día	It will be awesome
Será inolvidable	To eat seafood

2. Complete the words

a. U _ c _ st _ ll _   *A castle*

b. Un a _ berg _ e   *A hostel*

c. Ap _ si _ na _ te   *Exciting*

d. E _ vu _ l _   *The flight*

e. M _ gust _ r _ a   *I would like*

f. El ba _ ri _   *The neighbourhood*

g. Esp _ ct _ c _ lo   *Show*

h. In _ lvid _ ble   *Unforgettable*

i. Plat _ _ t _ picos   *Typical dishes*

j. U _ pa _ eo   *A walk*

k. _ l p _ e _ to   *The port*

3. Break the flow

a. EsteveranovoyairaCádiz.

b. Voyaviajarenavión.

c. Elvueloduratreshoras.

d. Megustaviajarenbarco.

e. EnCádizvoyaalojarmeenunhotel.

f. Elhotelestácercadelcascoantiguo.

g. Duranteelviajevoyacomermarisco.

h. Elprimerdíavamosairalparque.

i. Finalmentevoyavolveracasaentren.

4. Complete with the missing words (one is spare)

a. Este verano voy a ir a Cádiz con mi ____________.

b. El viaje a Cádiz dura tres ____________.

c. Me gusta viajar en ____________ porque es divertido.

d. No me gusta viajar en tren porque es ____________.

e. Vamos a ____________ en un albergue básico.

f. Voy a alojarme en un hotel ____________.

g. El hotel está ____________ del Puerto de Santa María.

h. El albergue no está cerca del ____________.

i. Durante el viaje, me gustaría probar ____________.

j. Durante el viaje, voy a ____________ el teatro romano.

k. El primer día, vamos a ir a la ____________.

l. Por la mañana voy a ir al ____________.

m. Creo que el viaje a Cádiz será la ____________.

n. Me hace ilusión visitar la Plaza de las ____________.

5. Spot and correct the nonsense sentences

a. Este verano voy a ir a marisco.

b. El vuelo a Cádiz dura un año.

c. Vamos a alojarnos en un hotel.

d. El hotel está en avión del centro.

e. Me gustaría comer al parque.

f. Voy a comer marisco en la catedral.

g. Finalmente, voy a volver a casa en tapas.

h. Creo que el viaje a Cádiz será la leche.

alojarnos	centro	museo	barato	lento
Flores	**marisco**	**horas**	**visitar**	**barco**
playa	**familia**	**leche**	**lejos**	**genial**

UNIT 13. A future trip to Cádiz: VOCAB BUILDING

6. Sentence puzzle

a. verano ir Este a familia Cádiz voy a con mi

b. a horas España El tres vuelo dura

c. en es Me coche porque gusta viajar cómodo

d. en un alojarme albergue básico Voy a

e. vamos Cádiz hotel en un a alojarnos En caro

f. de El lejos la hotel está de la playa Caleta

g. el Genovés Me visitar gustaría Parque

h. voy a típicos probar También platos

i. vamos El primer ir al museo día a

j. Cádiz será Creo viaje que el inolvidable a

8. Translate into English

a. Este verano…

b. Voy a viajar en tren.

c. El vuelo a España dura tres horas.

d. El viaje a España dura cinco horas.

e. Me gusta viajar en coche.

f. En Cádiz voy a alojarme en un hotel.

g. El hotel está cerca del casco antiguo.

h. Me gustaría comer platos típicos.

i. Por la mañana voy a ir al parque.

j. Creo que el viaje a Cádiz será inolvidable.

7. Gapped translation

a. Este verano voy a Cádiz.

___________ ___________ *I'm going to go to Cadiz.*

b. Voy a viajar en avión.

I'm going to _______________ *by* _____________.

c. El vuelo a España dura tres horas.

The _____________ *to Spain takes* _________ *hours.*

d. Viajar en barco es barato.

To travel by _____________ *is* _______________.

e. Voy a alojarme en un hotel caro.

I am going to __________ *in a* _______________ *hotel.*

f. El hotel está lejos del casco antiguo.

The hotel is __________ *from the* ___________ *town.*

g. Me gustaría visitar el jardín botánico.

I would like to __________ *the botanical* ___________.

h. Voy a probar platos típicos.

I am going to _____________ *typical* ___________.

i. El primer día voy a comer marisco.

On the __________ *day I am going to eat* ___________.

j. Voy a volver a casa en tren.

I am going to go back ____________ *by* _____________.

k. Creo que el viaje a Cádiz será la leche.

I believe the _________ *to Cádiz will be* ____________.

9. Guided translation

a. *Este verano voy a ir a Cádiz.*

Th _ _ summer I'm g _ _ _ _ to _ _ to Cádiz.

b. *El vuelo a España dura dos horas y media.*

The _ _ _ _ _ _ to Spain takes _ _ _ hours and a half.

c. *Me gusta viajar en tren porque es cómodo.*

I like to travel by train because it's _ _ _ _ _ _ _ _ _ _ _ .

d. *No me gusta viajar en coche porque es lento.*

I don't like to travel by _ _ _ because it's _ _ _ _ .

e. *En Cádiz, voy a alojarme en un hotel caro.*

In Cádiz, I'm going to stay in an _ _ _ _ _ _ _ _ _ hotel.

f. *El hotel está lejos del casco antiguo.*

The hotel is _ _ _ from the _ _ _ _ _ _ _ .

g. *Durante el viaje, me gustaría probar tapas.*

_ _ _ _ _ _ the _ _ _ _ , I'd like to _ _ _ tapas.

h. *También voy a dar un paseo por el parque.*

I'm _ _ _ _ going to _ _ for a _ _ _ _ in _ _ _ park.

i. *El primer día voy a ir a la playa.*

On the _ _ _ _ _ day, I'm going _ _ go to the _ _ _ _ _ .

j. *Finalmente, vamos a volver a casa en avión.*

Finally, _ _ are going to go _ _ _ _ home by _ _ _ _ _ _ .

1. Hola, me llamo Verónica. Soy de Barbastro, en el norte de España, pero vivo en Malasia. Este verano voy a ir de vacaciones a Cádiz, una ciudad en el sur de España. Voy a ir con mi mejor amiga, Alicia, así que, primero, tengo que viajar a Barbastro en avión. Después, vamos a viajar en autocar de Barbastro a Zaragoza y, luego, vamos a tomar el tren hasta Cádiz. ¡El tren rápido de España se llama AVE porque es tan rápido como un pájaro! El viaje en tren dura casi seis horas.

2. En Cádiz, vamos a quedarnos en un hostal básico en el centro de la ciudad, Hostal Rosa de los Vientos. Me gustaría alojarme en un hotel de lujo pero no puedo. El hostal está en la calle de la Rosa, cerca de la Torre Tavira y la Plaza de las Flores. La playa de la Caleta está a diez minutos. En la calle del hostal también hay varias tiendas y restaurantes donde comer.

3. El primer día por la mañana, vamos a dar un paseo por el parque en el barrio de la Viña. El parque es enorme y hay muchas cosas que ver. Sin embargo, lo que más me gusta es tomar el sol así que voy a tumbarme *(lie down)* en el parque un rato. Por la tarde vamos a ir a un restaurante local y vamos a comer unas tapas muy ricas. Me gustaría probar algunos platos típicos como el pescaíto frito *(fried fish)* o la tortillita de camarones *(fried prawns in batter)*. Para el postre, me gustaría probar algunos pestiños *(traditional pastry – aniseed twist)*.

4. El segundo día por la mañana, vamos a ir al Museo de Cádiz, el museo más conocido y más famoso de la ciudad. Me encanta la historia, la cultura y el arte así que tengo que visitarlo. La entrada es gratuita *(free)* y hay muchas cosas interesantes que ver. ¡Será involvidable! Luego, vamos a ir al barrio del Pópulo, el barrio más antiguo de la ciudad. Voy a visitar el Teatro Romano, uno de los teatros más grandes del mundo. Por la noche, vamos a comer tapas en el Faro de Cádiz, un restaurante muy bueno.

6. Finalmente, vamos a volver a casa en tren y autocar. El regreso a casa parecerá *(will seem)* más lento. Creo que voy a estar un poco triste. Sin embargo, estoy segura de que el viaje a Cádiz será la leche.

Verónica Palacín, 18 años. Barbastro, España

1. Answer the following questions

a. Where does Verónica live?

b. Who is Alicia?

c. How are they going to travel to Zaragoza?

d. What is the AVE and why is it called that?

e. Where in Cádiz are they going to stay?

f. What are they going to do in the morning and in the afternoon on the first day?

g. What are they going to do in the morning and evening on the second day?

h. What is said about the Cádiz Museum?

i. What is said about the Roman Theatre?

j. What is said about the journey home?

2. Complete the translation of paragraph 4

On the ______________ day, in the ______________, ________ are going to go to the Cádiz Museum, the city's most well known and ____________ museum. I love ______________, ______________ and art so I ________ to visit it. ____________ is free and there are ________ of interesting things to ________. It will be ________________! Later, we are going to go to the Pópulo ____________, the city's ____________ neighbourhood. I am going to ____________ the Roman Theatre, one of the ____________ theatres in the world. At ____________, we are going to ________ tapas at Faro de Cádiz, a ____________ good restaurant.

3. Find the Spanish equivalent in the text

a. As fast as a bird	j. Very delicious
b. Takes nearly	k. For dessert
c. A hostel	l. Some
d. 10 minutes away	m. Most famous
e. There are various	n. Entry is free
f. Go for a walk	o. Oldest
g. Is enormous	p. In the world
h. What I like most	q. Sad
i. A while	r. It will be awesome

UNIT 13. A future day trip to Cádiz: WRITING

1. Multiple choice: choose the correct translation

		1	2	3
a.	**Este verano**	Last summer	This summer	Next summer
b.	**Voy a viajar**	I travel	I travelled	I am going to travel
c.	**Dura ocho horas**	Takes five hours	Takes eight days	Takes eight hours
d.	**Viajar en avión**	Travel by boat	Travel by plane	Travel by car
e.	**Vamos a alojarnos**	I would like to stay	We are going to stay	I am going to stay
f.	**Un albergue caro**	An expensive hostel	A cheap hostel	A basic hostel
g.	**Cerca del puerto**	Near the door	Far from the port	Near the port
h.	**Probar marisco**	Eat seafood	Try seafood	Try shellfish
i.	**Dar un paseo**	Go for a walk	Give a pass	Try tapas
j.	**El segundo día**	A secure day	The second day	The third day
k.	**Voy a ir**	We are going to go	I want to go	I am going to go

2. Complete with the correct option

a. Voy a ______________ tapas.

b. Voy a __________ un paseo por el parque.

c. Voy a __________________ la catedral.

d. ______________ a alojarnos en un albergue.

e. Me ____________________ comer marisco.

f. El viaje a España ____________ cinco horas.

g. Voy a ______________ en un hotel barato.

h. Voy a ______________ en coche.

i. El primer día, vamos a ir a la ___________.

j. Por la ____________, vamos a ir al museo.

k. Voy a dar un paseo ________ el parque.

l. Finalmente, vamos a ______________ a
casa en tren.

gustaría	playa	por	volver
dar	alojarme	visitar	vamos
tarde	comer	viajar	dura

3. Spot and correct the grammar and spelling mistakes

a. Voy a viajo en coche.

b. Mi madre va comprar recuerdos.

c. Voy a como marisco en el Puerto de Santa María.

d. Voy a alojarse en un hotel.

e. El hotel es lejos de la catedral.

f. Durante el viaje, me gusto comer marisco.

g. El primer día, dar a voy un paseo.

h. El segundo día, vamos a fui a la playa.

i. Por la mañana, ir a ver un espectáculo.

j. Por la tarde, voy no a ir al museo.

k. Finalmente, volver a voy a casa.

l. Creo que el viaje a Cádiz voy a ser genial.

m. En mi opinión, el viaje ser la leche.

n. El viaje me hacer mucha ilusión.

o. Este verano, voy ir a Cádiz.

p. Voy a viaje en tren.

q. El vuelo duro cuatro horas.

r. En Cádiz vamos a alojarme en un hotel básico.

1. Me llamo Dylan y soy de Londres. Normalmente voy de vacaciones a Portugal con mi familia. Nos gusta porque siempre hace sol y buen tiempo. Viajamos en avión de Londres a Lisboa y luego tomamos un autocar hasta el Algarve, que está en el sur del país. Mis padres y yo siempre vamos a Tavira, y nos encanta porque la gente es muy amable y simpática y la comida está buenísima. En Tavira se puede ver un antiguo puente romano y se puede ir a la playa. Para mí, lo mejor son las calles típicas del casco antiguo y la comida local.

2. El mes pasado fuimos de vacaciones a Cádiz, en el sur de España. Viajamos en avión y el viaje duró dos horas y media. Nos quedamos tres días en un hotel cerca del centro de la ciudad. El primer día visitamos la Plaza de las Flores y dimos un paseo por el barrio de la Viña. ¡Muy curioso! El segundo día comimos en un restaurante cerca del Puerto de Santa María. Probé marisco pero no me gustó. Sin embargo, me encantaron las tapas. Finalmente, volvimos a casa y en mi opinión fue inolvidable. El viaje me hizo mucha ilusión; me encantó Cádiz.

3. El año que viene voy a viajar a Gibraltar con mi amigo Roberto. Gibraltar es una ciudad británica en el sur de España. Allí la gente habla inglés y también español. Es muy curioso, pero guay. Vamos a viajar en avión. El viaje desde Londres dura dos horas y media. Vamos a alojarnos en el *Rock Hotel*, uno de los mejores hoteles de la ciudad. Las habitaciones son cómodas y tienen vistas excelentes del estrecho.

4. El primer día por la mañana vamos a visitar el jardín botánico y luego vamos a tomar un café en el casco antiguo. Quiero visitar una cafetería que se llama *Sacarello's*, que es una de las cafeterías más antiguas de Europa. Por la tarde vamos a ir al Peñón *(the Rock)* para dar un paseo. Hay muchas cosas que hacer en el Peñón: se puede ver monos, sacar fotos de África y del estrecho *(the straits)* de Gibraltar, y se puede visitar la cueva de San Miguel, una cueva enorme. A Roberto y a mí también nos gustaría visitar las playas. Son muy bonitas y hay una que se llama la Caleta, ¡igual que en Cádiz! Creo que será un viaje muy apasionante y divertido.

Dylan, 19 años. Londres, Inglaterra

1. Find the Spanish equivalent in Dylan's text

a. It's always sunny

b. We take a coach

c. One can see

d. The typical streets

e. The trip lasted

f. We stayed

g. I tried seafood

h. I am going to travel

i. A British city

j. One of the best hotels

k. We are going to visit

l. There are many things to do

m. Take pictures of Africa and the straits

n. There is one which is called

2. Answer in English

a. Why does Dylan like Portugal?

b. Why do Dylan and his family like Tavira?

c. What can one see in Tavira?

d. What did they do in Cádiz on the 2nd day?

e. When is he going to go to Gibraltar?

f. What languages do they speak there?

g. What can you see from the hotel rooms?

h. Where are they going to have a coffee on the first day?

i. What is special about *Sacarello's*?

j. What three things can you do on the Rock?

k. What is "la Caleta"?

l. Where else can you find a "Caleta"?

3. Translate the following into English

a. El sur del país (1)

b. Lo mejor (1)

c. El mes pasado (2)

d. Nos quedamos (2)

e. El primer día (2)

f. Volvimos a casa (2)

g. La gente (3)

h. Tienen vistas excelentes al mar (3)

i. Para dar un paseo (4)

j. Será un viaje muy apasionante (4)

UNIT 13. A future day trip to Cádiz: WRITING & TRANSLATION

1. Complete the table

	English	Spanish
a.		Este verano
b.	A show	
c.	The old town	
d.		Un albergue
e.	Luxury	
f.	The botanical gardens	
g.		Por la mañana
h.	Go back home	
i.		En avión
j.	Awesome	
k.	Great	
l.	Uncomfortable	
m.		Rápido
n.		Finalmente

2. Complete with a suitable word

a. Este verano voy a __________ a Cádiz.

b. El ______________ a Cádiz dura cuatro horas.

c. Me gusta ______________ en coche porque es cómodo.

d. En Cádiz, vamos a __________________ en un hotel de lujo.

e. El hotel está lejos de _______ catedral.

f. Me gustaría __________ platos típicos.

g. Voy a __________ un paseo por el jardín botánico.

h. El primer día, _________ a ir al parque.

i. Por la tarde, voy a ir _________ museo.

j. Finalmente, vamos a volver a casa en ____________.

k. Creo que el viaje a Cádiz ____________ inolvidable.

l. El viaje me __________ mucha ilusión.

3. Slalom translation (left to right)

e.g. This summer I am going to go to Cádiz.

a. I am going to travel by plane.

b. The flight to Spain takes three hours.

c. The hotel is near the Caleta beach.

d. I would like to eat seafood and tapas.

e. We are going to stay in a cheap hotel.

f. I am going to go for a walk in the old town.

g. In Cádiz, I am going to stay in a luxury hotel.

h. We are going to try typical Spanish dishes.

i. I think the trip will be awesome.

Este	voy a	**voy a**	la playa	hotel de lujo
El hotel	**verano**	en	en	horas
Vamos a	comer	el viaje	y	barato
Creo	dar	dura	**ir**	españoles
Voy	a	cerca de	por	de la Caleta
Vamos	que	alojarme	tres	**a Cádiz**
El vuelo	alojarnos	marisco	en un	el casco antiguo
En Cádiz	a España	un paseo	típicos	tapas
Me gustaría	está	viajar	un hotel	avión
Voy a	a probar	platos	será	la leche

UNIT 13. A future day trip to Cádiz: WRITING & TRANSLATION

4. Complete the text below choosing from the options provided

Hola, me llamo Ainhoa y soy de Valencia. Normalmente __________ de vacaciones al extranjero *(abroad)* pero este verano voy a ir a Cádiz con mis _____________. ¡El viaje a Cádiz ___________ ocho horas y media en coche! Sin ________________, me gusta viajar en coche porque _________ divertido y _____________.

En Cádiz, vamos a alojarnos en _______ hotel de lujo. El hotel está _____________ de la playa de la Caleta. Durante el viaje, me gustaría _____________ marisco local y __________ un paseo por el barrio de la Viña.

cómodo	embargo	voy	dar	es
abuelos	un	cerca	probar	dura

5. Write the questions for the answers below

a. Este verano, voy a ir a Cádiz.

b. En Cádiz, vamos a alojarnos en un hotel de lujo.

c. Voy a visitar el barrio de la Viña.

d. Voy a viajar en avión porque es rápido.

e. Durante el viaje, me gustaría comer marisco.

f. En Cádiz, voy a alojarme en un albergue básico.

g. Por la tarde, voy a ir al parque.

h. Voy a viajar a Cádiz en barco porque es cómodo.

6. Gapped translation

a. *This year I'm going to Cádiz.* E______ v_____________ voy a ______ a Cádiz.

b. *I'm going to travel by plane.* V_______ a v___________ en av________.

c. *I like to travel by boat because it's fun.* Me g_____ v________ en barc_ porq___ es d________.

d. *We are going to stay in a cheap hotel.* V__________ a alojar_______ en un hotel b__________.

e. *The hotel is near the Port of Santa María.* El hotel e______ c______ del P_______ de Santa María.

f. *I would like to visit the Viña neighbourhood.* Me gust________ v___________ el b_______ de la Viña.

g. *In Cádiz, I'm going to try typical dishes* En Cádiz, v______ a p__________ pla_______ típicos.

h. *On the first day, I'm going to go to the park* El primer d______, v________ a ______ al par__________.

i. *We are going to go to the beach* V___________ a ______ a la pl__________.

j. *I believe the trip to Cádiz will be great.* Cr______ que el v______ a Cádiz s________ g________.

7. Translate into Spanish

a. This summer

b. We are going to go on holiday

c. To Cádiz

d. In the south of Spain

e. It is a beautiful city

f. On the coast

g. We are going to travel

h. By train

i. We are going to stay

j. I am going to stay

k. In a cheap hotel

l. In a basic hostel

m. It is near the centre

n. Far from the cathedral

o. We are going to go for a walk

p. In the old town

1. Hola, soy Emmanuel y vivo en Liverpool, una ciudad en el noroeste del país. Mis padres son de España aunque los padres de mi madre son colombianos.

2. El año pasado fui de vacaciones a Irlanda con mi mejor amigo, ya que su tía es irlandesa. Fuimos a Dublín, la capital del país. Está en el este de Irlanda, en la costa. Me quedé cinco días en casa de su tía. La casa era muy grande y había un salón de juegos, ¡qué chulo! Me gustó la casa porque era muy bonita y luminosa y estaba superlimpia.

3. La semana que viene voy a viajar a Barcelona con mis padres. Vamos a viajar en avión porque es rápido y cómodo. En Barcelona vamos a alojarnos en un hotel básico. El hotel está muy cerca de la playa.

4. Durante el viaje vamos a hacer muchas cosas. Me gustaría probar platos típicos y dar un paseo por el barrio Gótico. El primer día quiero ir al Parc Güell y tomar un café. Por la noche vamos a comer tapas en un restaurante típico. El segundo día vamos a visitar la Sagrada Familia, una basílica católica en Barcelona y la obra maestra de Gaudí. Luego, vamos a ver un espectáculo e ir a la playa.

5. En el futuro me gustaría ir de vacaciones a Sudamérica porque me gustan los países tropicales. Por ejemplo, me apetece viajar *(to travel)* a Colombia o Brasil, ya que siempre hace calor y se puede comer diversas frutas. Además, mi abuelo es colombiano así que me gustaría aprender *(to learn)* sobre su cultura y probar platos locales. Sin embargo, mi padre prefiere países europeos ricos en historia, arte y cultura como Italia, Egipto o Grecia.

6. Mi madre dice que este verano vamos a ir de vacaciones a Alemania. Vamos a pasar una semana en la capital, Berlín, y una semana en Múnich. Vamos a quedarnos en un hotel de lujo en Berlín, pero en Múnich nos vamos a quedar en un hotel barato. Me gustaría hacer turismo y comprar recuerdos de los museos y las galerías. Si tengo tiempo, voy a hacer senderismo en las montañas.

Emmanuel, 17 años. Liverpool, Inglaterra

1. Answer the following questions in English

a. Where is Liverpool?

b. Where did Emmanuel go on holiday last year?

c. Where is Dublin?

d. Where is Emmanuel going on holiday next week?

e. Where will he stay?

f. What will he do on the first day?

g. What will he do on the second day?

h. Where does his mum say they will go on holiday?

i. Where will they stay in Munich?

2. Find the Spanish equivalent in Emmanuel's text

a. My mother's parents (1)

b. On the coast (2)

c. Five days (2)

d. It is fast (3)

e. I want to go (4)

f. To watch a show (4)

g. I would like to go (5)

h. I fancy (5)

i. My mum says (6)

j. A week (6)

k. We are going to stay (6)

l. If I have time (6)

3. Complete the translation of paragraph 5

In the future, I would like to go on ________________

to South America _____________ I like tropical

____________. For _________, I fancy travelling to

Colombia or Brazil given that it's always _______ and

one   can   _______   diverse   ___________.

Furthermore, my ________________ is Colombian

therefore _____ would like to learn about his

________________ and try local ___________.

________________, my dad _____________ European

countries that are ___________ in history, art and

___________ like Italy, Egypt or ________________.

Andrés y su amiga Luna están hablando del verano pasado. Andrés fue de vacaciones, pero Luna no.

Andrés	¿Qué tal el verano, Luna? ¿Qué hiciste?
Luna	Bueno, no mucho. Me quedé aquí durante el verano porque voy a ir de vacaciones a Mallorca en diciembre. ¿Y tú?
Andrés	Fui de vacaciones a Italia con mis padres y mi hermana mayor. Fuimos a Venecia, una ciudad ubicada en el noreste de Italia.
Luna	¡Qué guay! Me encanta Venecia. ¿Qué hiciste allí?
Andrés	Pues hice mucho turismo ya que hay muchos museos y galerías de arte. También hay varias plazas muy bonitas.
Luna	Sí, ¿viajaste en góndola?
Andrés	Sí, me encantó pero fue muy caro. ¿Dónde vas a quedarte en Mallorca?
Luna	Voy a quedarme en un hotel de lujo en la costa de Mallorca.
Andrés	Qué chulo. ¿Cuánto tiempo vas a pasar en Mallorca?
Luna	Voy a pasar dos semanas allí con mi familia.
Andrés	¿Y qué vas a hacer en Mallorca?
Luna	Me imagino que voy a hacer muchas cosas, pero todos los días voy a tomar el sol en la playa y voy a hacer natación en el mar.
Andrés	¿Te gustaría hacer buceo o hacer vela?
Luna	Creo que sí. También me gustaría ir de compras y comprar algunos recuerdos.
Andrés	Comprar recuerdos es lo que más me gusta de ir de vacaciones.
Luna	A mí también.

4. True (T), False (F) or Not Mentioned (NM)?

Luna did not go on holiday in the summer.	
Luna stayed with her grandmother.	
Andrés went to Italy.	
Venice is in the north of Italy.	
Luna does not like Venice.	
Andrés went to many museums and galleries.	
Andrés didn't go to many beautiful places.	
Andrés went for a gondola ride.	
Luna will spend a week in Mallorca.	
Luna will sunbathe every day.	
Luna does not like to go swimming.	
Luna is looking forward to buying souvenirs.	
Andrés is also going to Mallorca.	

5. Complete the statements

a. _________________ went on holiday to Venice.

b. Andrés did a lot of _____________ in Venice.

c. Andrés thought the gondola ride was _____________.

d. __________ is going to Mallorca for ________ _____________.

e. Both agree that _____________ _____________ is the best thing about holidays.

END OF TERM 3 – QUESTION SKILLS

<table>
<tr><td>

1. Fill in the missing letters

a. ¿Q _ _ h _ _ _ _ _ _ _ el s _ b _ do?

b. ¿C _ _ q _ _ _ _ f _ _ _ _ _ ?

c. ¿C _ _ _ f _ _ ?

d. ¿Q _ _ v _ _ a hac _ _ este finde?

e. ¿Q _ _ v _ a h _ _ _ _ tu herman _ ?

f. ¿Q _ _ quie _ _ _ hacer est _ ma _ ana?

g. ¿T _ g _ _ _ _ _ _ _ ir al parque?

h. ¿A q _ _ hora q _ _ _ _ _ _ _ ?

i. ¿A _ _ _ _ _ v _ _ a i _ este veran _ ?

j. ¿C _ _ _ v _ _ a viaj _ _ ?

k. ¿D _ _ _ _ v _ _ a q _ _ _ _ _ _ _ ?

l. ¿Q _ _ v _ _ a h _ _ _ _ ?

m. ¿D _ _ _ _ _ e _ _ _ el hotel?

n. ¿Q _ _ lugares v _ _ a visit _ _ ?

</td><td>

2. Choose the option that you hear

a. El sábado fui al **centro / estadio / bosque**.

b. Fui con mi **hermana / hermano / mejor amigo**.

c. Fue **muy / un poco / bastante** aburrido.

d. Voy a hacer **deporte / los deberes / natación**.

e. Mi hermano va a ver **un partido / una película**.

f. Quiero **ir al cine / ir al parque / dar una vuelta**.

g. Sí, pero tengo que **trabajar / limpiar / estudiar**.

h. Quedamos a las **seis / cinco y cuarto / siete**.

i. Este verano voy a ir a **Cádiz / Sevilla / Madrid**.

j. Voy a viajar en **tren / avión / barco**.

k. Voy a alojarme en un **hotel / albergue / hostal**.

l. Voy a probar **marisco / platos típicos / tapas**

m. Está cerca del **centro / casco antiguo / puerto**.

n. Voy a visitar el **castillo / parque / teatro.**

</td></tr>
</table>

3. Listen and write in the missing information

a. El sábado pasado ____________ museos en el ____________ ____________ a las ________ __ ____________.

b. ____________ al casco antiguo con mi ________________ ____________ y su ____________, Raquel.

c. En mi ______________, fue ________________ ________________ pero un poco ________________.

d. Este fin de semana voy a ______________ ________________ en el ______________ con mi amigo.

e. Mi hermano va a ____________ al ________________ en el ________________ con sus amigos.

f. Esta ______________ me ______________ dar una ____________ en bici por el ______________.

g. Bueno, me gustaría, pero primero ________________ ________ hacer mis ______________.

h. Quedamos ______________ del ________________ ________________ a las ________ ___ ________.

i. Este ________________ voy a ________ a Cádiz en ______________ con mis ____________.

j. Voy a ____________ a Cádiz en ____________ porque es más ______________ que en ________.

k. Voy a ________________ en un ____________ ________________ y ________________.

l. Voy a dar una ____________ por el ______________ y por el ____________ de la Viña.

m. El ____________ está __________ ________________ del ________________ de Santa María.

n. Voy a ____________ el ________________ ________________ y vamos a ______ a muchos ____________.

END OF TERM 3 – QUESTION SKILLS

4. Fill in the grid with your personal information

Question	Answer
a. ¿Qué hiciste el fin de semana pasado?	
b. ¿Con quién fuiste?	
c. ¿Cómo fue?	
d. ¿Qué vas a hacer el próximo fin de semana?	
e. ¿Qué va a hacer tu hermano?	
f. ¿Qué quieres hacer esta mañana?	
g. ¿Te gustaría ir al parque?	
h. ¿A qué hora quedamos?	
i. ¿Adónde vas a ir este verano?	
j. ¿Cómo vas a viajar?	
k. ¿Dónde vas a quedarte?	
l. ¿Qué vas a hacer?	

5. Survey two of your classmates using the same questions as above and write down the main information you hear in Spanish

Q.	Person 1	Person 2
a.		
b.		
c.		
d.		
e.		
f.		
g.		
h.		
i.		
j.		
k.		
l.		

Term 3 Recap

Translate each part of the pyramid out loud with your partner, then write it into the spaces provided below.

a.
Three
days ago.

b. Three days ago I
went shopping.

c. Three days ago I went
shopping. Last Friday my
friend and I played
videogames.

d. Three days ago I went shopping. Last
Friday my friend and I played
videogames. Next weekend I am going to
go to a concert.

e. Three days ago I went shopping. Last Friday my
friend and I played videogames. Next weekend I am
going to go to a concert. Tomorrow I would like to go
to the park with my brother.

f. Three days ago I went shopping. Last Friday my friend and I
played videogames. Next weekend I am going to go to a concert.
Tomorrow I would like to go to the park with my brother. After, I
would like to eat seafood at a restaurant.

Write your translation here:

SOLUTION: *Hace tres días fui de compras. El viernes pasado mi amigo y yo jugamos a videojuegos. El próximo fin de semana voy a ir a un concierto. Mañana me gustaría ir al parque con mi hermano. Después, me gustaría comer marisco en un restaurante.*

No Snakes No Ladders

START	1 The day before yesterday	2 Yesterday I went to the cinema	3 Three days ago I did sport	4 The day before yesterday I visited art galleries	5 Yesterday I played football in the park	6 Last Friday I watched a film at the cinema	7 Yesterday I went shopping with my best friend
15 It will be a bit tiring but very cool	14 Next Sunday my brother is going to play basketball	13 Next Saturday my sister is going to go shopping	12 Next weekend	11 It was not boring at all	10 It was quite interesting	9 Last Friday I went to the stadium	8 Last weekend
16 What do you want to do today?	17 Today I would like to go to the cinema	18 However, I don't want to go to Pablo's house	19 I fancy it but I can't	20 It's ok we can stay at home	21 What time shall we meet at?	22 We will meet opposite the shopping mall at eight	23 Great, we will see each other later
FINISH	30 On the first day we are going to go to the museum	29 During the trip I am going to try seafood	28 The hotel is far from the beach	27 In Cádiz I am going to stay in a basic hostel	26 I like to travel by plane because it is comfortable	25 This summer I am going to go to Cádiz	24 This summer

No Snakes No Ladders

SALIDA

7 Ayer fui de compras con mi mejor amigo	**6** El viernes pasado vi una película en el cine	**5** Ayer jugué al fútbol en el parque	**4** Anteayer visité galerías de arte	**3** Hace tres días hice deporte	**2** Ayer fui al cine	**1** Anteayer
8 El fin de semana pasado	**9** El viernes pasado fui al estadio	**10** Fue bastante interesante	**11** No fue nada aburrido	**12** El próximo fin de semana	**13** El próximo sábado mi hermana va a ir de tiendas	**14** El próximo domingo mi hermano va a jugar al baloncesto
23 Genial, nos vemos luego	**22** Quedamos enfrente del centro comercial a las ocho	**21** ¿A qué hora quedamos?	**20** Está bien podemos quedarnos en casa	**19** Me apetece pero no puedo	**18** Sin embargo, no quiero ir a casa de Pablo	**17** Hoy me gustaría ir al cine
24 Este verano	**25** Este verano voy a ir a Cádiz	**26** Me gusta viajar en avión porque es cómodo	**27** En Cádiz voy a alojarme en un albergue básico	**28** El hotel está lejos de la playa	**29** Durante el viaje voy a probar marisco	**30** El primer día vamos a ir al museo

15 Será un poco agotador pero muy guay

16 ¿Qué quieres hacer hoy?

LLEGADA

The End

We hope you have enjoyed using this workbook and found it useful!

As many of you will appreciate, the penguin is a fantastic animal. At Language Gym, we hold it as a symbol of resilience, bravery and good humour; able to thrive in the harshest possible environments, and with, arguably the best gait in the animal kingdom (black panther or penguin, you choose). In Spanish, it is also the best example of the ü (dieresis); this is a symbol that helps distinguish "gui" (pronounced like the 'gi' in English "gift) and "güi"(pronounced like the 'gui' in "penguin"). The same occurs with 'gue' (ge) and 'güe' (gue).

Join us again on Spanish Sentence Builders – TRILOGY – Part III